RHETORICAL RENAISSANCE

Rhetorical Renaissance

THE MISTRESS ART AND HER MASTERWORKS

Kathy Eden

The University of Chicago Press CHICAGO AND LONDON

The University of Chicago Press, Chicago 60637
The University of Chicago Press, Ltd., London
© 2022 by The University of Chicago
Published 2022
Printed in the United States of America

31 30 29 28 27 26 25 24 23 22   1 2 3 4 5

ISBN-13: 978-0-226-82125-2 (cloth)
ISBN-13: 978-0-226-82126-9 (paper)
ISBN-13: 978-0-226-82127-6 (e-book)
DOI: https://doi.org/10.7208/chicago/9780226821276.001.0001

Library of Congress Cataloging-in-Publication Data

Names: Eden, Kathy, 1952– author.
Title: Rhetorical Renaissance : the mistress art and her masterworks /
Kathy Eden.
Description: Chicago : University of Chicago Press, 2022. | Includes
bibliographical references and index.
Identifiers: LCCN 2022005953 | ISBN 9780226821252 (cloth) | ISBN
9780226821269 (paperback) | ISBN 9780226821276 (ebook)
Subjects: LCSH: Rhetoric, Renaissance. | Rhetoric, Ancient—Influence. |
European literature—Renaissance, 1450–1600—Classical influences.
Classification: LCC PN183 .E34 2022 | DDC 808—dc23/eng/20220505
LC record available at https://lccn.loc.gov/2022005953
♾ This paper meets the requirements of ANSI/NISO Z39.48-1992
(Permanence of Paper).

To the more than four decades of students at Columbia
who have made teaching the delight of a lifetime

ἤ τέθνηκεν ἤ διδάσκε γράμματα (*Adagia* I.x.59)

CONTENTS

Introduction

My title, *Rhetorical Renaissance*, cuts two ways. Read along one bias, it invokes the rediscovery or rebirth—the renaissance—of a number of key rhetorical works from antiquity that changed the course of literary culture between the fourteenth and sixteenth centuries in Europe. According to Erasmus of Rotterdam, master rhetorician and rhetorical theorist of the period, these ancient authorities, largely unavailable to his predecessors, were the ones to follow, especially for those who sought not only advancement in church and state but basic competency "on any matter both in judgment and in speech."[1] Chief among these authorities was Cicero, whose late rhetorical works written between 54 and 46 BCE, including the complete *De oratore*, *Brutus*, and *Orator*, revolutionized the world of letters shortly after their rediscovery in 1421. In 1422 one prominent humanist, Guarino Veronese, credited another, Gasparino Barzizza, with bringing Cicero back to life (*renascens ad superos*) as the result of having a skilled paleographer copy the newly recovered manuscript containing these three works.[2] Copies like Barzizza's were so valued that yet another

1. *Collected Works of Erasmus* (Toronto, 1974–), 25: 34 (hereafter CWE). On the small number of ancient authorities, see *Adages* III.i.1, CWE 34: 172.

2. On the exchange between Barzizza and Guarino, see Remigio Sabbadini, *Le scoperte dei codici latini e greci*, 2 vols. (Florence, 1905, 1914), 1: 100, and G. W. Pigman III, "Barzizza's Studies of Cicero," *Rinascimento* 21 (1981): 123. On the discovery of these texts, see, for instance, K. Kumaniecki, "La tradition manuscrite du *De oratore*," *Revue des études latines*, 44 (1966), 204–18; L. D. Reynolds, ed.,

prominent humanist, Giovanni Aurispa, offered to lend Lorenzo Ghiberti his volume on siege machines if and only if the famous Florentine sculptor would part temporarily with *his* personal copy of Cicero's hitherto lost rhetorical works.[3] So momentous a rite of passage was reading these works in the early fifteenth century that Leon Battista Alberti not only openly refers to them in his ground-breaking treatise *On Painting* but proudly records having finished writing it on August 26, 1435, on the last page of *his* personal manuscript copy of Cicero's *Brutus*.[4] No one could hope to compete with the ancients for eloquence in writing or speaking, the self-congratulating humanist Alamanno Rinuccini could be heard to boast, before these paradigm-shifting works of Cicero were rediscovered.[5]

Also brought back to life and equally decisive in strengthening the grip of ancient rhetoric on the literary theory and practice of the Renaissance was Quintilian's *Institutio oratoria*, the early imperial handbook for the "complete orator." Large portions of its twelve books were still unavailable to Petrarch and his contemporaries at the end of the fourteenth century, motivating the so-called "father of humanism" to lament these lacunae directly to the Roman schoolmaster in a letter in the last book of his *Letters on Familiar Matters*. In 1416, more than forty years after Petrarch's death, Poggio Bracciolini finally remedied this loss with his spectacular find of a complete manuscript of

---

Texts and Transmission: A Survey of the Latin Classics (Oxford, 1983), 102–9; Ruth Taylor-Briggs, "Reading between the Lines: The Textual History and Manuscript Transmission of Cicero's Rhetorical Works," in *The Rhetoric of Cicero in Its Medieval and Early Renaissance Commentary Tradition*, ed. Virginia Cox and John O. Ward (Leiden, 2006), 101–7; Martin McLaughlin, "*Renascens ad superos Cicero*: Ciceronianism and Anti-Ciceronian Styles in the Italian Renaissance," in *The Afterlife of Cicero*, ed. Gesine Manuwald (London, 2016), 67–81; Colin Burrow, *Imitating Authors: Plato to Futurity* (Oxford, 2019), 169–70.

3. On this "codex swapping crowd," including the proposed exchange between Aurispa and Ghiberti, see E. H. Gombrich, *Norm and Form: Studies in the Art of the Renaissance* (London, 1966), 5–6.

4. For Alberti's reference to *Brutus*, esp. 70 and 71, see *On Painting*, trans. John R. Spencer (New Haven, 1956; rpt. 1966), 82, 98; and see Michael Baxandall, *Giotto and the Orators: Humanist Observers of Painting in Italy and the Discovery of Pictorial Composition, 1350–1450* (Oxford, 1971), 126n11, for commemoration of its completion.

5. Gombrich, *Norm and Form*, 1–2 and 139–40.

Quintilian at St. Gall.[6] And Tacitus's *Dialogue on Orators*, an equivocating response to Cicero's late rhetorical theory written shortly
thereafter and preserved in a single manuscript, lay unnoticed somewhere in a library in southern Germany until a lucky set of circumstances brought it to Rome in the 1450s.[7]

While the details regarding the recovery of these and other ancient rhetorical works are too well known to require retelling, they
do, as we will see, constitute an especially important chapter of this
book's backstory—as does the other bias along which its title, *Rhetorical Renaissance*, can be read.[8] For the intellectual movement we continue to call the Renaissance was profoundly rhetorical because the

6. On Poggio's discovery, see Sabbadini, *Le scoperte*, 1: 77–78, and Reynolds,
Texts and Transmission, 332–34. See also Michael Winterbottom, "Fifteenth-
Century Manuscripts of Quintilian," *Classical Quarterly* 17 (1967): 339–69, and
Priscilla Boskoff, "Quintilian in the Late Middle Ages," *Speculum* 27 (1952): 71–
78. On Petrarch's letter to Quintilian in the last book of his *Familiares* (24.7), see
Kathy Eden, *The Renaissance Rediscovery of Intimacy* (Chicago, 2012), 47–48.

7. On the rediscovery of Tacitus's *Opera minora*, including his *Dialogus de oratoribus*, see Sabbadini, *Le scoperte*, 1: 108–9 and 2: 254; L. D. Reynolds and N. G.
Wilson, *Scribes and Scholars: A Guide to the Transmission of Greek and Latin Literature* (Oxford, 1968), 123; Rudolf Pfeiffer, *History of Classical Scholarship, 1300
to 1850* (Oxford, 1976), 30–31; Francisco della Corte, "La scoperta del Tacito minora," in *La Fortuna di Tacito dal Sec. XV ad Oggi*, ed. Franco Gori and Cesare
Questa (Urbino, 1978), 13–45.

8. In an epilogue to his field-shaping *Rhetoric in the Middle Ages: A History of
Rhetorical Theory from Saint Augustine to the Renaissance* (Berkeley, 1974) entitled
"Rediscovery and Implications" (357–63), James J. Murphy sums up the consensus
claim that "within only five years, 1416 to 1421, Italian humanists located complete
texts . . . whose application to contemporary life helped to institute major changes
in Western society" (361). In "Humanism and Rhetoric," *Renaissance Humanism:
Foundations, Forms, and Legacy*, ed. Albert Rabil Jr., 3 vols. (Philadelphia, 1988),
3: 171–235, John Monfasani opens with a reaffirmation of this claim: "From one
perspective the history of Renaissance rhetoric is the story of the recovery of classical texts and the integration of classical rhetoric within contemporary education
and practice." Regarding the rediscovery of the Ciceronian texts lost in part or as
a whole, George A. Kennedy writes in a similar vein, "The dissemination of these
works among the humanists sparked a renaissance of Ciceronian and rhetorical
studies, first in Italy and then through western Europe generally. In 1465, *De oratore* was the first book to be printed in Italy on the introduction there of the new
technology" ("Cicero's Oratorical and Rhetorical Legacy," *Brill's Companion to
Cicero: Oratory and Rhetoric*, ed. James M. May [Leiden, 2002], 491). See also
Brian Vickers, *In Defence of Rhetoric* (Oxford, 1988), 254–93.

sibling rivalry among the three discursive or "trivial" arts—grammar, dialectic and rhetoric—reached a new equilibrium, in and out of the classroom, with the *ars rhetorica* ascendant.[9] The very same humanists who negotiated for manuscript copies of Cicero's newly discovered rhetorical works and distinguished their own literary production from that of their recent predecessors on the grounds that they had access to these ancient works wholeheartedly supported a renewed attention to rhetorical studies. Coming of age in a world of printed as well as manuscript copies, Erasmus himself dates the first pangs of this rebirth of literary culture to Petrarch's accomplishments as a rhetorician—accomplishments unthinkable apart from Petrarch's admiration for the ancient rhetoricians whose works he could read only in mutilated versions.[10] Unlike Erasmus, then, Petrarch sometimes had to find a mediated path to ancient rhetoric. For this mediation, as no few scholars have noted, he often turns to Augustine, who had himself given up a career as teacher of rhetoric to become not only a Christian but the singularly most influential church father.[11]

9. On this rivalry and the gradual ascension of rhetoric, see, for instance, Paul Oskar Kristeller, *Renaissance Thought and Its Sources*, ed. M. Mooney (New York, 1979); Monfasani, "Humanism and Rhetoric"; Daniel Kinney, "More's Letter to Dorp: Remapping the Trivium," *Renaissance Quarterly* 34 (1981): 179–210; Brian Vickers, "Rhetoric and Poetics," in *Cambridge History of Renaissance Philosophy*, ed. Charles Schmitt and Quentin Skinner (Cambridge, UK, 1988), 715–45; Quentin Skinner, *Reason and Rhetoric in the Philosophy of Hobbes* (Cambridge, UK, 1996), 26–40, 100–110; Peter Mack, *A History of Renaissance Rhetoric, 1380–1620* (Oxford, 2011); and see L. D. Green and J. J. Murphy, *Renaissance Rhetoric Short-Title Catalogue 1460–1700* (Aldershot, 2006). In *Rhetoric and Renaissance Culture* (Berlin, 2004), Heinrich F. Plett concludes that "rhetoric regained an importance in the timespan from about the middle of the fourteenth to about the middle of the seventeenth century, which it did not possess before or after" (13–14).

10. For Erasmus's estimation of Petrarch as "leader in the rebirth of eloquence in Italy," see CWE 28: 414.

11. For Augustine's influence on Petrarch, the subject of a vast bibliography, see, for instance, B. L. Ullman, *Studies in the Italian Renaissance* (Rome, 1955); Carol Everhart Quillen, *Rereading the Renaissance: Petrarch, Augustine, and the Language of Humanism* (Ann Arbor, 1998); Albert Rabil Jr., "Petrarch, Augustine, and the Classical Christian Tradition," in *Renaissance Humanism*, 1: 95–114; W. J. Bouwsma, "The Two Faces of Humanism: Stoicism and Augustinianism in Renaissance Thought," *Itinerarium Italicum: The Profile of the Italian Renaissance in the Mirror of Its European Transformations*, ed. H. A. Oberman and T. A. Brady Jr. (Leiden, 1975), 3–50. For Petrarch's knowledge of the *Orator*, including

From the end of the fourteenth to the end of the sixteenth century, through some combination of direct and indirect means, Rhetorica regained a royal status she had not enjoyed since the late antique Martianus Capella, Augustine's contemporary, compared her to "a queen with power over everything" in his *Marriage of Philology and Mercury* (5.427). As portrayed visually by Andrea Mantegna in the fifteenth century (see cover) as well as verbally by Martianus Capella in the early fifth, Rhetorica Regina seemed to the Renaissance to bring under her control not only "cities but armies in battle."[12] She was not just a queen but a warrior queen. Had not Cicero himself in *De oratore* (2.187) described her as a soul-bending ruler with the bravery of a general?

Of course, not everyone agreed to Rhetorica's elevated status. Some, like northern humanist Rudolf Agricola, continued to consider Dialectica the mistress art—*dux illa directrixque artium*—even while rhetoricizing her content.[13] Others sought instead to diminish Rhetorica's rising fortunes by reviving old allegations of her promiscuity, taking "mistress" in a very different sense. In an effort to salvage her reputation in his *Defense of Poetry*, Philip Sidney briefly repeats the rumors of a Rhetorica (here honey-tongued Eloquence) "apparelled, or rather disguised in a courtesan-like painted affectation."[14] But this figure too—Rhetorica meretrix—looks back to the antiquity

---

through Augustine's *De doctrina christiana*, see Pierre Blanc, "Petrarque lecteur de Cicéron. Les scolies pétrarquiennes du *De oratore* et de l'*Orator*," *Studi Petrarcheschi* 9 (1978): 109–66, and Rabil, "Petrarch, Augustine, and the Classical Christian Tradition," 110–12.

12. Martianus Capella, *The Marriage of Philology and Mercury*, in *Martianus Capella and the Seven Liberal Arts*, trans. William Stahl and Richard Johnson, 2 vols. (New York, 1977), 2: 156. On the iconology of the period for a Rhetorica Regina, see Plett, *Rhetoric and Renaissance Culture*, 502–52.

13. On the rhetoricizing of dialectic in Agricola's *De inventione dialectica*, see J. R. McNally, "Dux Illa Directrixque Artium: Rudolf Agricola's Dialectical System," *Quarterly Journal of Speech* 52 (1966): 337–47; Lodi Nauta, "Lorenzo Valla and the Rise of Humanist Dialectic," in *The Cambridge Companion to Renaissance Philosophy*, ed. James Hankins (Cambridge, UK, 2007), 193–210; Monfasani, "Humanism and Rhetoric," 196–97; Peter Mack, *Renaissance Argument: Valla and Agricola in the Traditions of Rhetoric and Dialectic* (Leiden, 1993) and *History of Renaissance Rhetoric*, 56–75.

14. *Sidney's "Defence of Poesy" and Selected Renaissance Literary Criticism*, ed. Gavin Alexander (London, 2004), 49.

that Renaissance humanists worked to revive. For their revival included the renowned courtesan (*hetaera*) Aspasia, who was no less famous for brazenly overthrowing her male opponents in debate than for being the mistress of the rhetorically gifted statesman Pericles. Renaissance rhetoricians like Erasmus rehearse her unceremonious takedowns of such high-profile adversaries as Xenophon with her Socratic-style cross-examinations.[15]

Not to be overshadowed by his outspoken lover, Pericles too contributes to the singular authority of rhetoric as the ruling discipline in the Renaissance. In a fragment from the *Demoi*, a lost play of the comic dramatist Eupolis, a contemporary of Aristophanes, the goddess Peithō (Persuasion) is said to sit enthroned on Pericles' lips. Borrowing this compliment from *De oratore*, *Brutus*, the *Institutio oratoria*, or possibly all three, Erasmus has his mouthpiece Bulephorus in the satiric *Ciceronianus* apply these words of praise to the rigid Ciceronian Nosoponus in an effort to gain his confidence before undertaking to cure him of his debilitating obsession with writing like the master of Roman oratory.[16] Another crucial chapter in the backstory of this book, then, is the formation of an intellectual culture in Europe thoroughly saturated with rhetorical principles and practices that shape its education, its professional training, its politics, and even its leisure activities. Like the history of the rediscovery of ancient texts in the Renaissance, the social and institutional history of rhetoric's impact on early modernity is well known.[17]

---

15. Erasmus, *De copia*, CWE 24: 624. Her skill is treated in more detail by, for instance, Cicero (*De inv.* 1.51–52) and Quintilian (5.11.27–29). On her life and legacy, see Madeleine M. Henry, *Prisoner of History: Aspasia of Miletus and Her Biographical Tradition* (Oxford, 1995).

16. For Erasmus's appropriation of the compliment, see CWE 28: 344; and see *De oratore* 3.138, *Brutus* 59, and Quintilian 10.1.82, the last of these appropriated to refer to Xenophon.

17. See, for instance, T. W. Baldwin, *William Shakspere's 'Small Latine & Lesse Greeke'*, 2 vols. (Urbana, IL, 1944); Hanna H. Gray, "Renaissance Humanism: The Pursuit of Eloquence," *Journal of the History of Ideas* 24 (1963): 497–514; D. R. Kelley, *Foundations of Modern Historical Scholarship: Language, Law, and History in the French Renaissance* (New York, 1970); Marc Fumaroli, *L'âge de l'éloquence: Rhétorique et 'res literaria' de la Renaissance au seuil de l'époque classique* (Paris, 1980); John W. O'Malley, *Praise and Blame in Renaissance Rome* (Durham, NC, 1979); Victoria Kahn, *Rhetoric, Prudence and Skepticism in the Renaissance* (Ithaca, 1985); Debora K. Shuger, *Sacred Rhetoric: The Christian Grand Style in the*

But what about particular practices and principles and their peculiar impact on particular texts, especially those that are themselves very well known, both in their own time and in ours? The double premise of this book is that, on the one hand, some of the most widespread practices and principles enshrined in ancient rhetoric are far less familiar to us than they should be, even though, on the other hand, they inform many of the most widely read literary works of the period.[18] Four of these underappreciated practices, accordingly, are the subject of the four chapters that follow. Each of these four chapters, more precisely, focuses on a single principle or practice that figures prominently in literary production because it forms the backbone of rhetorical training in the Renaissance—a training rooted in the traditional architecture of the most influential rhetorical manuals. This architecture routinely divides both inventional from stylistic matters and invention proper, first of the five traditional rhetorical *partes* or *officia*, from disposition or arrangement, the second of the five.[19] In keeping with this architecture and the book's double focus

English Renaissance (Princeton, 1988); Robert Black, *Humanism and Education in Medieval and Renaissance Italy* (Cambridge, UK, 2001); Peter Mack, *Elizabethan Rhetoric: Theory and Practice* (Cambridge, UK, 2002); Ronald G. Witt, *The Two Latin Cultures and the Foundation of Renaissance Humanism in Medieval Italy* (Cambridge, UK, 2012).

18. Two notable examples of recent scholarship that perform precisely this task of analyzing particular literary texts in light of particular rhetorical practices are Quentin Skinner's *Forensic Shakespeare* (Oxford, 2014) and Lorna Hutson's *Circumstantial Shakespeare* (Oxford, 2015). Their titles were admittedly the provocation for my own. See also Skinner's now classic discussion of *paradiastolē* in *Reason and Rhetoric in the Philosophy of Hobbes*, 138–80.

19. For the foundational division in the manual tradition between proof and style—a division that goes back at least as far as Aristotle's *Rhetoric* and continues well into the seventeenth century—see, for instance, Quintilian 3.3.7, on the authority of Cicero (*De orat.* 2.120), and 8 Pr 13, and Ben Jonson, who divides writing into "the Invention and the Fashion," identifying the latter with "the Qualities of your style" (*Timber, or Discoveries*, in *The Poems, the Prose Works*, ed. C. H. Herford Percy and Evelyn Simpson, 11 vols. [Oxford, 1925–52], 8: 629–30). On Jonson's division, following John Hoskyns, see Eden, *Renaissance Rediscovery of Intimacy*, 1. On the five traditional *officia*, including invention (*inventio*), disposition or arrangement (*dispositio*), elocution or style (*elocutio*), memory (*memoria*), and delivery (*pronuntiatio, actio*), see George Kennedy, "Classical Rhetoric," in *Encyclopedia of Rhetoric*, ed. Thomas O. Sloane (Oxford, 2001), 111–12, and Vickers, *In Defence of Rhetoric*, 62–67.

on not just rhetorical theory but its impact on literary production, chapter 1 turns to the beginning of the beginning, the starting point of invention, with the so-called *status* system: the series of questions designed to locate the principal issue in any legal conflict and thereby the arguments needed to resolve it. Cicero's Antonius in *De oratore* states unequivocally that his first task as an orator is always to determine the *status* of any case he agrees to argue (2.114). In *De copia*, the most widely read early modern rhetorical textbook, Erasmus appropriates this standard for his advice to schoolmasters. For their young schoolboys, as we will see in chapter 1, are discouraged from putting pen to paper until, like Antonius, they have located the *status* of their compositions (CWE 24: 605). And Erasmus's own most prolific student, Philip Melanchthon, extends this advice not only to preachers but to those who hear their sermons since no speech is either skillfully composed or properly understood, whether delivered from the pulpit, the courtroom, or the assembly hall, unless its composition or interpretation radiates from a central point, its *status*.[20] Behind Melanchthon's principle of coherence, in other words, is a most basic rhetorical practice, and this practice of locating the *status*, as we will also see, lies behind such literary masterworks as Petrarch's *Secret* and Castiglione's *Book of the Courtier*.

But these and other major literary works of the period take their shape from rhetoric's dispositional as well as inventional directives; and chief among these directives is the demand that an orator demolish the arguments of his adversary. Fourth of the traditional five parts of an oration, refutation meets this demand. As the dismantling of opposing arguments, it is the focus of chapter 2.[21] More to the point, ref-

---

20. For Melanchthon on *status*, which he identifies with the *scopus*, see Robert E. Stillman, *Philip Sidney and the Poetics of Renaissance Cosmopolitanism* (Aldershot, 2008), esp. 91–92, and Kathy Eden, *Hermeneutics and the Rhetorical Tradition: Chapters in the Ancient Legacy and Its Humanist Reception* (New Haven, 1997), 79–89. For Melanchthon on a coherence closely aligned with *status*, see Francis Goyet, *Le sublime du "lieu commun": L'invention rhétorique dans l'Antiquité et à la Renaissance* (Paris, 1996), 499–512. And see Kees Meerhoff, "The Significance of Philip Melanchthon's Rhetoric in the Renaissance," in *Renaissance Rhetoric*, ed. Peter Mack (London, 1994), 46–62.

21. While there are minor differences among the manuals regarding the number of parts of an oration, I, like Kennedy in "Classical Rhetoric" (111), follow

utation (*refutatio, confutatio, refellatio*) is at once the least theorized part of the speech and the most valued. Cicero and his followers, ancient as well as early modern, insist that refuting an opponent makes or breaks an orator's case, even if the rules governing this adversarial practice are hard to formulate. Often, as we will see, textbook formulations simply recommend reversing the procedures for constructing proofs, the work of the confirmation (*confirmatio, probatio*) as the third part of a speech. Meanwhile, orators are warned to keep an eye out for an adversary's inconsistencies and contradictions, the bread and butter of refutation. When it comes to Renaissance literary practice, in contrast, refutation has no trouble finding its footing. Like so many literary works of the Renaissance, the masterworks featured in chapter 1, including Petrarch's *Secret* and Castiglione's *Book of the Courtier*, prove, as we will also see in chapter 2, to be fundamentally refutative in structure. So do some of Erasmus's most popular dialogues and Montaigne's essays. Following ancient practice, moreover, some of these works discover in the refutative agenda an opportunity for self-refutation.

If the first half of *Rhetorical Renaissance* addresses two key weapons in the orator's arsenal of inventive practices that leave more than a superficial imprint on Renaissance literary production, its second half, still in keeping with the architecture of the rhetorical manuals, turns to style—but not, for good reason, all at once. For these same manuals, ancient as well as early modern, emphasize certain "crossover" strategies—those that contribute to both the invention of arguments or proofs and their verbal expression, their style. Chief among these is the similitude (*similitudo, parabola, collatio*), which, as we will see in chapter 3, not only takes inductive proof as its point of departure but comes eventually to characterize the style of the sixteenth century— a style as characteristic of Erasmus and Castiglione at the start of the century as of John Lyly and Michel de Montaigne at its end. While not nearly as flamboyant or easily recognizable as Euphues' clustered similitudes in Lyly's raucous novel, Ludovico's famous comparison of the bee to the successful courtier in Castiglione's best-selling dia-

---

Quintilian (3.9.1) in holding to five: introduction (*exordium*), narration (*narratio*), confirmation (*confirmatio*), refutation (*refutatio*), conclusion (*peroratio*). See also Vickers, *In Defence of Rhetoric*, 67–72.

logue owes no less to this "crossover" strategy, with its signature two-part structure. "And even as [*come*] the Bee in greene medowes fleeth always about the grasse, choosing out flowers," Ludovico elaborates as if following textbook instructions, "So [*così*] shall our Courtier steale his grace from them that to his seeming have it, and from eche one, that parcell that shall be most worthie prayse."²² Counting on not only its inductive logic but its vividness, which helps readers visualize what is expressed verbally, Ludovico, like all aspiring stylists of the period, leverages the particularity and familiarity that underwrite the similitude's probative and stylistic power to persuade.

As late as 1589, George Puttenham praises this same figure for both beautifying and enlarging an argument, claiming that "no one thing more prevaileth with all ordinary judgments than persuasion by similitude."²³ This persuasiveness, as mentioned above, was thought to sit on Pericles' lips; but it makes its way into Renaissance literature, as we will see in chapter 3, not through the lost speeches of the great Athenian statesman but through both the instructions of the rhetorical manuals and the newly accessible dialogues of the philosopher Plato, reputed in some authoritative quarters to be the greatest stylist of antiquity.²⁴ No small part of this greatness, as we will also see, is attributed to the "free-flowing and agreeable" (*fusus ac iucundus*) quality of his style, achieved, according to Erasmus, through simil-

---

22. Baldassare Castiglione, *The Book of the Courtier*, trans. Thomas Hoby (1563; rpt. London, 1959), 1.26, 45; *Il libro del Cortegiano*, ed. Bruno Maier (Turin, 1955), 123 (hereafter cited in the text with book, chapter, and page number as Hoby and Maier). On the selectivity of the bee as the subject of numerous similitudes, including those in Erasmus's collection *Parabolae sive similia*, see Jürgen v. Stackelberg, "Das Bienengleichnis: Ein Beitrag zur Geschichte der literarischen *Imitatio*," *Romanische Forschungen* 68 (1956): 271–93, and Jacques Chomarat, *Grammaire et rhétorique chez Érasme*, 2 vols. (Paris, 1981), 2: 802–3. At 4.10 (Hoby 265, Maier 456), Ottaviano uses the equally familiar Lucretian similitude of the "sweete licour" around the rim of the cup (*De rerum natura* 1.936–42), so identified by Quintilian (3.1.4).

23. George Puttenham, *The Art of English Poesy*, ed. Frank Whigham and Wayne A. Rebhorn (Ithaca, 2007), 326. On the long-standing belief in the power of similitudes to effect more than persuasion, see Caroline Walker Bynum, *Dissimilar Similitudes: Devotional Objects in Late Medieval Europe* (New York, 2020).

24. On Plato as the *summus orator*, see, for instance, *De oratore* 1.47, and Helen North, "Combing and Curling: 'Orator Summus Plato,'" *Illinois Classical Studies* 16 (1991): 201–19.

itudes (*per similitudines*)—what the Dutch humanist characterizes even more precisely as *similitudines Socraticae*.[25]

Willing to share the similitude with invention on the authority of antiquity, especially Quintilian, Renaissance stylistic theory is not about to be upstaged by it. And why should it be, when Cicero's late rhetorical works, especially *Brutus* and *Orator*, credit an orator's style with making or marring his career? On the contrary, style so threatens to overwhelm invention that some early modern theorists, like Rudolf Agricola, mentioned above, and his admirer Peter Ramus, are eager to decouple the two, cornering invention for dialectic while reducing rhetoric to stylistic matters alone.[26] Like other important bits of the backstory of a rhetorical renaissance, this one is well known; so is the runaway interest during the Renaissance in rhetorical figures, a featured part of *elocutio* often called "figures of speech."[27] Less well known, however, is either how or how much newly recovered rhetorical works, like Cicero's *Brutus* and Tacitus's *Dialogue on Orators*, coupled with newly edited and translated texts, like Aristotle's *Rhetoric*, transform the sixteenth-century understanding of style, in contrast to invention, as not just a historical artifact, conditioned by time and place, but a theoretical epicenter of what later centuries come to call *historicism*.[28] This transformation in the Renaissance understanding of

25. CWE 68: 489; *Opera omnia Desiderii Erasmi Roterodami* (Amsterdam, 1969–), V-4, 264 ll. 420–22 (hereafter ASD), and CWE 41: 633; *Ausgewählte Werke*, ed. Hajo Holborn (Munich, 1933), 260 (hereafter H).

26. On this decoupling see, for instance, Mack, *History of Renaissance Rhetoric*, 56–75, 136–48, and Walter Ong, *Ramus: Method and the Decay of Dialogue* (Cambridge, MA, 1958).

27. See, for instance, Lee Sonnino, *A Handbook to Sixteenth-Century Rhetoric* (London, 1968); Sylvia Adamson, Gavin Alexander, and Katrin Ettenhuber, eds., *Renaissance Figures of Speech* (Cambridge, UK, 2007); Mack, *History of Renaissance Rhetoric*, 208–27; and Vickers, *In Defence of Rhetoric*, 322–39.

28. On renewed interest in Aristotle's *Rhetoric* in the fifteenth and sixteenth centuries, see, for instance, Marvin T. Herrick, "The Early History of Aristotle's *Rhetoric* in England," *Philological Quarterly* 5 (1926): 242–57; James McConica, "Humanism and Aristotle in Tudor Oxford," *English Historical Review* 94 (1979): 291–317; Monfasani, "Humanism and Rhetoric," 182–83; Lawrence D. Green, "The Reception of Aristotle's *Rhetoric* in the Renaissance," in *Peripatetic Rhetoric after Aristotle*, ed. William W. Fortenbaugh and David C. Mirhady (New Brunswick, NJ, 1994), 320–48, and *John Rainolds's Oxford Lectures on Aristotle's "Rhetoric"* (Newark, NJ, 1986), 9–56; Skinner, *Reason and Rhetoric in the Philosophy of Hobbes*, 35–38; and Mack, *History of Renaissance Rhetoric*, 169–71.

style is the focus of chapter 4; and like the three chapters before it, this chapter too features the impact of rhetorical—here, more precisely, stylistic—theory on literary production, including such high-profile literary products as *The Book of the Courtier* and the *Ciceronianus*.

On the one hand, then, *Rhetorical Renaissance* relies on only a few literary masterworks to make its case, opting for depth of analysis over breadth in the hopes that readers will broaden the field of vision with their own examples. On the other hand, even this small sample of well-known Renaissance works from north and south of the Alps sets in high relief how the four rhetorical principles and practices featured here were understood to reinforce one another in the interests of a coherence that Melanchthon and his contemporaries would applaud—a coherence that overcomes the architectural divide between invention and style from the rhetorical manuals in favor of an integrated literary architecture. Both this integration and the architecture that upholds it were of particular concern to Melanchthon's teacher. In a preface to the multivolume first edition of Jerome's *Letters* (1516), for instance, Erasmus makes explicit his identification of this integrated literary architecture with the *stilus* or style he finds on display in the desert father's best epistolary writing.

If Castiglione's Ludovico famously insists in the *Book of the Courtier* that no one can define style (1.39, Hoby 64, Maier 152), Erasmus offers in this preface to his edition of Jerome the next best thing in the form of a fulsome enumeration. "The term style [*stilus*]," Erasmus explains,

> comprehends all at once a multiplicity of things—manner in language and diction [*sermonis habitum, & dictionis . . . figuras*], texture, so to speak [*quasi filum*], and, further, thought and judgment [*consilium, iudicium*], line of argumentation [*argumentationis genus*], inventive power [*inventionem*], control of material [*tractationem*], emotion [*affectus*], and what the Greeks call ἦθος—and within each one of these notions a profusion of shadings, no fewer, to be sure, than the differences in talent, which are as numerous as men themselves.[29] (CWE 61: 78)

29. For the Latin of this edition, here and in the conclusion, I have used *Hieronymi opera omnia* (Basel, 1516), vol. 2, part 1, 3D–4A.

The first few items on this list—language, diction, and even texture—
are predictable enough in an early sixteenth-century discussion of
style or *elocutio* as the third of the five rhetorical *officia*. But what
about those elements more applicable to what Aristotle's *Rhetoric*
and Cicero's later rhetorical works include under *logos*, like line of
argumentation, inventive power, and control of material, followed by
pathos and *ēthos*?[30] Surely Erasmus is thinking of *stilus* or style here as
not only more capacious than mere *elocutio* but more integrated into
the *ars rhetorica* as a whole. In keeping with this capaciousness as well
as integration, as we will see in conclusion, Erasmus also offers a literary analysis of one particular letter by Jerome that illustrates for his
Renaissance readers just how masterfully the skilled writer executes
his *stilus* by interweaving the very building blocks featured throughout this book: *status*, refutation, and the similitude.[31] With the help
of this closing testimony by Erasmus, I rest my case for the signal importance of these building blocks in a renascent rhetoric—*Rhetorica
renascens*—animating a rhetorical Renaissance.

30. On the Aristotelian legacy of *ēthos*, *logos*, and *pathos* as the sources of persuasion, including its promotion by Cicero, see Friedrich Solmsen, "Aristotle and
Cicero on the Orator's Playing upon the Feelings," *Classical Philology* 33 (1938):
390–404, and "The Aristotelian Tradition in Ancient Rhetoric," *American Journal
of Philology* 62 (1941): 35–50, 169–90. And see Jakob Wisse, *Ethos and Pathos from
Aristotle to Cicero* (Amsterdam, 1989). On Erasmus's claim regarding an individuality of style, see Eden, *Renaissance Rediscovery of Intimacy*, 81–89, 119–24.

31. For an influential forerunner of Erasmus's literary analysis, including its
focus on the practices and principles featured here, see, for instance, Antonio
Loschi's studies of Cicero's orations in his *Inquisitio artis in orationibus Ciceronis*,
in Pigman, "Barzizza's Studies of Cicero," 130–31; Monfasani, "Humanism and
Rhetoric," 188–89; and Mack, *History of Renaissance Rhetoric*, 33–34.

✳ 1 ✳

Status

RHETORICAL THEORY AND PRACTICE

In *De oratore*, Cicero's dialogue on the ideal orator, Crassus, one of two principal interlocutors during two days of discussion at his villa in Tusculum, recalls the rhetorical curriculum of his early education. Among these schoolboy recollections Crassus includes learning the so-called *status* system, a series of questions—usually three—designed to locate the point of contention in a controversy (1.139).[1] Traditionally ascribed to the Hellenistic rhetorician Hermagoras (second cen-

---

1. For the dismissive attitude of *De oratore* toward the rhetorical handbooks, see Jakob Wisse, "*De oratore*: Rhetoric, Philosophy, and Making of the Ideal Orator," *Brill's Companion to Cicero*, ed. May, 375–400, who speculates that "contemporary readers must have been surprised by how little space is given to status theory, which formed the backbone of many of the standard accounts" (387). In "The Intellectual Background of the Rhetorical Works" in the same volume, Wisse gives status theory equally little attention (357). More detailed discussions of status theory include *De oratore libri III*, ed. Anton D. Leeman and H. Pinkster (Heidelberg, 1981–) (hereafter Leeman-Pinkster), 3: 27–33; Hanns Hohmann, "The Dynamics of Stasis: Classical Rhetorical Theory and Modern Legal Argumentation," *American Journal of Jurisprudence* 34 (1989): 171–97, and "Stasis," *Encyclopedia of Rhetoric*, ed. Sloane, 741–45; Lucia Calboli Montefusco, *La dottrina degli "status" nella retorica greca e romana* (Hildesheim, 1986); Malcolm Heath, "The Substructure of Stasis-Theory from Hermagoras to Hermogenes," *Classical Quarterly* 44 (1994): 114–29; D. A. Russell, *Greek Declamation* (Cambridge, 1983), 40–73; George Kennedy, *Greek Rhetoric under Christian Emperors* (Princeton, 1983), 73–86, and *The Art of Persuasion in Greece* (Princeton, 1963), 306–13; Otto A. L. Dieter, "Stasis," *Speech Monographs* 17 (1950): 345–69; Ray Nadeau, "Classical Systems of Stases in Greek: Hermagoras to Hermogenes," *Greek, Roman and Byzantine Studies* 2 (1959): 51–73.

tury BCE) and reflecting their legal pedigree, these three questions routinely address (1) whether an act was committed; (2) how the act should be defined (as murder, for instance, rather than homicide, or theft rather than sacrilege); and (3) how the act should be qualified (as just, for instance, rather than unjust). Assuming his guests have been through the same rhetorical training, Crassus reminds them that "the question always posed is either whether or not the deed was done, or, if it was, what its nature is, or again, by what name it should be called, or, as some add, whether or not it seems to have been done justly."[2] This training offered by the rhetorical handbooks, belittled here and throughout *De oratore*, labels these three *status* questions *conjectural, definitive* (or *legal*), and *qualitative* (or *juridical*). The first asks "did it happen?" (Lat. *sitne?*), the second "what happened?" (*quid sit?*), and the third "what kind of act was it?" (*quale sit?*).[3]

Among the devalued handbooks treating the *status* system is Cicero's own *De inventione*. In this early effort at rhetorical theory focused on invention, Cicero anticipates the words if not the dismissive attitude of his more philosophically inclined Crassus by remarking in his own adolescent voice that "Every subject which contains in itself a controversy to be resolved by speech and debate involves a question of fact, or about a definition, or about the nature of the act."[4] In the *Institutio oratoria*, a complete education for the orator in twelve books, the imperial schoolmaster Quintilian passes this lesson on to his first-century students with a lively give-and-take that begins by distinguishing the *conjectural* from the *definitive* status as part of a dialogue between two interlocutors: "'You did it,' 'I did not,' 'Did he do it?'" as opposed to "'You did this,' 'I did not do this,' 'What did

2. Cicero, *On the Ideal Orator*, trans. James M. May and Jakob Wisse (Oxford, 2001), 1.139. All further references are to this edition and in the text. For the Latin I have used the edition by K. Kumaniecki (Leipzig, 1969). May and Wisse provide a brief introduction to status, where they maintain that the "most conspicuous difference between the standard doctrine and its echoes in *De oratore* is Cicero's avoidance of technicalities" (34).

3. For these three questions, see also *Orator* 45, *De partitione oratoria* 33, and *Institutio oratoria* 5.10.53. On an early distinction between the first and third question, *ti esti* and *poion ti*, see *Gorgias* 448E, and for the need to answer the definitive before the qualitative question, 463C; and see Gerard Watson, "Plato's *Gorgias* and Aristotle," *Maynooth Review* 14 (1989): 51–66.

4. Cicero, *De inventione*, trans. H. M. Hubbell (Cambridge, MA, 1949; rpt. 1976), 1.8.10. All further references are to this edition and included in the text.

he do?'"⁵ Eventually adding the *qualitative* status to this exchange, Quintilian cautions his reader that a single *causa* or case may call into question more than one *status*:

> When the accused says "Admitting that I did it, I was right to do it," he makes the *basis* one of *quality* [*qualitatis . . . statu*]; but when he adds "but I did not do it," he introduces an element of *conjecture* [*coniecturam*]. But denial of the facts is always the stronger line of defense, and therefore I conceive the *basis* [*statum*] to reside in that which I should say, if I were confined to one single line of argument. (3.6.10)

In keeping with this acknowledgment that questions of *status* may overlap (cf. 7.10.1–4), Quintilian further insists that they reach beyond the confines of the courtroom, catering to the needs of deliberative and epideictic as well as forensic orators (3.6.1, 3.6.81).

In registering this insistence, Quintilian takes his cue from Cicero's *De oratore* (and not *De inventione*), where both Crassus and his conversational sparring partner, Antonius, agree that the law court is far too narrow a purview for *status*. Indeed, its *conjectural, definitive,* and *qualitative* issues serve to pinpoint the controversy not only in the particularized cases (*quaestiones definitae* or *causae*) traditionally handled by the orator but in the general questions (*quaestiones infinitae*) debated by philosophers (2.104–5, 2.132, 3.111–17).⁶ The

---

5. Quintilian, *Institutio oratoria*, trans. H. E. Butler, 4 vols. (Cambridge, MA, 1921; rpt. 1976), 3.6.5. All further references to this work are included in the text. On Quintilian's overview of the history of status in book 3 and his own system in relation to this history, see Erling B. Holtsmark, "Quintilian on Status: A Progymnasma," *Hermes* 96 (1968): 356–68.

6. In the *Orator*, Cicero similarly aligns *status* with the *quaestio infinita* as well as with the *causa*, but he then goes on to distinguish the rhetorical from the philosophical general question: "To use these distinctions an orator . . . always should divert the controversy, if he can, from consideration of specific persons and circumstances, since one can speak more broadly about the general than about the specific and take what is proved about the former to serve as proof about the latter. An inquiry converted from specific persons and circumstances to a generalized discussion is called a 'thesis.' Aristotle used this to inculcate in the young not the philosophical habit of precise discussion but the rhetorical abundance that enables one to argue both sides of an issue elaborately and richly" (trans. Robert Kaster [Oxford, 2020], 45–46). On the relation of general to specific questions,

agreement of not only Cicero's Crassus and Antonius but Cicero and Quintilian on this broad applicability, as we will see throughout this chapter, leaves its mark on Renaissance literature—a mark equally visible in Renaissance rhetorical theory.

In the singularly popular *De copia*, for instance, Erasmus advises the schoolboy to begin composing his themes only after he has considered "the precepts of the rhetoricians concerning the main types of issue, which Quintilian calls *status*, the Greeks στάσεις" (CWE 24: 605; ASD I-6, 228 l. 796). In *Ecclesiastes sive de ratione concionandi* (1535), his rambling manual for the preacher written late in his life, Erasmus similarly advises those charged with addressing a congregation that every sermon, like every other type of oration, has an essential point, a *status*, "to which the speaker refers everything and which the listener has particularly in view" (CWE 68: 581). Aligning the *status* with the "target" or *scopus* of the sermon and reminding the preacher of both its forensic origin and its crucial role in Cicero's *Pro Milone*, Erasmus insists on its usefulness in preventing the sermon from veering off course (CWE 68: 581–82).[7]

For those who have progressed from simpler themes to orations of any kind, including sermons, Thomas Wilson in his *Arte of Rhetorike*

---

see also Leeman-Pinkster, 5: 42–57. On Hermagoras as possibly the first to assign the philosophical question or *thesis* to the student of rhetoric, see Kennedy, *Art of Persuasion in Greece*, 305, who in *Greek Rhetoric under Christian Emperors* notes that "Rhetoricians often claimed that stasis theory was applicable to all kinds of oratory" (85). For Valla's following Quintilian's lead in the broadening of the status questions from forensic oratory to all kinds of inquiry, see Charles McNamara, "*Certum atque confessum*: Lorenzo Valla on the Forensics of Certainty," *Rhetorica* 36 (2018): 244–68. On the extension of the three questions of *status* to the judge in contemporary procedure, see Antoine Braet, "The Classical Doctrine of *Status* and the Rhetorical Theory of Argumentation," *Philosophy and Rhetoric* 20 (1987): 79–93. In *Muses of One Mind: The Literary Analysis of Experience and Its Continuity* (Princeton, 1982), 366–67, Wesley Trimpi aligns the three *status* questions with the formal, cognitive, and judicative intentions of literary discourse.

7. On the relation between *scopus* and *status*, especially in Erasmus's student Melanchthon, see Stillman, *Philip Sidney and the Poetics of Renaissance Cosmopolitanism*, 74–75 and 91–101; he notes that "Melanchthon was not the first in Renaissance Europe to revive the vocabulary of *scopus* and *status*: Erasmus appears to have set the precedent, but it was Melanchthon who developed that vocabulary into a systematic hermeneutic—into a new institutionalized practice of reading and writing" (91). On *scopus* in Melanchthon, see Eden, *Hermeneutics and the Rhetorical Tradition*, 79–89.

similarly defines *status* or "the state" as "the chief ground of a matter and the principal point, whereunto both he that speaketh should refer his whole wit, and they that hear should chiefly mark."[8] Wilson then divides the "states" or "issues" into the *conjectural, legal,* and *juridical,* which answer the questions, respectively, "whether the thing be or no," "what it is," and "what manner of thing it is."[9] Like the orator-in-training, then, both the early modern schoolboy and the preacher-in-training are encouraged to take *status* as the starting point of their rhetorical inventions.

But *status* theory, as we will also see in this chapter, does not always find its way so directly into the Renaissance mainstream. Sometimes its route is more indirect, as when it enters through early Christian theology; and Augustine, a founding father of this theology, offers a particularly telling example of *status* theory's unacknowledged ubiquity. When he famously considers the marvels of human memory in book 10 of the *Confessions,* for instance, Augustine explains that it houses many assumptions or concepts (*res*) untethered to any image rooted in sense perception. Among such *res* or concepts he includes not only literature (*litteratura*) and disputation (*peritia disputandi*) but the different kinds of question (*genera quaestionum*), which, without further comment, he numbers at three:

> When I hear that there are three kinds of question, viz. "Does P exist? What is P? What kind of a thing is P [*an sit, quid sit, quale sit*]?" I retain images of the sounds which constitute these words. I know that they have passed through the air as a noise, and that they no longer exist. Moreover, the ideas [*res ipsas*] signified by those sounds I have not touched by sense-impression, nor have I seen them independently of my mind. I hid in my memory not their images but the realities [*ipsas*].[10]

8. Thomas Wilson, *The Art of Rhetoric,* ed. Peter E. Medine (University Park, PA, 1994), 122.

9. Wilson, *Art of Rhetoric,* 123.

10. Saint Augustine, *Confessions,* trans. Henry Chadwick (Oxford, 1991); for the Latin, I have used the LCL edition, trans. William Watts, 2 vols. (Cambridge, MA, 1912; rpt. 1979), 10.9.16–17. All further references are to these editions and included in the text. The ubiquity of the *status* questions is also illustrated by Augustine's answer to the inquisitive Nebridius in ep. 11 regarding the perplexing relations among the Persons of the Trinity, which, Augustine explains, is analogous to

The originally legal division of questions into *conjectural, definitive,* and *qualitative,* in other words, is so deeply engrained in the minds of both this teacher of rhetoric converted to Christianity and his earliest readers that he invokes them to illustrate his point about human memory without feeling the need to situate them in any context, legal or otherwise.[11] On the contrary, he takes for granted that these three *status* questions are as familiar to his audience as both the poets they read and reread as young boys and the rudiments of dialectic they learned not long thereafter.

Fully in keeping with this rudimentary task of making dialectical divisions, moreover, each of the three familiar questions of the *status* system is eventually divided in turn into a number of topics or places of argument readily available to speaker or writer.[12] While these topical divisions display considerable variability, seeming to multiply over time, their DNA is discernible not only in the most influential

---

the inevitable interaction, noted by Quintilian above, of the three *status* questions (*Nicene and Post-Nicene Fathers,* trans. J. G. Cunningham and ed. Philip Schaff, 14 vols. [Buffalo, 1887], 1: 229–30): "But if you see that whatever is must immediately be *this* or *that,* and must *remain* so far as possible in its own generic form, you see that these Three do nothing in which all have not a part . . . in the three kinds of question above mentioned, although the question raised be whether a thing is or is not, this involves necessarily also both *what* it is (this or that), for of course it cannot be at all unless it be something, and whether it ought to be approved or disapproved of, for whatever *is* is a fit subject for some opinion as to its *quality*; in like manner, when the question raised is *what* a thing is, this necessarily involves both that it *is* and that its quality may be tried by some standard; and in this way, when the question raised is what is the *quality* of a thing, this necessarily involves that the thing *is* and is *something,* since all things are inseparably joined to themselves— nevertheless, the question in each of the above cases takes its name not from all the three, but from the special point towards which the inquirer directs his attention." For Augustine's application of the *status* questions to the Trinity in this letter, see Trimpi, *Muses of One Mind,* 357–61.

11. That current readers do indeed need this context explained is set in high relief both by Chadwick's overly logical translation and by his note (Saint Augustine, *Confessions,* 199), which vaguely identifies the three questions as "evidently three standard questions in the schools, interestingly different from those of Aristotle's *Posterior Analytics* 2.1."

12. Although *De oratore* avoids the more schematic divisions of the handbooks, *Ad Herennium,* for instance, indulges them. As they affect the *status* system, see *Ad Herennium* 1.11.18–1.15.25. On the divisions in Hermagoras's system, see Kennedy, *Art of Persuasion in Greece,* 308–12.

versions of the *status* system, like Cicero's and Quintilian's, but even in its prototypes. Aristotle's *Rhetoric*, for instance, indicates that a defendant might admit to having committed an action without conceding either that he has acted unjustly or that the action fits "the specific terms of an indictment."[13] He might confess, Aristotle points out, "to have 'taken' something but not to have 'stolen' it . . . to have had sexual relations but not to have committed 'adultery' . . . for this reason, [in speaking we] should give definitions of these things: what is theft? . . . what is adultery?" (1.13.9, p. 104).[14] Without fully theorizing the three *status* questions, Aristotle explicitly advises the forensic orator to address the very issues they raise.

In keeping with these prototypical divisions, Aristotle also anticipates the two principal topics of the conjectural status. In the second book of the *Rhetoric*, while considering the commonplaces of past action, he registers the widely accepted view that "if a person had the capacity and the will [to do something] [*kai ei edynato kai ebouleto*], he has done it; for all act when ability to do so coincides with desire; for nothing hinders them" (2.19.18, p. 177). And the same holds true for future action because "that will be for which there is both capacity and motivation [*en dynamei kai boulēsei*]" (2.19.22, p. 177). Will (*boulēsis*) and power (*dynamis*), according to Aristotle, are the conditions of agency;[15] and determining agency is key to asserting or denying that something happened—that is, to answering the first *status* question: *sitne?*

13. Aristotle, *On Rhetoric: A Theory of Civic Discourse*, trans. George A. Kennedy (Oxford, 1991), 1.3.6, p. 49; 1.13.9, p. 104. All subsequent references to this work are cited in the text. For the Greek, I have used *The Rhetoric of Aristotle*, ed. Edward Meredith Cope, 3 vols. (Cambridge, UK, 1877; rpt. New York, 1973).

14. On an Aristotelian *status* system *avant la lettre*, see also 3.17.1, Aristotle, *On Rhetoric*, trans. Kennedy, 265; Cope, *Rhetoric of Aristotle*, 250–51; Ray Nadeau, "Some Aristotelian and Stoic Influences on the Theory of Stases," *Speech Monographs* 26 (1959): 248–54; and Wayne N. Thompson, "Stasis in Aristotle's Rhetoric," *Quarterly Journal of Speech* 58 (1972): 134–41.

15. That will and power continue to define agency well into the eighteenth century is demonstrated by Rousseau in *On the Social Contract*: "Every free action has two causes that come together to produce it. The one is moral, namely, the will that determines the act; the other is physical, namely the power that executes it. When I walk toward an object, I must want to go there. Second, my feet must take me there. A paralyzed man who wants to walk or an agile man who does not want to walk will both remain where they are" (trans. Donald A. Cress [Indianap-

Aristotle's advice to forensic orators regarding the best way to make their cases for and against the occurrence of some past action finds confirmation in rhetorical practice, and especially in the practice of Greece's most famous rhetorician. Putting his widely acclaimed powers of persuasion on display, Gorgias in the person of the hapless Palamedes defends himself against Odysseus's accusation that he conspired with the Trojans against his fellow Greeks. The case is clearly conjectural as Palamedes asserts unequivocally that "I have done no such thing."[16] The arguments in support of his denial focus by his own account on two points (chap. 5): will and power. "For I could not if I wished," he insists, "nor would I if I could [*oute gar boulētheis edynamēn an oute dynamenos ēboulēthēn*], put my hand to such works as these." Turning first to what was in his power—"the capability of performing the action charged" (chap. 6)—Gorgias's Palamedes offers in evidence his lack of opportunity to conspire, including his inability to communicate in a foreign language and to give or receive a pledge (chaps. 7–10). He then turns to his lack of motivation. Discounting one by one potential arguments for wanting power, wealth, honor, or security (chaps. 13–17), he concludes the proof portion of his speech by reaffirming that in regard to betraying his countrymen, "I would not [if I could, nor could if I would]" (*out'an eboulomēn [dynamenos out'an boulomenos edynamēn]*, chap. 21).[17]

Already taking hold in the late fifth- and fourth-century legal arguments for agency, the coupling of *would* and *could*—will and power—resonates throughout the Roman rhetorical manuals most read by early modern Europe. In *De inventione*, for instance, Cicero advises the prosecutor to make the case either that no one other than the defendant had sufficient motive (*causa*) for acting or, if others did have a motive, that no one else had the ability or opportunity to do it. "But if

olis, 2011], 3.1, p. 191). For Nietzsche's treatment of the *status* system, see *Friedrich Nietzsche on Rhetoric and Language*, ed. and trans. Sander L. Gilman, Carole Blair, and David J. Parent (New York, 1989), 94–105.

16. Gorgias, "A Defense on behalf of Palamedes," trans. George Kennedy, in *The Older Sophists*, ed. Rosamond Kent Sprague (Columbia, SC, 1972), chap. 5. All subsequent references to this work are cited in the text. For the Greek, I have used *Die Fragmente der Vorsokratiker*, ed. Hermann Diels and Walter Kranz (Berlin, 1952), 2: 294–303.

17. In *Greek Declamation*, 46n21, D. A. Russell notes the topics of will and power in Gorgias's "Palamedes."

it seems that others, too, had a reason for the crime," Cicero explains, "it must be shown that others lacked the power [*potestas*], or the opportunity [*facultas*], or the desire [*voluntas*]" (*De inv.* 2.7.24). Seconding Cicero's attention to opportunity, Quintilian folds it into the other two principal topics, especially when dealing with legal cases:

> Such considerations [of resources or *facultates*] arise both in deliberative and forensic oratory: in the latter they occur in relation to two questions, namely, whether some given person had the will, and whether he had the power to do the deed [*an voluerit quis, an potuerit*]. (*Instit. orat.* 5.10.50)

And when he returns to conjectural cases in book 7, Quintilian devotes one section to the various elements of *voluntas*, including character, before turning to another on *potestas*, including opportunity; and he does so because "we first ask what the accused intended to do [*voluerit*], next what he was in a position to do [*potuerit*], and lastly what he actually did [*fecerit*]" (7.2.27; cf. 7.2.44). As theorized in Roman rhetoric, then, conjectural cases turn on the two key topics of will and power—*voluntas* and *potestas*—to resolve a controversy over the facts, where a *fact*, from Latin *facere*, pertains to whether or not an agent did or did not do something.

But will and power combine to determine agency in Roman rhetorical practice as well as theory. And the best illustration of this decisive combination in practice, in Quintilian's judgment, is Cicero's *Pro Milone*, the forensic speech most admired by not only ancient but also Renaissance readers.[18] For Cicero begins his defense of his friend

---

18. In *Fam.* 12.8 (*Letters on Familiar Matters*, trans. Aldo S. Bernardo, 3 vols. [Albany, 1975–85; rpt. New York, 2005], 2.154; further references in the text), where Petrarch figures his books as friends, he includes Milo among those who made their "rural sojourn" peaceful, pleasant, and happy. For Petrarch on his books as friends, see Eden, *Renaissance Rediscovery of Intimacy*, 65–69. For the singular popularity of *Pro Milone* among Renaissance readers, who were drawn to its use of *status* by the commentaries, see Mack, *History of Renaissance Rhetoric*, 29–34, 43, 123; C. Joachim Classen, "The Rhetorical Works of George of Trebizond and Their Debt to Cicero," *Journal of the Warburg and Courtauld Institutes* 56 (1993): 75–84, esp. 77–78; and Lorna Hutson, *The Invention of Suspicion* (Oxford, 2007), 124–25. On Melanchthon's commentary, which features the topics of *will* and *power*, see Goyet, *Le sublime du "lieu commun,"* 211–24 and 499–512.

Milo, accused of ambushing and murdering his enemy Clodius, by flagging the *qualitative* basis of the case, even comparing his client to Orestes, whom the Areopagus famously acquitted for justifiably slaying his mother (*Pro Milone* 8).[19] "[T]he point before the court today," Cicero insists, "is not, was Clodius slain—for we admit it—but was the act justifiable or not—an issue which has often been raised in many cases."[20] The justification in this case, however, links back, as Quintilian suggested it might, to a conjectural issue, to establishing the facts: namely, who laid the ambush for whom? Was the perpetrator Milo or Clodius? "Is there then," Cicero asks, "any other question before the court than this—which of the two plotted against the other? Obviously none; if my client plotted against Clodius, let him not go unpunished; if Clodius against Milo, let us be acquitted" (31). With obvious admiration for Cicero's mastery of the art, Quintilian alerts his own readers to the effective shift in *status*; and he does so with the admission that "in the case of Milo, I do not consider that the conflict is raised by the opening questions; but only when the orator devotes all his powers to prove that Clodius lay in wait for Milo and was therefore rightly killed" (*Inst. orat.* 3.6.12; cf. 3.6.93–94). The question of the quality of Milo's act, in this case, depends on a conjecture about a particular fact: did Milo lie in wait for Clodius or didn't he? Cicero's chief strategy for proving this question of agency—that Milo was not the perpetrator of the ambush—is to establish that his client lacked both the *voluntas* and the *potestas* to act, while Clodius, in contrast, was willing and able.

Cicero locates Clodius's willingness to act in his desire to be a praetor unhampered by Milo's restraining consulship. Clodius's praetorship, on the other hand, had no bearing on Milo's political career. Compounding Clodius's unrestrained political ambition was his widely acknowledged hatred for Milo, while Milo, Cicero maintains, harbored no such personal animus against Clodius (35). And while

---

19. On the case of Orestes as paradigmatic for treatments of the *status* system, see, for instance, Quintilian, who claims to "see no reason why I should not use the same example to illustrate this point that has been used by practically all my predecessors" (3.11.4).

20. Cicero, *Pro Milone*, trans. N. H. Watts (Cambridge, MA, rpt. 1979), chap. 31. All subsequent references to this work are cited in the text. For Cicero's use of an argumentative technique found in Gorgias, see Christopher P. Craig, "The Structural Pedigree of Cicero's Speeches *Pro Archia, Pro Milone* and *Pro Quinctio*," *Classical Philology* 80 (1985): 136–37.

Milo's enemies have misleadingly portrayed him as violent, leveraging the assumption shared by the rhetorical manuals that our characters have an impact on our intentions (36), Cicero attests from personal experience to Clodius's Catiline-like recklessness (36–37).[21] Had Milo been motivated to kill Clodius, Cicero conjectures in a shift from will to power, he [Milo] had no shortage of occasions to serve his turn; and these occasions were much more promising than a cumbersome expedition by coach with his wife and her entire retinue (28).[22] As Cicero transitions from the first topic of agency to the second, he lets a single contrary-to-fact protasis about *voluntas* generate a series of apodoses regarding *potestas* in the form of five rhetorical questions, all beginning with the Latin "Potuitne?"—"Could he not have?"

had [Milo] chosen [*voluisset*] to slay [Clodius], how many, how great, how glorious, were his opportunities [*occasiones*]! When he was defending his home and his household gods against Clodius' attacks, could he not have [*Potuitne*] taken a justifiable vengeance? Could he not have done so [*Potuitne*], when that noble citizen and gallant gentleman, Publius Sestius, his colleague, had been wounded? Or [*Potuitne*] when the worthy Quintus Fabricius, proposing a measure for my restoration, was ejected, and a ghastly massacre took place in the forum? Or [*Potuitne*] when the house of that upright and courageous praetor, Lucius Caecilius, was besieged? Could he not have done so [*Potuitne*] on that great day when the law concerning me was proposed, when all Italy, summoned by my welfare and mustered in her thousands, would gladly have acclaimed the glory of such a deed, so that even had Milo been its real author the whole state would have evermore assumed the renown of it as its own? (38)

If Milo had had the *voluntas*, the will or intention, to kill Clodius, Cicero hammers home, time and place would have afforded countless opportunities—opportunities Cicero sums up with *quotiens potestas*

---

21. On the impact of our characters on our intentions and so on our actions, see, for instance, Quintilian 7.2.32–41.

22. At 7.2.42–45, Quintilian invokes Cicero's emphasis on Milo's being so inconveniently accompanied to illustrate the importance of motive as well as opportunity. On their role in *conjectural* questions, see Montefusco, *La dottrina degli "status,"* 60–77, esp. 75.

fuit (41): how great was his power to do so.[23] Following his own rhetorical advice to apprenticing orators, as it were, Cicero undertakes to establish Milo's innocence as well as Clodius's guilt by zeroing in on the two principal topics of the conjectural *status*: will and power. One index of the staying power of these two key topics of conjecture, as mentioned above, is the role they continue to play in rhetorical training well into the sixteenth century.[24] In *The Arte or Crafte of Rhetoryke* (1524), which leans heavily on *Pro Milone* for its illustrations, Leonard Cox explains that "The confyrmacyon of the accuser is fetched out of these places/ wyl/ and power. For these two thynges wyll cause the person that is accused to be greatly suspecte that he had wyl to do the thing that he is accused of/ and that he might well enough bring it to pass."[25] Thomas Wilson's *Art of Rhetoric* lists the same two "places of confirmation to prove things by conjecture": the "will to do evil" and the "power to do evil."[26] And so does Richard Sherry's *A Treatise of Schemes and Tropes.* "Facultie is a power to do the thynge that is taken in hand," Sherry explains, "and in coniectures two thinges speciallye be considered: whether he could or wold."[27] Another index of the staying power of the rhetorical topics of conjecture, will and power, as also mentioned above, is their prominent

23. In *Le sublime du "lieu commun,"* Goyet reminds us regarding Cicero that "la longueur des développements oratoires est nettement proportionelle aux résistances que rencontre l'orateur" (525).

24. For their continued role in legal procedure, see Barbara Shapiro, "Presumptions and Circumstantial Evidence in the Anglo-American Legal Tradition, 1500–1900," in *The Law of Presumptions: Essays in Comparative Legal History*, ed. R. H. Helmholz and W. David H. Sellar (Berlin, 2009), 153–87, who, in her discussion of Lambarde's *Eirenarcha* (1581), a manual for English justices of the peace, claims that "Offenses were to be treated as a 'conjectural state of a cause, to be weighted by precedent, present or subsequent matter.' Each was divided into 'the will to do the act' and the 'power to commit the act' and then subdivided to consider the character and behavior of the accused's parents, his education, and personal characteristics, such as quarrelsomeness" (161–62). For the influence of rhetorical theory, and especially the concept of *voluntas*, on early modern continental legal theory, see Adolfo Giuliani, "Civilian Treatises on Presumptions, 1580–1620," *Law of Presumptions*, 21–71.

25. Leonard Cox, *The Arte or Crafte of Rhetoryke*, ed. Frederic Ives Carpenter (Chicago, 1899), 75. For Cox's illustrations from "Myloes cause," see 44, 48, 71–73, 76–80.

26. Wilson, *Art of Rhetoric*, 125.

27. Richard Sherry, *A Treatise of Schemes and Tropes* (Gainesville, 1961), 85.

place in theological discourse, and especially in the Augustinian theology that underwrites so much Renaissance literature. One iconic example of this Augustinian impact — including the staying power of the topics of conjecture—on the thinking and writing of Renaissance humanists is Petrarch's *Secret*.

AUGUSTINIAN WILL AND POWER IN PETRARCH'S *SECRET*

Sometime between 1342 and 1353, Petrarch wrote a dialogue in three books that details his worldly addictions and the psychological toll they take on him.[28] His interlocutor in this dialogue is Augustine of Hippo, whose *Confessions* Petrarch, on his own account, carried with him wherever he went.[29] In conversation with his favorite church father, Petrarch admits to having two cravings: one is for Laura's love; the other for the constant approbation of his reading public. He also admits to feelings of dejection—we would call them bouts of depression—occasioned by his unfulfilled and ultimately unfulfillable desires. In the course of the conversation, Petrarch has Augustine, his "Augustinus," characterize these cravings as sins, and more precisely as the sins of lust and pride. Encouraged by Augustinus to meditate

28. On the controversy over the dating of the *Secretum*, see Francesco Petrarca, *My Secret Book*, trans. Nicholas Mann (Cambridge, MA, 2016), xiv–xv. All translations of this work are from Mann's edition and are cited in the text. For the Latin, I have used the bilingual text of Ugo Dotti (Rome, 1993), who discusses the dating at vii–x. Part and parcel of this controversy over the date of composition is the double dimension of the dialogue, Stoic and Augustinian. On this question, see Hans Baron, *Petrarch's Secretum: Its Making and Its Meaning* (Cambridge, MA, 1985), esp. 36–37, who finds "islands of Stoicism in a primarily [and originally] Augustinian text." See also Alexander Lee, who, addressing the issue of dating, 70–72, emphasizes Augustine's indebtedness to Stoic philosophy, especially in his earlier works, *Soliloquia* and *De vera religione*, which "as conscious adaptations of Stoic thought, recommend themselves most strongly as potential sources for Petrarch's argument in the first pages of the *Secretum*" (*Petrarch and Saint Augustine: Classical Scholarship, Christian Theology and the Origins of the Renaissance in Italy* [Leiden, 2014], 78). On Stoicism and Augustinianism more generally in the Renaissance, see Bouwsma, "Two Faces of Humanism."

29. On the constant companionship of Petrarch and his Augustine, see *Fam.* 4.1 and *Seniles* 15.7.

on his sinful condition, Petrarch, called "Franciscus" in the dialogue, fully acknowledges his misery.

What Franciscus refuses to acknowledge, however, despite Augustinus's encouragement, is that he, Franciscus, wills his misery. From the beginning of the dialogue to its very last words three books later, Franciscus insists, on the contrary, that he *would* repent and reform if he *could*, that he is indeed a sinner but an unwilling one; and this unwillingness to be miserable, he insists further, is something he shares with every other sinner. "It is well known," Franciscus reports, "that everyone has wanted to lay down this burden of misery, but that very few have succeeded in doing so" (*Hanc miserie sarcinum omnes quidem deponere voluisse, rarissimos autem potuisse, notissimum est, Secretum* 1.2.1). The key distinction in Franciscus's report (obscured somewhat in translation) is between the two perfect infinitives *voluisse* and *potuisse*—between being willing to do something and being able to do it, that is between *will* and *power*: *voluntas* and *potestas*.

Augustinus flatly rejects this would/could distinction. "As for the words that I want you to use," he instructs Franciscus, "they are these: instead of saying 'I can do no more' you should say 'I don't want to do any more'" (*Verba vero, quibus uti te velim, hec sunt: ut ubi 'ultra te non posse' dixisti 'ultra te nolle' fatearis, Secretum* 1.5.3). The problem is not *potestas*, Augustinus asserts, but *voluntas*. As the three days of conversation draw to a close with Franciscus still affirming that he cannot put aside the worldly desires that derail his psychic health and jeopardize his salvation, Augustinus concludes with some amount of frustration tempered by affection, "We are back where we started our argument: you describe your will as weakness" (*In antiquam litem relabimur, voluntatem impotentiam vocas, Secretum* 3.18.8; cf. 1.8.4, 3.4.1). What is actually a failure of will or *voluntas*, Augustinus repeats one last time, Franciscus continues to mistake as a lack of power or *potestas*, as *impotentia*.

Petrarch's literary representation of a divided self plagued by anxiety and depression and paralyzed to the point of inaction builds, in other words, on the topics of the conjectural *status*, with its longstanding forensic analysis of agency. Petrarch's rhetorical and legal training would have familiarized him with this analysis, readily available in Cicero's *De inventione* and the "mutilated" Quintilian.[30] But

---

30. On Petrarch's seven years of legal training, first at Montpelier and then at Bologna, at his father's insistence, see *Sen.* 18.1.7. In *Sen.* 16.1, Petrarch recalls his

Petrarch deploys the conjectural topics in the *Secretum* in ways that also reflect a similar deployment by the rhetorician turned church father in whom he confides his misery. In his monumental *City of God*—which Petrarch's Augustinus takes for granted Franciscus has read (3.16.3)—Augustine addresses the very psychological distress featured in the Petrarchan literary dialogue. Book 14 of the *City of God*, in fact, transforms the Stoicized *aegritudo* of Cicero's *Tusculan Disputations* into its Christianized equivalent, often called *accidia* in Petrarch's day (2.13.1).[31] Whereas the Stoics, on Augustine's account, trace the psychological disturbances that estrange and destabilize us to the ill effects of the body (*City of God* 14.5, 14.7), Augustine himself, preserving the potential purity of the body for its postresurrection prestige, locates the cause of human misery in the will (14.6)—and more precisely in the misalignment or incommensurability of will and power.[32]

This incommensurability, Augustine reminds his readers, was occasioned by the first act of willfulness or disobedience when Adam and

---

father's rescuing two books from a bonfire of his own making, one of which was Cicero's *Rhetorica*, valued as "a prompt for your law studies" (*Letters of Old Age*, trans. Aldo S. Bernardo, Saul Levin, Reta A. Bernardo, 2 vols. [Baltimore, 1992], 2: 601). It is not incidental that this manual provided one of the most influential treatments of the *status* system. In a number of passages, including 3.5.14, 3.6.50, 3.6.58–59, and 3.6.64–65, Quintilian refers to Cicero's *De inventione* as his *rhetorica*. While Quintilian's treatment of *status* in the third and fifth books of the *Institutio oratoria* would have been available to Petrarch, those in the seventh book would not. See P. Lehman, "Die Institutio oratoria des Quintilianus im Mittelalter," *Philologus* 89 (1934): 349–83, esp. 355.

31. At *Secretum* 2.13.1, Augustinus explains that the "dreadful sickness of the spirit" that the *moderni* call *accidia*, the *veteres* or ancients called *egritudo*. On the relation between these two psychological disturbances and Petrarch's role in connecting them, see Siegfried Wenzel, "Petrarch's *Accidia*," *Studies in the Renaissance* 8 (1961): 36–48, and Charles Trinkaus, *The Poet as Philosopher: Petrarch and the Formation of Renaissance Consciousness* (New Haven, 1979), 37–41.

32. In *Aurelii Augustini de rhetorica liber* (*Rhetores Latini Minores*, ed. C. Halm [Leipzig, 1963], 137–51), the author outlines the Hermagorean status system, including the conjectural *status*, but does not detail its two key topics of will and power. On the late Latin rhetorical handbooks that preserve these topics, see Montefusco, *La dottrina degli "status,"* 76–77. In *De spiritu et littera*, chap. 53 (*Later Works*, trans. John Burnaby [Philadelphia, 1955], 237), Augustine stresses the distinction between will and power: "Willing is one thing, ability another; willing does not necessarily imply ability, nor ability willing: we sometimes will what we are not able to do, and sometimes are able to do what we do not will. The Latin words make it plain that will [*voluntas*] is derived from *velle*, power [*potestas*] from

Eve set up their own wills in opposition to God's. In their prelapsarian state, in contrast, Adam and Eve had the power to do whatever they willed (*City of God* 14.5). *Voluntas* was perfectly aligned with *potestas*, and this alignment accounted for our first parents' contentment. "In fact, to put it briefly," Augustine explains:

> in the punishment of that sin the retribution for disobedience is simply disobedience itself. For man's wretchedness is nothing but his own disobedience to himself, so that because he would not do what he could [*noluit quod potuit*], he now wills to do what he cannot [*quod non potest velit*]. For in paradise, before his sin, man could not, it is true, do everything [*non omnia poterat*]; but he could do whatever he wished [*poterat omnia quae volebat*] just because he did not want to do whatever he could not do [*quidquid tamen non poterat, non volebat*]. Now, however, as we observe in the offspring of the first man, and as the Bible witnesses, "man has become like nothingness." For who can list all the multitude of things that a man wishes to do and cannot [*multa quae non potest velit*], while he is disobedient to himself, that is, while his very mind and even his lower element, his flesh, do not submit to his will [*voluntati*]? (14.15)[33]

Like the Roman rhetoricians before him, the converted rhetorician Augustine analyzes agency—here pre- and postlapsarian agency—in terms, familiar from Quintilian, of being willing to do something, being able to do it, and actually doing it. And Augustine extends this rhetorical analysis to our postresurrection condition as well.

For the soul that is saved at the Last Judgment recovers not only its

---

posse: he who wills has *voluntas*, he who is able has *potestas*." On this passage, see Neil W. Gilbert, "The Concept of Will in Early Latin Philosophy," *Journal of the History of Philosophy* 1 (1963): 17–35.

33. *Concerning the City of God against the Pagans*, trans. Henry Bettenson (London, 1972; rpt. 1984), 575–76. For the Latin, I have used the LCL in seven volumes, trans. William M. Green (Cambridge, MA, 1963). For the centrality of the will to Augustinian theology, including the controversies over his view of free will, see, for instance, Albrecht Dihle, *The Theory of Will in Classical Antiquity* (Berkeley, 1982), 123–49, and Eleonore Stump, "Augustine on Free Will," in *The Cambridge Companion to Augustine*, ed. Eleanor Stump and Norman Kretzmann (Cambridge, UK, 2001), 124–47.

fleshly body in all its original purity but, no less paradoxically, its will once again in perfect alignment with its power: it has neither the will nor the power to sin. This everlasting freedom of the postresurrection will is paradoxical, in other words, because, unlike our first freedom in Eden, it lacks the ability to disobey: "The first freedom of will, given to man when he was created upright at the beginning, was an ability not to sin, combined with the possibility of sinning. But this last freedom will be more potent, for it will bring the impossibility of sinning" (22.30, p. 1089). Sandwiched between two states predicated on having a power commensurate with our will, the human condition as lived experience is defined, in contrast, by the constant tension between will and power—the conflict at the root of Petrarch's misery and our own.

But Augustine leverages the two key topics of the conjectural *status* to do more than characterize the human condition. He also invokes will and power to distinguish humanity from divinity—a distinction more central to his analysis in the *City of God* than the one fostered by the ancient philosophers between mortality and immortality. For Augustine insists that God is all-powerful or *omnipotens* precisely in the sense that "he does what he wills, and does not suffer what he does not will" (*faciendo quod vult, non patiendo quod non vult*, 5.10, p. 194). For divinity, then, will and power are commensurate, while humanity is reduced to "nothingness" because we continually will what we are not able to do.

This distinction between divine and human agency underwrites in turn the double causality that Augustine enlists in book 5 of the *City of God* to counter a potentially crippling dilemma. For either God is all-powerful in the so-called chain of causes and humans thereby lack the free will that makes them morally responsible for their actions, or humans genuinely exercise free will and therefore God is not all-powerful. The Ciceronian solution to this dilemma, Augustine reminds us, is to preserve human agency by limiting divine omnipotence, including omniscience. Augustine insists that Christians must reject this solution in favor of one that recalibrates the dynamic between will and power:

> In [God's] will rests the supreme power [*In eius voluntate summa potestas est*] . . . Just as he is the creator of all natures, so he is the giver of all power of achievement, but not of all acts of will [*ita*

omnium potestatum dator, non voluntatum] . . . But all bodies are subject above all to the will of God, and to him all wills also are subject, because the only power they have is the power that God allows them . . . Thus our wills have only as much power as God has willed and foreknown. (5.9, pp. 193–94)

Part and parcel of the incommensurability of human will and power, in other words, is our vulnerability to powers greater than our own. This inability to enforce our will, however, in no way negates the reality of our willing. That willing is rightly our own, while the power of execution belongs to God:

Our wills are ours and it is our wills that affect all that we do by willing, and which would not have happened if we had not willed. But when anyone has something done to him against his will, here, again, the effective power is will, not his own will, but another's. But the power of achievement comes from God. For if there was only the will without the power of realization, that will would have been thwarted by a more powerful will. Even so, that will would have been a will, and the will not of another, but of him who willed, although it was incapable of realization. Hence, whatever happens to man against his will is to be attributed not to the wills of men, or angels, or any created spirits, but to the will of him who gives the power of realization. (5.10, p. 195)

Once again like the Roman rhetoricians before him, Augustine acknowledges that the realization of any action requires will and power. Unlike these rhetoricians, however, Augustine subordinates human agency to divine agency by decoupling the two key factors and distributing them for any action between the divine and human agent. While humans can rightly be considered the agents of their actions through willing them, what Augustine calls the "power of realization" belongs to God. Every action, then, entails at once divine and human causality, including the actions that culminated in the fall of the Roman Empire. Augustine's analysis of this momentous historical event, the focus of the first five books of the *City of God*, undertakes to establish not only that Roman political power lasted only so long as it was backed by God's power but also that God empowered Rome only so long as its willed objectives or intentions deserved this backing. There is one act performed by humans, however, that mirrors divine agency in that will and power are commensurate, and this is the act featured in another Augustinian work informing Petrarch's *Secret.*

In the eighth book of the *Confessions*, Augustine recounts a number of conversions, including his own, that demonstrate that turning toward God is an act unlike any other; and he has one of his converts, the nameless companion of Ponticianus, imply this singularity when he asserts on the brink of converting, "if I wish [*si voluero*] to become God's friend, in an instant I may become that now [*ecce nunc fio*]" (8.6.15). With this assertion, the nameless companion tellingly reduces the three stages of agency featured in Quintilian—being willing, being able, and actually doing—to a single stage that not only excludes *potestas* altogether since will and power are indistinguishable but also collapses willing and doing since the act of conversion is entirely an act of will.

To draw out the implications of this important assertion, Augustine focuses on his own experience, which began in the garden as a conflict of wills—his old will or *vetus voluntas* burdened by bad habits and his new will, a *nova voluntas*, eager to devote itself to serving God (*Confessions* 8.5.10). This conflict within himself Augustine, like Petrarch after him, diagnoses as an *aegritudo animi* (8.9.21), a psychological malady that regularly afflicts the children of Adam (8.9.21, 8.10.22). "Such was my sickness [*Sic aegrotabam*] and my torture," Augustine recalls, "as I accused myself [*accusans memet ipsum*] even more bitterly than usual" (8.11.25). Holding up for scrutiny his morbid psychological condition, Augustine offers a full analysis of this condition in terms of the decisive factors of will and power. For the Christian convert exercises a peculiar agency that is comprehensible only in these fundamentally rhetorical terms.[34]

To showcase this peculiarity, Augustine contrasts the act of con-

34. Without disputing the key factors for Augustine of *will* and *power*, my student Kara Schechtman, in an email correspondence, understands them to operate somewhat differently in regard to both double causality and their commensurability in conversion. Double causality, she argues with support from *City of God* 12.9ff., pertains not to our evil intentions or *mala voluntas*, but only to *bona voluntas*, for which God is the efficient and we the formal cause; and conversion, instead of rendering *power* commensurate with *will*, inverts our normal

version with every other act, especially those involving some bodily motion:

> If I tore my hair, if I struck my forehead, if I intertwined my fingers and clasped my knee, I did that because to do so was my will [*quia volui, feci*]. But I could have willed this and then not done it if my limbs had not possessed the power to obey [*potui autem velle et non facere, si mobilitas membrorum non obsequeretur*]. So I did many actions in which the will to act was not equaled by the power [*tam multa ergo feci, ubi non hoc erat velle quod posse*]. Yet I was not doing what with an incomparably greater longing I yearned to do, and could have done the moment I so resolved. For as soon as I had the will, I would have had a wholehearted will [*et mox, ut vellem, possem, quia mox, ut vellem, utique vellem*]. At this point the power to act [*facultas*] is identical with the will [*voluntas*]. The willing itself was performative of the action [*et ipsum velle iam facere erat*]. Nevertheless it did not happen. The body obeyed the slightest inclination of the soul [*voluntati animae*] to move the limbs at its pleasure more easily than the soul obeyed itself, when its supreme desire [*voluntatem suam magnam*] could be achieved exclusively by the will alone [*in sola voluntate*]. (*Confessions* 8.8.20)

Yet again like the Roman rhetoricians, Augustine understands agency in terms of the conjectural *status*, that is in terms of *velle*, *posse*, and *facere*: having the will to do something, being able to do it, and doing it. Only in the case of conversion, the turning itself is so exclusively voluntary that the instant the whole will, the *tota voluntas* (8.9.21), undertakes the act, power is no longer a factor. Or, to put it another way, as soon as the agent has the will, he has the power, and the act is performed. The *magna voluntas* of conversion, Augustine concludes, requires *sola voluntas*, only the will.

Human agency in this act alone resembles divine agency, defined as the commensurability between *voluntas* and *potestas*. So Augustine, who famously models his own physical and intellectual wanderings after those of Aeneas, draws the distinction between the spiritual

---

condition of limitless will and limited power to a will limited to an alignment with God's will, in effect increasing our power and occasioning a reverse incommensurability.

journey to God and all other epic journeys, including the one that founded Rome:[35]

> But to reach that destination one does not use ships or chariots or feet. It was not even necessary to go the distance I had come from the house to where we were sitting. The one necessary condition, which meant not only going but at once arriving there, was to have the will to go—provided only that the will was strong and unqualified [*nihil erat aliud quam velle ire, sed velle fortiter et integre*]. (8.8.19)

Augustine's analysis of this singular act of spiritual conversion, then, takes as its point of departure his analysis of all the other actions performed by the sons and daughters of Adam in its concentration on will and power. Inheriting this concentration from ancient rhetoric, Augustine adapts it to his theological agenda. And this theological adaptation underwrites Petrarch's literary dialogue.

Early in the first book of the *Secret*, Petrarch has Augustinus rehearse this famous episode in the garden in the interest of ministering to Franciscus's psychological distress. He reminds Franciscus of how miserable he, Augustine, was, how he tore his hair, beat his breast, clasped his knees, and wept until a deep meditation settled his will. "From that moment onward," Augustinus recalls,

> since I wanted it, I could do it instantly [*Itaque postquam plene volui, illicit et potui*] and so was transformed happily, and remarkably quickly into another Augustine, whose unfolding story you know, unless I'm mistaken, from my *Confessions*. (*Secretum* 1.5.5)

The story Augustinus retells here is one of a fragmented will becoming whole and a whole will becoming power—a story of the full commensurability between *voluntas* and *potestas* in the act of turning toward God. But neither Augustine's original account nor Augustinus's

---

35. On Augustine's use of the *Aeneid*, see John O'Meara, "Augustine the Artist and the Aeneid," in *Mélanges offerts à Mademoiselle Christine Mohrmann*, ed. L. J. Engels et al. (Utrecht, 1963), 253–61, and Camille Bennett, "The Conversion of Vergil: The *Aeneid* in the *Confessions*," *Revue des Études Augustiniennes* 34 (1988): 47–69.

retelling redirects the outcome of Petrarch's literary dialogue, which portrays Franciscus firmly in the grip of fragmentation and so failing to grasp the theologically recalibrated dynamic between being willing and being able. Franciscus continues to misapprehend the salvific relation between *would* and *could*.[36]

The depth of this misapprehension is reflected in turn in Franciscus's continued misdiagnosis of the problem. "I consider that the punishment I have been given because I didn't want to stand up when I could [*quia dum stare possem nolui*]," Franciscus laments, "is to find that now that I do want to get up again, I can't [*assurgere nequeam dum velim*]" (*Secretum* 1.5.1). Augustinus responds to this misunderstanding by engaging Franciscus in the complexities of willing. One aspect of this complexity concerns the will's unusual relation to temporality. For there is no difference, Augustinus insists, between willing (*velle*) and having willed (*voluisse*), despite the shift in tense (1.5.2).[37] When the will is firm, it withstands without alteration the passage of time. On the other hand, willing comes in various degrees of intensity, from the halfhearted or weak will, which lacks constancy, to one that is whole, strong, and unchanging.

At the end of the first book of the *Secret*, Augustinus characterizes this whole will as *desiderium* and assures Franciscus that it is a necessary ingredient in the cure for what ails him:

> But two elements are in play in human actions [*sed in actionibus humanis duo versantur*], and if one of them is missing, any outcome

36. In "The Figure of the Reader in Petrarch's *Secretum*," *PMLA* 100 (1985):154–66, Victoria Kahn similarly locates the source of Franciscus's failure in his divided will but goes on to locate the source of this division in turn in his reading practice. Unlike Augustine, who represents the ideal, passive reader, the "Petrarchan persona" represents "the willful (mis)reader who fails to imitate his master" (142). In *The Unrepentant Renaissance: From Petrarch to Shakespeare to Milton* (Chicago, 2011), 61–62, Richard Strier reads the *Secretum* as the failure of Socratic ethics and as Petrarch's "resistance to moral education."

37. In the same email correspondence noted above (n. 34), Schechtman reads this puzzling exchange differently, with support from the episode under the fig tree, to feature two shifts: one from a "temporality-independent" weak will fixated on the past in contrast to a strong will rooted in the present/future; the other from objects of desire subject to time to those belonging, in contrast, to eternity.

is bound to be blocked. Therefore your will [*voluntas*] should be at the ready, and so strong that it may rightly earn the name of desire [*desiderii vocabulam*]. (*Secretum* 1.14.3)

While explicitly identifying here one of the two necessary elements for the performance of an action, Augustinus neglects to mention the other. One plausible explanation for this oversight is that he takes for granted, as Augustine himself did regarding the three *status* questions in the *Confessions* (see above), that Franciscus (and we) need no reminder that human agency requires not just will but power.[38] Both the rhetorical tradition and an Augustinian theology rooted in that tradition, as we have seen, confirm this requirement.

Whereas the rhetoricians consider these two topics of the conjectural *status*, will and power, complementary, however, Augustine realigns them in light of God's omnipotence, including His saving grace.[39] If only Franciscus can muster the will, Augustinus would have him believe, God will assuredly grant him the power (*Secretum* 1.14.2). But Franciscus fails to summon this belief. Until the very end

38. On E. Fenzi's observation that Augustinus's claim looks back to Boethius, *De cons. phil.* 4.2.4 ("Duo sunt, quibus omnis humanorum actuum constat effectus, voluntas scilicet ac potestas, quorum si alterutrum desit, nihil est, quod explicari queat"), see Ugo Dotti, *Secretum* (Rome, 1993). For a different reading of the two elements, see Robert R. Edwards, "Petrarchan Narratives: Representation and Hermeneutics," *Modern Language Notes* 130 (2015): 1–23, who identifies them as will and desire (15–16), even though he emphasizes the influence of Boethius's *Consolatio* on the *Secretum*. On Franciscus's *noluntas*, see Dotti, xiii–xv. At *Fam.* 17.10 (trans. Bernardo, 3.32–33), Petrarch rehearses *Confessions* 8.8.20 before voicing his anxiety that "I may not want wholly what I wish in part and, unless I am mistaken, what I desire to will fully." See also Seneca, *Ep.* 116.8, who warns, "nolle in causa est, non posse praetenditur."

39. Indeed, one might have expected "the two elements in play" in a work about the human condition written in Europe during the fourteenth century to be faith and grace, but as Trinkaus notes in *The Poet as Philosopher* regarding this dialogue (61), "Petrarch has not talked of grace. Here he presents the *desiderium virtutis* as something that must have great power and depth within the soul so as to drive out all other desires." In *In Our Image and Likeness: Humanity and Divinity in Italian Humanist Thought* (2 vols. [Chicago, 1970], 1: 28–41), on the other hand, Trinkaus sees Petrarch on a continuum between Augustine and Luther on the question of grace. In *Petrarch and Saint Augustine* (91–93), Lee rejects this position, identifying Petrarch with the early, pre-Pelagian Augustine.

of the conversation, he perseveres in his misguided understanding of *would* and *could*. He insists that he *can't*, rather than that he *won't*, put off his worldly addictions. Despite both what he has read about Augustine's conversion and what he has just heard from Augustinus himself, Franciscus still does not grasp the decisive shift in the two principal topics of conjecture. In other words, he lacks faith in the saving dynamic of a will turned to power. Franciscus's inability to understand this shift, however, does not prevent Petrarch, whose Augustinus urgently advances this understanding, from making it a centerpiece of his literary exploration of the self-imposed miseries of the human condition as reflected in his own.[40]

CICERONIAN *STATUS* IN *DE ORATORE* AND *BOOK OF THE COURTIER*

Cicero's *De inventione* and Quintilian's *Institutio oratoria*, as we have seen, are among the ancient rhetorical manuals available to Petrarch that feature the two conjectural topics of will and power.[41] Cicero's more mature *De oratore*, on the other hand, refrains from openly showcasing these and other details of *status* theory in an effort to distance itself, as noted earlier, from the kind of rhetorical handbook dismissed by Crassus as too trivial to require attention. Despite Crassus's refusal to belabor the obvious, however, he and Antonius do return on a number of occasions to the *status* system and especially to its three fundamental questions. With each return, as suggested above, they substantially enlarge the purview of these questions.

In book 2, for instance, Antonius makes the case for expanding the *status* system to include not only deliberative and epideictic as well as forensic concerns but also general or indefinite as well as definite

---

40. In *Petrarch's Secretum* (248), Baron advises reading the dialogue as "a book of intimate confessions" rather than as "a piece of literary art," while Nicholas Mann, "From Laurel to Fig: Petrarch and the Structure of the Self," *Proceedings of the British Academy* 105 (2000): 17–42, cautions against underestimating the literariness of even the most seemingly autobiographical works of the so-called "father of humanism."

41. On the availability of these two texts, see the introduction above and Burrow, *Imitating Authors*, 141–46.

questions.[42] "For everything that can be a matter of dispute between people," Antonius asserts,

> whether the case turns on a criminal charge as when it involves some wrongdoing, or on a civil controversy as when it involves an inheritance, or on deliberation as when it involves war, or on a personality as when it involves praise, or on a theoretical discussion as when it involves the way to live—the question must either be about what was done, is being done, or will be done; or about the character of the matter involved; or about the name that should be applied to it [*aut quid factum sit, aut fiat, futurumve sit, quaeratur, aut quale sit, aut quid vocetur*]. (2.104)

Serving well beyond the confines of the law courts, in other words, the three status questions settle points of contention in the Senate, in the Assemblies, and even in the schools of the philosophers. Among the philosophical questions they address, Antonius tellingly flags one that preoccupies the entire company assembled at Crassus's villa: what is an art (*quid sit ars*) (2.108)? This *quaestio*, as we will see, sets the course for no small part of the conversation.

Fully attuned to Antonius's more capacious view of *status* theory in book 2, Crassus revisits it in book 3, concluding his own reformulation with the unconvincing reassurance that "our two treatments are identical" (*eadem enim sunt membra in utriusque disputationibus*, *De orat.* 3.119). In fact, Crassus reformulates *status* theory (3.111–19) in keeping with his own earlier statement in book 1 about what all arts have in common: their dialectical divisions into genus and species— the very divisions that underwrite definition. "Nearly all subjects that are nowadays covered by a systematic art were once disconnected and scattered," Crassus claims, before going on to explain what belongs to the art of oratory in particular and how that art was first formed:

> in our subject here (the theory of speaking [*ipsa ratione dicendi*]), devising what to say, style, arrangement, memory, and delivery, were once, it seems, in disorder and scattered far and wide. And

---

42. For the difference between the historical Antonius's *libellus* on *status*, mentioned by Quintilian (3.1.19), and the *status* theory of Cicero's Antonius, see Leeman-Pinkster, 5: 51.

so a certain art was invoked from outside, from some different branch of knowledge that the philosophers claim is entirely theirs, in order to cement together material that has previously been disjointed and kept apart, and to tie it together with the help of a certain method [*ratione quadam*]. (1.187–88)

Like all arts, in other words, the *ars oratoris* (also called the *ratio dicendi*) owes its architecture, including the five fundamental *officia*, to the organizational art of the dialectician.[43] In keeping with this appreciation in book 1 of the crucial role of the genus and species of dialectic, Crassus's treatment of *status* in book 3 divides each of the three questions into kinds and subkinds, without forfeiting, by its own account, what he calls the "individual branches" or *membra*, by which he means presumably the three principal kinds of question: *conjectural, definitive*, and *qualitative* (*De orat.* 3.119).[44]

But Cicero's *De oratore* does more than offer its interlocutors the leisurely opportunity to exchange views of this essential part of rhetorical training as theorized in the handbooks and practiced by the orators. As the two days of conversation unfold, these same interlocutors assembled at Crassus's villa demonstrate how effectively the three *status* questions combine to explore the controversies closest to their hearts: is there an art of oratory? how is it defined? what kind of art is it? Keeping firmly in mind the inevitable overlap and even interplay of these three questions, Cicero's Crassus and Antonius do their best to meet the challenges of their young admirers Sulpicius and Cotta to shed some light on the very art to which they have all committed not only their livelihoods but, in some cases, their lives.[45]

43. At *De oratore* 1.162–65, Scaevola invokes the architectural metaphor to describe Crassus's rhetorical theory.

44. At 5: 9, Leeman-Pinkster provides a schematic of Crassus's version of *status* theory. For the appropriation by philosophers of rhetorical *status*, see Leeman-Pinkster, 5: 49–57, where they refer to Crassus's kinds and subkinds as "status-based subdivisions" (57). On dialectic as the bond that holds all the arts together, see Trimpi, *Muses of One Mind*, 282–84.

45. According to May and Wisse (Cicero, *On the Ideal Orator*, 23), (1) whether or not rhetoric is an art was of little concern to Cicero in *De oratore* and (2) his demand that the orator "should have philosophical knowledge has no moral background" (25). For reasons that should be clear by the end of this chapter, I do not agree with either of these claims. In addition, at 2.17.36, Quintilian cites *De oratore* 2.30 on the question of whether or not rhetoric is an art. In *The State of Speech*:

Taking his cue from Antonius, Sulpicius puts the *conjectural* question to Crassus in its clearest form, wondering early in the dialogue, "what is your opinion about the point Antonius discussed just now? Do you believe there is such a thing as an art of speaking [*artem aliquam esse dicendi*]?" (1.102). Moments earlier (1.85) Antonius introduced the *conjectural* question in the context of a debate he had heard years ago in Athens between the Academic philosopher Charmadas and the politician Menedemus. Taking his own cue from Plato's strategy of setting his discourse at several removes, Cicero has Antonius recall Charmadas's persuasive argument for the extreme position that "an art of speaking did not exist at all" (*nullam artem esse dicendi*, 1.90).[46] In response to this dispute on *conjectural* grounds—is there or isn't there an art of oratory?—Crassus demurs, setting in motion key claims that he and others will champion as the dialogue continues:

> I believe that there is no art of speaking at all [*dicendi aut nullam artem*], or only a very insubstantial one; but that the entire con-

---

Rhetoric and Political Thought in Ancient Rome (Princeton, 2007), Joy Connolly considers this one of the two central questions of *De oratore*, "dramatically posed in the prologues and opening scenes" (116). Similarly, Charles Guérin, in "Définir l'*ars dicendi*: enjeux et méthode de la réflexion cicéronienne dans le *De oratore*," *La rhétorique au miroir de la philosophie*, ed. Barbara Cassin (Paris, 2015), 175–90, notes that "La question de l'existence de l'*ars* et de son statut va donc être reprise tout au long du traité" (181). In *The Roman World of Cicero's* De oratore (Oxford, 2004), Elaine Fantham briefly alludes to the homology between Crassus's three theoretical questions and the Hermagorean *status* questions: "Crassus distinguishes three forms of theoretical question which correspond fairly closely to the three Hermagorean issues (Greek *staseis*, Latin *status*) of the law courts: questions of fact, 'does wisdom exist in man?' or definition, 'what is it?' or of implication, 'is it ever the act of a good man to lie?'" (258). And in "Platonic Elements in the Structure of Cicero's *De oratore* Book 1," *Rhetorica* 6 (1988): 237–58, Eckart Schütrumpf suggests, without mentioning the *status* system, that Cicero is aware of the *quid-quale* distinction, which nevertheless, he argues, plays a lesser role in *De oratore* than in the *Gorgias* (245–46).

46. On the Platonic elements in *De oratore*, see, for instance, Fantham, *Roman World of Cicero's* De oratore, 49–77; W. Görler, "From Athens to Tusculum: Gleaning the Background of Cicero's *De oratore*," *Rhetorica* 6 (1988): 215–35; Vittorio Hösle, "Cicero's Plato," *Weiner Studien* 121 (2008): 145–70; William Stull, "Deus ille noster: Platonic Precedent and the Construction of the Interlocutors in Cicero's *De oratore*," *Transactions of the American Philological Association* 141 (2011): 247–63.

troversy is one between learned men, based on a fight over a mere word. For if art is defined in the way that Antonius described a little while ago, as consisting of matters that are thoroughly scrutinized and clearly known, and that are beyond the control of mere opinion, but grasped by exact knowledge, then it seems to me that an art of oratory [*ars oratoris*] does not exist. After all, every aspect of our judicial and political speaking is variable and adapted to an ordinary and popular way of thinking. If, however, the procedures that have been followed in the actual practice of speaking have been observed and recorded by skilled and experienced people, and described through definitions, and clarified by division into classes and subclasses—and all this has obviously been possible,—I don't see why this shouldn't be called an art, if not according to that precise definition [*illa subtili definitione*], then at least in the ordinary sense in which we use the word. At any rate, whether this is an art or just a semblance of an art, we must certainly not neglect it, but at the same time we should realize that certain other things are more important for the attainment of eloquence. (1.107)

Crassus's answer to the *conjectural* question (*sitne?*) regarding the art of oratory, then, is at once yes and no.[47]

With his demurral in book 1, Crassus anticipates not only his later defense of dialectical division—here "classes and subclasses" (*genera* and *partes*)—but Antonius's more capacious view of *status*, linking the *conjectural* to the *definitive* status and the particular to the general question. For any inquiry into whether or not there is an art of oratory requires asking what that art might be—asking, that is, for a definition. *Sitne*, in other words, gives way to *quid sit?* At the same time, such an inquiry into whether or not an art of oratory—that is, a particular art—exists requires asking whether or not in a more general sense there is such a thing as an art. Furthermore, Crassus's demurral raises the related question, addressed by Socrates in his conversation with Phaedrus, regarding whether art is a sufficient or merely

---

47. At 1.246, as part of his refutation of Crassus's position on the role of civil law in oratory, Antonius mocks this demurral: "you talk about the easiness of this art [of oratory], while you concede it is still really no art at all, but some day will become an art, if someone will at some time first have learned another art in order to be able to fashion this into art."

a necessary condition of eloquence. On this open question, Crassus suggests that natural talent and practice are among the things he considers more important.[48]

In book 2, Antonius builds on this suggestion as he resumes the focus on oratory as an art. Taking as his point of departure a variation on the Socratic triad of art, natural talent, and practice, Antonius "grants pride of place to natural ability" or talent (*De orat.* 2.147–48) before further subordinating art to an assortment of practices he sums up as *diligentia* (2.149–50)—a diligence that should be concealed. "Indeed, between natural ability [*ingenium*] and diligence [*diligentiam*]," he concludes, "there is very little room left for art" (2.150)—a conclusion that does not stop Antonius from offering a definition that would garner Crassus's approval. For Crassus has already insisted that good definitions pinpoint "features that are proper to the object we wish to define" (1.189). Accordingly, Antonius defines the art of oratory in terms of what it does not share with any other art—that is, in terms of what belongs to it alone:

> For if there is any other art that professes knowledge of either creating or choosing words; or if anyone but the orator is said to shape discourse and give it variety and distinction with, as it were, special features of thought and speech; or if any method is taught except by this art alone for finding arguments or thoughts or finally for the distribution and ordering of material—then let us admit that what is professed by this art of ours belongs to, or is shared in common with, some other art. But if the teaching of such methods is characteristic only of this art, then it is the property of this art alone; and this is no less true because some representatives of other arts have expressed themselves well. (2.36)

Reaffirming both Crassus's recollection of his lessons at school (1.139) and his account of the fragmentary pieces of oratory first assembled by dialectic (1.187–88), Antonius reverts to the traditional precepts of the handbooks, with their attention to invention, disposition, and

---

48. On this foundational triad that looks back to Plato's *Phaedrus* (269D), see Paul Shorey, "Phusis, Melete, Episteme," *Transactions of the American Philological Association* 40 (1909): 185–201, and May and Wisse, in Cicero, *On the Ideal Orator*, 27.

style, when considering the definitive question—*quid sit?*—in regard to the *ars oratoris*.[49]

In *De oratore*, then, not only do the principal interlocutors comment on *status* theory as the part of the orator's art that determines the point of contention between litigants, but they put this theory into practice in an effort to settle two controversial questions concerning the art of oratory itself: does it exist? how is it defined? Whereas books 1 and 2 focus on conjecture and definition, book 3 sets its sights on the question of quality: what kind of art is it? just or unjust, worthwhile or worthless? In keeping with the inevitable overlap of these questions and the unsystematic flow of conversation, however, Antonius first raises the issue of quality in book 2 in the conventional terms associated with Cato's orator: the good man experienced in speaking (*vir bonus dicendi peritus*). Such a man, Antonius affirms, confers value on the entire community (2.85). At the end of book 2, Antonius also anticipates the unconventional way Crassus will approach the issue of quality in book 3; and he does so by making a move to erase two basic divisions that the handbooks enforce. Whereas they routinely treat confirmation and refutation as two separate parts of the speech, Antonius questions this separation (2.331). He also challenges the division between deliberative and epideictic oratory. While the handbooks as far back as Aristotle's *Rhetoric* consider them separately, Antonius looks to minimize the difference between them (2.333). In preparation for Crassus's turn to the third *status* question in book 3, Cicero has Antonius blunt the edges of the handbooks' distinctions, finding common ground instead.

Like Antonius, Crassus too, on one occasion, reverts to the Catonian formula, tethering the faculty of eloquence to the moral fiber of the speaker. "And the greater the power [*vis*] is," Crassus warns on behalf of the *vir bonus*:

49. Crassus's definition of the orator, as distinct from his art, relies on this same division of the activity into five *officia*: "Accordingly, then, if we want to capture the true meaning of the word 'orator' in a complete definition, it is my opinion that an orator worthy of this grand title is he who will speak on any subject that occurs and requires verbal exposition in a thoughtful, well-disposed, and distinguished manner, having accurately memorized his speech, while also displaying a certain dignity of delivery" (1.64). According to May and Wisse, in Cicero, *On the Ideal Orator*, Cicero's emphasis on the orator rather than the "discipline" characterizes the "special nature of his position" (26).

the more necessary it is to join it to integrity [*probitate*] and the highest measure of good sense [*prudentia*]. For if we put the full resources of speech at the disposal of those who lack these virtues, we will certainly not make orators of them, but will put weapons in the hands of madmen. (3.55)

Elsewhere (in fact, everywhere else), Crassus replaces this traditional position with a more unorthodox approach that addresses the question of quality in terms of wholeness or integration (rather than integrity or *probitas*). In support of this approach, Crassus contends that we can understand a thing's quality only by imagining its perfected form (*vis enim et natura rei nisi perfecta ante oculos ponitur, qualis et quanta sit intelligi non potest*, 3.85). This contention underwrites not only Crassus's understanding of quality in book 3 but Cicero's portrait of the *orator perfectus* throughout the dialogue.

Crassus prepares his audience for this novel approach by opening book 3 with a commonplace in praise of the unity or wholeness that extends to everything in the universe, including speech (3.19–24). "For, as I said yesterday," Crassus reminds his listeners, "and as Antonius indicated at several points in the morning's conversation, eloquence forms a unity [*una est enim . . . eloquentia*], into whatever realms or areas of discourse it travels" (3.22–23). Part and parcel of this all-pervasive unity is the integration of *res* and *verba*, wisdom and eloquence, philosophy and rhetoric.[50] In his own discursive practices, Socrates exemplifies this integration, effecting that "amazing sort of communion [*societas*] between speaking and understanding" (3.73). But Socrates also deserves blame for dismantling this "communion" since he "split apart the knowledge of forming wise opinions [*sapienter sentiendi*] and of speaking with distinction [*ornate dicendi*], two things that are, in fact, tightly linked" (3.60). Holding Socrates responsible for the rupture "between the tongue and the brain" (3.61), Crassus invites his listeners to imagine a time before Socrates when the liberal arts (*bonae artes*) were unified not only among themselves but with the virtues (3.136).

---

50. For the integration of philosophy and rhetoric in the ideal orator as a Ciceronian innovation, see Leeman-Pinkster, 4: 97–101 and 5: 50–54. For the quarrel between the philosophers and the rhetoricians, see May and Wisse, in Cicero, *On the Ideal Orator*, 20–26.

To assess the quality of the art of oratory—that is, to judge it as good or bad, worthy of praise or censure—one must, according to Crassus, consider its fully integrated form. Like the orator himself, in other words, the art of oratory derives its quality from its perfection. Far from ignoring the ethical dimension of the *ars oratoris*, then, Crassus's more integrative approach to the *qualitative* question deepens this dimension beyond the shallow precepts of the handbooks. Whereas the art of oratory they teach can be reduced to a handful of technical dos and don'ts, the activity that emerges from the two days of conversation at Tusculum is meant to transcend anything that Crassus learned in school. "The real power of eloquence," he proclaims regarding this transcendence,

> is so enormous that its scope includes the origin, essence, and transformations of everything: virtues, moral duties, and all the laws of nature that govern human conduct, characters, and life. It establishes traditions, laws, and legal arrangements, governs the state, and addresses with distinction and copiousness all questions belonging to any area whatever. (3.76)

Taking an admittedly extreme position regarding oratory's remit, Crassus nevertheless offers it as the choiceworthy alternative to both the Socratic rejection of rhetoric in the *Gorgias* and its trivialization in the manuals. Neither Socrates nor the handbooks acknowledge orators as "the real owners of the things that these people say about justice, about moral duty, about establishing and governing communities, actually about the whole of the conduct of life, and yes, even about the explanation of nature" (3.122). If there is an art of oratory, Crassus seems to say, it becomes worthwhile or even justifiable only insofar as it enables its practitioners to understand deeply and express skillfully whatever pressing issues they encounter. The joint effort of Antonius and Crassus in Cicero's dialogue to deploy the *status* system in an expansive way unheard of in the young Cicero's rhetorical theory marks one notable instance of the more capacious view of the *ars oratoris* in *De oratore*.[51]

---

51. In *Muses of One Mind* (251), Trimpi notes the agreement of Crassus and Antonius on an issue as an index of the shift in attitude from *De inventione* to *De*

Openly modeled on Cicero's *De oratore*, Castiglione's *Book of the Courtier* takes its final shape in four books as a full embrace of this more expansive view of the *status* system both practiced and preached in the Ciceronian dialogue.[52] Distancing itself, like *De oratore*, from the many handbooks that peddle precepts ("the which for the most part is woont to bee observed in teaching of any thing whatsoever it bee" [Hoby 16]), the *Book of the Courtier* focuses instead on the fully integrated, perfected form of courtiership.[53] With his suggestion for the evening's entertainment, Federico Fregoso makes this focus on perfection, on the ideal, explicit. "I would have such a pastime for this night," he suggests,

> that of the company might bee picked out, who should take it in hand to shape in words a good Courtier, specifying all such conditions and particular qualities, as of necessitie must bee in him that deserveth this name [*di formar con parole un perfetto cortegiano, esplicando tutte le condicioni e particular qualità che si richieggono a chi merita questo nome*]. (1.12, Hoby 19, Maier 100)

---

oratore—in this case on the relevance of the indefinite question to rhetorical inquiry: "The close agreement in thought and phrasing between Cicero's two chief protagonists on the kinds of indefinite questions proper to rhetoric makes clear what he has added to the views expressed in the *De inventione*. In distinguishing practical theses, which presuppose a relationship between definite and indefinite questions, from speculative theses, which ignore it, Cicero has not only continued to reject the mutual exclusiveness of questions with regard to their respective subject matters. He has also provided a method of moving from one type of question to the other within any *single* subject matter, thereby turning a 'material' distinction into a 'methodological' one." See also 247–48.

52. On the addition of a fourth book, see Amedeo Quondam, "On the Genesis of the *Book of the Courtier*," trans. Paul Bucklin, in Baldesar Castiglione, *The Book of the Courtier*, ed. Daniel Javitch (New York, 2002), 283–95. On *De oratore* as the model for the *Book of the Courtier*, see Hoby, who affirms that "Castilio hath followed Cicero" (3), and Wayne A. Rebhorn, *Courtly Performances: Masking and Festivity in Castiglione's "Book of the Courtier"* (Detroit, 1978), 154–55. On the differences between these two dialogues, see Daniel Javitch, *Poetry and Courtliness in Renaissance England* (Princeton, 1978), 18–49.

53. On the handbooks for courtly behavior that form the backdrop of Castiglione's dialogue, see Rebhorn, *Courtly Performances*, 12–13. And see Brian Vickers, "Some Reflexions on the Rhetoric Textbook," in *Renaissance Rhetoric*, ed. Mack, 81–102.

With this suggestion, Federico Fregoso recalls Crassus's reminder, noted above, that we can more readily understand the quality of anything if we can imagine its perfected form. Like Crassus, in other words, Federico aligns the ideal with the question of the third *status*: *quale sit?* Also like Crassus, Federico acknowledges the frequent overlap of the *status* questions—in this case, *what* a thing is or its definition and *what kind* of thing it is, its quality.[54] Routinely labeled a Ciceronian dialogue by virtue of its historical setting and characters as well as its disputatious structure in search of an ideal, the *Book of the Courtier* owes at least some portion of its Ciceronian pedigree to its expansive view and subtle use of *status*.

Unlike the interlocutors in Cicero's dialogue, however, those at the court of Urbino do not take up *status* theory as a topic of conversation. Their total neglect of this issue is not only not surprising; it is predictable in light of the *decorum* that underwrites the art of courtiership they practice. For indecorous behavior, which includes not only raising inappropriate topics but also pursuing fitting ones in an overly specialized way, routinely provokes censure from Emilia Pia and the others.[55] But if Castiglione's interlocutors do not debate the fine points of Hermagorean *status*, they do, like their counterparts in *De oratore*, discuss in some detail whether or not there is an art of courtiership and, if so, how this art should be defined. They do, in other words, address directly both the *conjectural* and the *definitional* dimensions of the subject of their collective inquiry.

The defining property of courtiership, Ludovico assures the assembled company, is grace, prompting Cesare Gonzaga to wonder whether it can be achieved through the industry of art or whether it

54. At 2.15.1–2, Quintilian directly addresses this overlap in the context of the paradigmatic art of rhetoric: "The first question which confronts us is 'What is rhetoric?' Many definitions have been given; but the problem [*quaestionem*] is really twofold. For the dispute [*dissentio*] turns either on the quality [*qualitate*] of the thing itself or on the meaning of the words in which it is defined. The first and chief disagreement on the subject is found in the fact that some think that even bad men may be called orators, while others, of whom I am one, restrict the name of orator and the art itself to those who are good." On the overlap of the *status* questions and the alignment of quality with form, see Augustine's letter to Nebridius, discussed above (n. 10).

55. On this censure of inappropriate, including overly specialized, topics, see Rebhorn, *Courtly Performances*, 156. On decorum, see Rebhorn, *Courtly Performances*, 118–19.

is, pure and simple, a gift of nature (1.24). This opposition between art and nature (Lat. *ars/ingenium, natura*; Ital. *arte/ingenio, natura*), so familiar from *De oratore*, inevitably, here as in the ancient dialogue, raises the *conjectural* question: is there an art of courtiership given that "it bee (in maner) in a proverbe, that Grace is not to be learned?" (1.25, Hoby 44, Maier 122). Without denying the importance of natural talent, Ludovico posits that there is such an art and offers a number of rules or precepts for its practice. These rules are brazenly appropriated from the very rhetorical handbooks that are so freely disparaged.

Among these precepts is imitation (1.26), and especially imitation of multiple models, treated at length by Cicero and Quintilian.[56] No less important is *sprezzatura*. Although the term is new, this *regula universalissima* against affectation (1.26, Hoby 46, Maier 124) is grounded in two ancient rhetorical precepts: the paradox of art concealing art (*ars celare artem*) and the oxymoron of diligent negligence (*diligens negligentia*), understood as "to minde any other thing than that a man is in hand withall" (1.27, Hoby 47, Maier 125–26).[57] Both Ludovico and Federico agree that the courtier must dissemble "the studie and paines that a man must needs take in all thinges that are well done" (2.12, Hoby 100, Maier 208). The first precept reaches as far back as Aristotle's *Rhetoric* (3.2.4); the second rehearses Cicero's instructions in the *Orator* (78). Ludovico's two exemplars of *sprezzatura*, coyly referred to as "some most excellent Orators" (1.26, Hoby 46, Maier 124), are none other than Cicero's Crassus and Antonius in *De oratore*. Recognized by Ludovico and everyone else as a master of *diligens negligentia*, Cicero's Antonius, as we have seen, goes so far as to wonder if the orator's *ingenium* and *diligentia* render art unnecessary. In *De oratore* as in the *Book of the Courtier*, in other words, the *conjectural* question continues to dog the conversation.

The third rhetorical principle underwriting the art of courtiership,

---

56. On the dispute over imitating a single model in contrast to multiple models, see Martin L. McLaughlin, *Literary Imitation in the Italian Renaissance: The Theory and Practice of Literary Imitation in Italy from Dante to Bembo* (Oxford, 1995; rpt. 2001), esp. 5–7 and 191–227, and Burrow, *Imitating Authors*.

57. On the two rhetorical principles and their relation to *sprezzatura*, see Eduardo Saccone, "*Grazia, Sprezzatura* and *Affettazione* in the *Courtier*," in *Castiglione: The Ideal and the Real in Renaissance Culture*, ed. Robert W. Hanning and David Rosand (New Haven, 1983), 45–67. On its relation to imitation, see Burrow, *Imitating Authors*, 183–91.

already noted above, is *decorum*.[58] In the second book of Castiglione's dialogue, Federico leaves no doubt about the affiliation of this unnamed rule to that of the rhetorical handbooks. After reinforcing Ludovico's call for *sprezzatura*, Federico promotes both speaking and acting decorously as taking into account all the particularities of the occasion. "Afterwarde let him consider well what the thing is he doth or speaketh," Federico advises concerning the courtier:

> the place where it is done, in presence of whom, in what time, the cause why he doth it, his age, his profession, the end wherto it tendeth, and the meanes that may bring him to it: and so let him apply him selfe discreetly with these advertisements to what soever hee mindeth to doe or speake. (2.7, Hoby 95, Maier 200)

Federico's rule that there is no hard and fast rule rehearses Cicero's brief treatments of *decorum* in *De oratore* and *Orator*. For the Ciceronian orator must "know what is appropriate to a particular occasion" (*De orat.* 3.212), adapting his speech to "fit all conceivable circumstances" (*ad id quodcumque decebit poterit accommodare orationem*, *Orator* 123). The frustrated Morello da Ortona challenges this rehearsal when he complains that Federico's unhelpful rule reminds him of the "circumstances" taught by the friars at confession (2.8, Hoby 95, Maier 200)—a charge that Federico embraces. "And for my part," Federico remarks about the courtier's duty to engage in conversation, "I am not able in this behalfe to give him other rules than the aforesaide, which our maister Morello learned of a child in confessing himselfe" (2.17, Hoby 105, Maier 215). Federico agrees, in other words, that *le circonstanzie* play a decisive role in speaking and acting appropriately.[59] His understanding of these circumstances in terms of

58. For a thorough discussion of *decorum*, see Trimpi, *Muses of One Mind*, 83–240. For the interlocking roles of *decorum*, *sprezzatura*, and conversation in Castiglione's dialogue, see Jennifer Richards, *Rhetoric and Courtliness in Early Modern Literature* (Cambridge, UK, 2003), 43–64.

59. On the circumstances in rhetorical argument and dramatic structure, see Hutson, *Circumstantial Shakespeare*. See also D. W. Robertson Jr., "A Note on the Classical Origin of 'Circumstances' in the Medieval Confessional," *Studies in Philology* 43 (1946): 6–14, and Kathy Eden, "Forensic Rhetoric and Humanist Education," in *The Oxford Handbook of English Law and Literature, 1500–1700*, ed. Lorna Hutson (Oxford, 2017), 27–28.

times, places, persons, motives, means, and so on, however, relies as much on Quintilian's complete handbook for the aspiring orator as on Cicero's more philosophical discussions of the *ars rhetorica*.

While taking Cicero's brief remarks in *De oratore* and *Orator* as the starting points for his own fuller treatment of *decorum* in book 11 of the *Institutio oratoria* (11.1.4), Quintilian introduces the circumstances as early as the third book, where he aligns them with both *conjectural* and *qualitative* questions. For when we inquire into whether or not an act was committed, as well as when we assess the kind of act it was, we must investigate the particularities of the act. These particular details—who committed the act; where, when, how, and why he committed it—constitute the *circumstantiae*, which, Quintilian tells us, translates the Greek *peristaseis*, literally "the things that stand around" (5.10.104). These *circumstantiae*, Quintilian also tells us, "must always be regarded as coming under *conjecture* or *quality*, as, for instance, when we ask with what purpose, or at what time, or place something was done" (*Qua mente? et Quo tempore? et Quo loco*, 3.6.90). Time, place, manner, and motive, he adds in book 5, frequently affect "the quality of an action, for the same action is not always lawful or seemly [*aut decorum est*] under all circumstances" (5.10.40). Returning yet again to *status* in book 7, Quintilian invokes Cicero's brilliant handling of the circumstances in *Pro Milone* to highlight their decisive role in determining cases (7.2.43–44).

In the course of their days-long conversation, the courtiers at Urbino have ample opportunity to discuss not only what the perfect courtier should do but how and why, when and where, he should do it—that is, the quality of his courtiership. On one of these many occasions, Gaspar Pallavicino contests Federico's defense of the courtier's skill in dissembling his skills, for the courtier sometimes goes so far as to promote those skills he lacks at the expense of those he possesses. Whereas Federico attributes such dissembling to art, Gaspar Pallavicino considers it deceit, thereby raising the question at the heart of both *De oratore* and the *Book of the Courtier*: not, in the end, does the art under discussion exist or how is it defined but, most pressingly, is it worthy of praise or blame? By identifying the courtier's artful behavior with deceit, pure and simple, Gaspar Pallavicino judges it blameworthy (2.40, Hoby 132, Maier 252–54). Federico rejects this judgment not by denying that there is an element of deception in the art of courtiership but by qualifying it in a way that renders it praiseworthy, shifting the question from conjecture to quality. Granting that the courtier dissembles, Federico undertakes to justify (which is to say, qualify) the dissimulation.[60] The courtier's skill at dissembling, Federico argues not wholly convincingly, resembles the goldsmith's artistry in placing a precious jewel in a setting that enhances its beauty. Like the master craftsman, the courtier adds grace and adornment in order to give pleasure.

Federico's response to Gaspar Pallavicino's charge against art in book 2 reprises Ludovico's lengthy discussion in book 1, where attention pivots from asking if there is an art of courtiership to defining this art and, even if only briefly, to qualifying it, especially by investigating the courtier's intentions. For the third *status* question, *quale sit*, requires, as we have seen, considering *qua mente*—in what frame of mind the art is practiced. With his emphasis on grace, Ludovico promotes the courtier's intention to please (1.14)—and, above all, to please his prince.

But neither Ludovico nor Federico gets the last word on the quality of courtiership as determined by the courtier's intentions. The revised structure of the dialogue into four books provides the occasion for Ottaviano, Federico's older brother, to ask once again, and much more emphatically, why the courtier should take such pains (albeit disguised by *sprezzatura*) to achieve grace.[61] For the art of courtiership is worthwhile, according to Ottaviano, only if it is performed with a worthwhile motive or end; and, in his judgment, pleasing the prince, with or without dissembling, does not qualify. On the other hand, Ottaviano contends, if courtiers aim to educate a prince in the interests of the peace and security of his people, these efforts are "most profitable, and deserve infinite prayse" (4.4, Hoby 261, Maier 450). Promoting as expansive a view of courtiership as Cicero's of oratory, both of which exploit a capacious view of *status*, Castiglione has Ottaviano include Plato and Aristotle among this praiseworthy cohort (4.47, Hoby 299, Maier 508). He also has the Magnifico Giuliano

60. On the role of dissimulation in the *Book of the Courtier*, see Eduardo Saccone, "The Portrait of the Courtier in Castiglione," *Italica* 64 (1987): 1–10, rpt. *Book of the Courtier*, ed. Javitch, 328–39.

61. On the heightened rhetoric of book 4, see Rebhorn, *Courtly Performances*, 175. On the *status qualitatis* as the "kingdom" of the orator because it gives full rein to his eloquence, see Quintilian 7.4.23–24 and Trimpi, *Muses of One Mind*, 265–66.

push back against Ottaviano's overgeneralization and in doing so enlist the definitive *status*. For "he that instructeth a Prince (I believe) ought not to bee called a Courtier," the Magnifico counters (4.44, Hoby 296, Maier 504), "but deserveth a farre greater and a more honourable name." Like Cicero and Quintilian, Giuliano appreciates the way one *status* question implicates another.

Despite Ottaviano's commitment to an ideal, however, he is far from naïve about the difficulty and even danger of undertaking the honorable task of educating a prince; and it is here that "those honest qualities that Count Lewis and Sir Fredericke have given him" come in handy (4.5, Hoby 264, Maier 450). For the *grazia* that derives from the artfully concealed or dissembling art that the courtier practices can and should "purchase him the good will, and allure unto him ye mind of his Prince" (4.9, Hoby 264, Maier 456), who, drawn to the "veil of pleasure," like the child drawn to the honey around the rim of a medicinal draft, is beguiled into imbibing the lessons he would revile without this device (4.10, Hoby 265; Maier 457–58). Reaffirming Federico's defense of the deceptions of art in book 2, Ottaviano's highly conventional analogy in book 4, dating back to Lucretius, aligns the courtier's intentions with those of the literary artist, including Castiglione himself: like Plato, Xenophon, and especially Cicero before him, Castiglione relies on the indirection of fiction to communicate the lessons he would impart. In the prefatory letter to Don Michel de Silva (chap.3, Hoby 13, Maier 76), he boldly advertises his alignment with these other fiction writers.

Like the third and final book of *De oratore*, then, the fourth and final book of the *Courtier* focuses attention on the quality of the art it investigates. This focus on the third *status* question, *quale sit*, theorized by Cicero and elaborated by Quintilian, highlights three discrete but related dimensions of quality. One of these dimensions, as we have seen, pertains to the general nature or form of the subject under investigation. In *De inventione*, the young Cicero refers to this *status* as the *constitutio generalis* (1.10). In keeping with this alternative designation, Quintilian reminds his readers not only that every definite question or *causa* contains indefinite or general questions but that "wherever the notion of quality comes into question, there is a certain intrusion of the abstract" (*generale sit*, 3.5.10). Here as elsewhere, Quintilian turns to *Pro Milone* for illustration; for Cicero's defense of Milo on qualitative grounds, Quintilian insists, rests not on the singular event of his fatal encounter with Clodius but on "the general question as to whether we have the right to kill a man who lies in wait for us" (*Inst. orat.* 3.5.10). Further in keeping with Quintilian's reminder, Cicero also has Crassus insist, as we have seen, that the quality of anything is set in high relief in its perfected form. Accordingly, Castiglione has Federico devise a game that features the ideal. Another dimension of quality, as we have also seen, is intentionality or motive. When Quintilian turns in book 7 to what the agent intended to do (*an voluerit*) as one of the two key topics of the *conjectural status*, he notes that "such considerations [of motive (*causa voluntatis*)] lessen the guilt of a crime when regarded from the point of view of its quality [*in qualitate*]" (7.2.40). In the *Courtier*, both Federico and Ottaviano turn to the intention of the courtier to mitigate the charge against him of dissimulation—a potentially dishonorable practice that figures so prominently in his art. In the appended fourth book, in fact, Ottaviano rests his case on behalf of courtiership on the *qualitative status*, justifying the courtier's conduct on the basis of his praiseworthy motive. But any effort to qualify the courtier's actions as just or unjust, worthwhile or worthless, according to Quintilian, will inevitably entail not only generality or abstraction and motivation but fiction (*fictio*), defined at the end of the discussion of *status* in book 5 as the proposition of something that, if true, would resolve the question (5.10.96). Both the idealized portrait of the court of Urbino painted with words in Castiglione's dialogue and the composite ideal proposed by his interlocutors, including Ottaviano, constitute just such *fictiones.*[62]

Although the *Book of the Courtier*, as we have seen, avoids explicit mention of the arid legalities of the *status* system in the interest of *decorum*, Castiglione closes his dialogue with a witty exchange between the Prefect and Emilia Pia that borrows its lexicon from the law courts. In a playful response to the Prefect's offer to see the litigation (*lite*) adjudicated between Gasparo Pallavicino and the Magnifico (regarding the status of women), Emilia insists that the misogynist Gasparo poses a flight risk and so must post bond to stand trial (4.73, Hoby 324, Maier 544). In another Renaissance dialogue modeled on

---

62. On the relation between the qualitative *status* and fiction, which involves both generality and motivation, see Trimpi, *Muses of One Mind*, 245–305, esp. 255–58.

De oratore—this one conceived even if never executed in four books—
Erasmus not only openly leverages the language of the law but also
subtly structures the discourse of the principal speaker according to
the dictates of *status* theory.

CODA ON ERASMUS'S *ANTIBARBARIANS*

Only partially completed and even more partially preserved, the *Antibarbarians* offers a defense of the liberal arts (*artes liberales* or *bonae
literae*) in the form of a dialogue among friends at a country retreat.[63]
Fully aware of the Platonic and Ciceronian dimensions of their setting
(CWE 23: 39; ASD I-1, 64–65), the interlocutors are also aware of the
disputatious nature of their conversation, regularly referring to the
questions they debate in legal terms.[64] Jacob Batt, whose speech takes
up much (too much, according to some) of the only surviving book
of the projected four, calls his speech a *causa* and the act it defends an
alleged crime (CWE 23: 41; ASD I-1, 67 ll. 1–7). "Here am I, a young
man and a layman," he freely confesses, "engaged in public affairs,
and with a declared interest in literature which is itself secular [*literas
ipsas prophanas*], and they arraign me [*in ius vocant*], they put me on
trial as guilty of a nefarious crime [*nephandi criminis reum agunt*],
because I freely spend my time reading ancient philosophy, early history, and writings of the poets and orators" (CWE 23: 104; ASD I-1,
123 ll. 13–17). Batt's offense, in other words, is the act of reading. More
precisely, it entails reading that promotes a certain kind of learning or
eruditio. Accordingly, his *apologia*, as we will see in the next chapter,

63. On the projected four-book structure, see M. M. Phillips, CWE 23: 3: "After the refutation of the enemies of humanism the second book was to provide an
answer to this, in which a fictitious character used all the powers of eloquence
to pour scorn on eloquence; the third book was to be a refutation of the second, and the fourth a defense of poetry." On the book's gradual formation and
partial disappearance, see CWE 23: 3–8 and ASD I-1, 7–32 and Ep. 1110, CWE
23: 16–17.

64. On *De oratore* as model for the *Antibarbari*, see Kazimierz Kumaniecki,
ASD I-1, 20–21. For the advice of close friend Robert Gaguin in a letter to Erasmus to follow in the footsteps of Plato and Cicero, see Ep. 46, CWE 1: 93, where
Gaguin also finds fault with "the leading role given to Batt on the ground that his
monologue is somewhat too protracted."

undertakes to refute the charges against not only such erudition but, by extension, those who cultivate it.

In keeping with Erasmus's advice to schoolboys in *De copia*, noted earlier, to consider the three *status* questions before beginning their compositions, Batt's answer to his adversaries addresses whether or not such erudition—or, indeed, any erudition—exists (*sitne?*). Dismissing the so-called *eruditio* of these adversaries as too narrow to be considered erudition at all (CWE 23: 62; ASD I-1, 85 ll. 14–15), Batt applies the *conjectural* question to his own conception of learning. "In my opinion," he asserts, "there is no erudition in existence [*nullam esse eruditionem*] except what is secular (this is their name for the learning of the ancients) or at least founded on and informed by secular literature" (CWE 23: 62; ASD I-1, 84 ll. 28–29). Here as in *De oratore*, then, whether or not something exists can depend on how it is defined. Like Crassus and Antonius, Batt appreciates the inevitable overlap of the *status* questions. Whereas his opponents define real knowledge as the kind that comes directly from heaven (CWE 23: 62; ASD I-1, 85 l. 17), Batt insists, on the contrary, that the erudition offered by the liberal arts comes exclusively from the ancients, especially the Greeks and Romans. He further insists that these *artes liberales* "all concern Christ" (*ad Christum autem omnes referuntur*), even if "they neither treat of Christ nor were invented by Christians" (CWE 23: 90; ASD I-1, 110 ll. 14–16).

While the disagreement between Batt and his adversaries addresses *conjectural* and *definitive* questions, the crux of their dispute rests, as it did in the founding case of Orestes before the Areopagus, on the issue of quality. Can the *eruditio* that derives from the liberal arts be justified or not? Is it worthwhile or worthless? In the *Antibarbarians*, as in *De oratore*, justification hinges on integration. In the ancient dialogue, as we have seen, Cicero gives his Crassus the challenge of making the case for eloquence by uniting it with wisdom or *sapientia*. Adapting this challenge to his own time and place, Erasmus tasks Batt with defending the union not of wisdom and eloquence but of wisdom (or erudition) and piety. For Batt's opponents, the *religiosi*, categorically deny that *pietas Christiana* is compatible with *literaria secularis* (CWE 23: 75; ASD I-1, 96 ll. 30–31).

As we will see in more detail in the next chapter, one of Batt's chief argumentative strategies in this effort is to place in evidence proof-texts from Scripture, including the Book of Wisdom or *Sapi-*

entia 7:17–21, which calls for "no confused or barren erudition, but one which is polished and rich, and founded in high antiquity" (*non perturbata quaedam et ieiuna eruditio, sed polita et copiosa . . . antiquitate condita*, CWE 23: 99–100; ASD I-1, 119 ll. 16–18). Another is to neutralize the Pauline dictum, weaponized by the opponents of learning, that "Knowledge [*Sapientia*] puffs up; charity builds" (1 Cor. 8:1), with the help of an arsenal of exegetical tools that Erasmus treats in great detail elsewhere, and especially in the *Ratio verae theologiae*.[65] With the support of these texts, Batt will defend, not learning pure and simple, but a certain kind or quality of learning—one that enables Christians to appreciate more fully all that Christ has done for them. For in His love for them He has ensured that "the best religion should be adorned and supported by the finest studies" (CWE 23: 60; ASD I-1, 83 ll. 16–17).

With the *status* system as treated by the most influential ancient rhetoricians, including those turned church fathers, Renaissance writers inherit a set of questions, along with their topics, originally designed to establish the point of contention in legal cases. As we have seen in this chapter, this inheritance proves not only basic to the inventional or creative process but flexible enough to structure very different literary products, among them some of the most acclaimed works of the period—arguably its masterworks. But Petrarch, Castiglione, and Erasmus share more from their favorite rhetorical manuals than a common inheritance of rhetorical *status*. For these same ancient manuals also encourage Renaissance writers to hone their skills in refutation. The rhetorical instructions institutionalizing this encouragement and the responsiveness of these writers in the same masterworks to this instruction are the subject of the next chapter.

---

65. On the rules of interpretation in the *Ratio verae theologiae*, see Manfred Hoffmann, *Rhetoric and Theology: The Hermeneutic of Erasmus* (Toronto, 1994); Eden, *Hermeneutics and the Rhetorical Tradition*, 64–78; Robert Sider, CWE 41: 185–90.

✳ 2 ✳

Refutation

RHETORICAL THEORY

When Erasmus began writing the *Antibarbarians* in 1494, he clear-headedly conceived of it in rhetorical terms as a refutation, a *refellatio*. Both its original title and a preview of its content to a close friend featured its refutative agenda.[1] By so labeling his new literary creation, Erasmus was joining the ranks of his humanistically inclined readers, who, like Erasmus himself, would have learned the dos and don'ts of demolishing the arguments of an adversary in court or elsewhere from a short list of Roman rhetorical handbooks, including *Ad Herennium*, Cicero's *De inventione*, and Quintilian's *Institutio oratoria*. Despite its dismissive attitude toward such handbooks, even *De oratore* had advice to give on refuting an opponent (1.143, 2.80–83, 2.315–32).

Before encountering this advice, the average early modern schoolboy would have already tried his hand at refutation as part of his earliest training in composition. Aphthonius's so-called *Progymnasmata*, the most widely used composition textbook for beginners in North-

---

1. Eventually settling on the streamlined *Antibarbarorum liber primus autore Des. Erasmo Roterodamo*, Erasmus entitled the first version *Liber apologeticus Desiderii Herasmi Roterodami, in quo refelluntur rationes inepte barbarorum contra poesim et literaturam secularem pugnantium.* For both the change of title and other changes between the first and second versions, see ASD I-1, 7–32, esp. 14–15 and 23. In a 1494 letter to Cornelis Gerard (Ep. 37, CWE 1: 71–72, *Opus epistolarum Desiderii Erasmi Roterodami*, ed. P. S. Allen et al., 12 vols. [Oxford, 1906–58] 1: 136 ll. 12–13), Erasmus confirms the refutative agenda: "The first book will be almost entirely concerned with refuting the absurdities perpetrated by the barbarians (*in refellendis ineptis barbarorum rationibus*)."

ern Europe, not only includes refutation (Gr. *anaskeuē*) as the fifth of fourteen exercises but considers it *the* exercise for assessing the promise of young writers because it "includes in itself all the power of the art [of rhetoric]."[2] Like the Roman rhetoricians, Aphthonius couples refutation with confirmation (Gr. *kataskeuē*); but unlike them, he puts refutation before confirmation in his textbook presumably on the grounds that it is easier to dismantle an argument than to assemble one. In the rhetorical manuals, in contrast, proving one's case precedes demolishing the proofs of one's opponent. Accordingly, the confirmation (*confirmatio*) is traditionally the third part of an oration, after the introduction and narration, while the refutation is fourth, followed by the conclusion.[3] Also unlike Aphthonius, Quintilian follows Cicero in finding it easier to accuse than defend—just as it is easier to inflict a wound than to heal one (*Inst. orat.* 5.13.3). Even more to the point, all defenses are refutations of the accusations that provoke them (5.13.1–3).[4]

Quintilian also agrees with Cicero—here the young Cicero of *De inventione*—that refuting is as difficult as it is important. For there is no winning an argument without it. When it comes to specific strategies for disproving what an opponent has undertaken to prove, however, Cicero's handbook on invention is both vague and apologetic.

2. *Progymnasmata: Greek Textbooks of Prose Composition and Rhetoric*, trans. George A. Kennedy (Atlanta, 2003), 101; *Rhetores Graeci*, ed. L. Spengel, 3 vols. (Leipzig, 1854), 3: 28. On the prominent place of Aphthonius in the sixteenth-century curriculum, see Baldwin, *William Shakspere's Small Latine & Lesse Greeke*, 288–354; Anthony Grafton and Lisa Jardine, *From Humanism to the Humanities* (Cambridge, MA, 1986), 129–36; and Eden, "Forensic Rhetoric and Humanist Education," 35–36. On invective (*psogos*), the ninth exercise in the sequence, see *Progymnasmata*, trans. Kennedy, 111–13; he notes that "a major feature of the exercises was stress on learning refutation or rebuttal: how to take a traditional tale, narrative, or thesis and argue against it" (x). On the relation of refutation to invective, see Quintilian 5.13.38–39; *De oratore* 2.349; Anthony Corbeill, "Ciceronian Invective," in *Brill's Companion to Cicero*, ed. May, 197–217; and Marc Laurays, "Per una storia dell'invettiva umanistica," *Studi umanistici piceni* 23 (2003): 9–30, esp. 22–23, who cites Quintilian 6.4.10 and 12.9.8–13.

3. For the arrangement of the parts of the speech (*partes orationis*), see, for instance, *De inventione* 1.14.19, *Ad Herennium* 1.3.4, and Wisse, "The Intellectual Background of Cicero's Rhetorical Works," in *Brill's Companion to Cicero*, ed. May, 355–57, and above, p. 7.

4. As part of preliminary exercises, Quintilian also puts the *anaskeuē* before the *kataskeuē* (2.4.18).

All the methods for confirming an argument, Cicero suggests, can be used for refuting one (*De inven.* 1.42.78). Sometimes we should attack our opponent's assumptions, at other times, his conclusions. At still other times, we should point out the fallacies in his arguments (1.42.79). "But the theoretical mastery of this art is so difficult," Cicero concedes, "that it cannot be appended to any chapter of rhetoric, but demands for itself alone a long period of profound and arduous thought. Therefore this will be treated by us at another time and in another work, if opportunity shall offer" (1.45.86).

While no such opportunity was forthcoming for Cicero, who set his sights elsewhere in his later rhetorical works, Quintilian devotes considerable attention to refutation in book 5 of his *Institutio oratoria*.[5] Far from denying Cicero's assertion that probative and refutative strategies overlap (*Instit. orat.* 5.13.1), Quintilian tethers refutation to the three *status* questions as the backbone of invention.[6] Regarding the arguments put forward by one's adversary, Quintilian notes that they "may be demolished either by conjecture, when we shall consider whether they are true, by definition, when we shall examine whether they are relevant to the case, by quality, when we shall consider whether they are dishonorable, unfair, scandalous, inhuman, cruel, or deserve any other epithet coming under the head of quality" (5.13.19). Elsewhere (5.13.7) Quintilian merely alludes to *status* theory when he advises his reader simply to deny the facts when he can, and when he can't, to justify them.

Focusing on the possible weaknesses of an opponent's arguments, he counsels this same reader to be on the lookout for irrelevance, overstatement of similarity to other cases, ambiguity, and most damaging of all, inconsistency and outright contradiction (*Instit. orat.* 5.13.16, 5.13.23–24, 5.13.35). For only a consummate practitioner can discover inconsistencies (*quae contra semetipsa pugnent*) in the arguments of an adversary (5.13.30). Other arguments open to attack, Quintilian notes, are those that take what is disputable as indisputable, what is controversial as admitted, and what is common to a class of cases as peculiar to the case under consideration (5.13.34). Finally, he cautions against attacking the pleader (*actor*) instead of refuting

---

5. For Cicero's overriding preoccupation with style in his late rhetorical works, see chap. 4 below.

6. For a full discussion of these three *status* questions, see above, chapter 1.

his case (*causa*)—that is, against so-called *ad hominem* arguments (5.13.37).

Long before the heyday of either the *progymnasmata* or even the Roman rhetorical manuals most familiar to Erasmus and his humanistically trained contemporaries, Plato's Socrates draws attention to the central role of refutation in Greek rhetorical theory and practice. In addition to offering at the beginning of *Phaedrus* a refutation of Lysias's speech in favor of nonlovers over lovers, his so-called palinode (243B), Socrates includes at the end, in an overview of the arts of rhetoric he rejects, the work of one Theodorus on the refutation or *elenchus* of both accusation and defense (*Phaedrus* 267A).[7] Aristotle references this same Theodorus in his treatment of the parts of the oration at the end of his own art of rhetoric; and he does so to contrast it with his strongly preferred, simpler division of a speech into statement and proof—*prothesis* and *pistis* (*Rhetoric* 3.13.4). Those who insist on introductions, statements, proofs, refutations, conclusions, and so on are pegged as wrongheaded followers of Theodorus and his

---

7. Although the earliest context for the verb *elenchein* and its derivatives, including the noun *elenchos*, is arguably not the law courts or legal rhetoric, by Plato's day, as *Phaedrus* 267A makes clear, the method of "testing" was routinely associated with the adversarial "cross-examination" that aimed to disclose inconsistencies and contradictions in the claims and arguments of one's opponent. In the *Gorgias*, as we will see below, Socrates himself identifies the kind of elenchus embraced by Polus as a legal practice, which Cicero, in turn, will identify with Socrates when he records in *Brutus* (31) Socrates' skill at refuting (*refellere*) the sophists. For the legal dimension of *elenchos* as refutation or cross-examination, see Hayden W. Ausland, "Forensic Characteristics of Socratic Argumentation," in *Does Socrates Have a Method? Rethinking the Elenchus in Plato's Dialogues and Beyond*, ed. Gary Alan Scott (University Park, PA, 2002), 36–60. In "Parmenidean Elenchus" in the same volume (19–35), James Lesher puts "the first signs of a 'legalized' form of *elenchus*, a 'cross-examination'" (25) in Aeschylus's plays. For the forensic dimension of *elenchos* in the *Gorgias*, see Harold Tarrant, "Socratic Method and Socratic Truth," in *A Companion to Socrates*, ed. Sara Ahbel-Rappe and Rachana Kamtekar (London: Blackwell, 2005), 254–72. In *Plato's Earlier Dialectic* (Oxford: Clarendon, 1953), 7, Richard Robinson distinguishes between a wider and a narrower meaning of "elenchus." The former he characterizes as "examining a person with regard to a statement he has made, by putting to him questions calling for further statements, in the hope that they will determine the meaning and the truth-value of his first statement," while the latter is characterized as "a form of cross-examination or refutation." He concludes, however, that "we may almost say that Socrates never talks to anyone without refuting him."

school (*Rhetoric* 3.13.4–5). In Aristotle's view, on the contrary, not only will defendants often need to open their speeches by refuting the accusations of their opponents (3.14.7, 3.17.15), but the probative value of a strong refutation (*tōn de enthymēmatōn ta elengtika*) is so great that it belongs wherever it can do the most damage (*Rhetoric* 3.17.13).

Among the most effective ways to damage an opponent's case, according to Aristotle as well as Quintilian, is to expose its inconsistencies, whether they are brought to light in a counterspeech or through interrogation (*erotēsis*) (*Rhetoric* 3.17.13, 3.18.3). To illustrate the proper technique for interrogating a witness, Aristotle cites Socrates' refutation of Meletus in Plato's *Apology* (3.18.2). Quintilian seconds this admiration for Socratic refutation when he sends his young orator-in-training to Plato's dialogues for a "first-rate preparation for forensic debates and the examination of witnesses" (*Institutio oratoria* 10.1.35–36). From its earliest examples, then, ancient dialogue fully embraces this adversarial dimension, while ancient rhetoricians appreciate Plato's mastery of the refutative art.

THE MASTER REFUTER IN ERASMUS'S *ANTIBARBARIANS*

By the time Erasmus finishes the *Antibarbarians* and is preparing it for publication in 1520, he is not only reading Plato and Aristotle as well as Cicero and Quintilian on demolishing the arguments of an opponent but refining the very skills of refutation he will turn on Reformist and Catholic critics alike in the 1520s and 1530s.[8] More to the point, Erasmus structures the *Antibarbarians*, which evolves over the course of three decades from a monologue into a dialogue able to present both sides of an issue, as a series of disputations heavily tilted toward dismantling rather than assembling the cases argued.[9] And

---

8. For Erasmus's attacks on his critics, see Erika Rummel, *Erasmus and His Catholic Critics*, 2 vols. (Nieuwkoop, 1989), and James D. Tracy, *Erasmus of the Low Countries* (Berkeley, 1996), esp. 127–82.

9. On the gradual evolution of the *Antibarbari*, see CWE 23: 3–15 and ASD I-1, 7–32. For the requirement of being able to argue for and against any issue, including the importance of the arts, see CWE 25: 43–44; ASD I-2, 263–64.

he makes Batt, the principal interlocutor whose combative nature is reflected in his name, a master refuter (CWE 23: 48). In keeping with this role, Batt speaks after the other guests at the country retreat open the conversation by taking turns addressing a controversial question: why the cultivation of *bonae literae* has declined since antiquity. Rejecting their various explanations, including the impact of Christianity, the alignment of the stars, and the natural aging of the physical world and everything in it, Batt offers the decline of education as the major contributing factor and accuses the burgomaster Conrad of failing in his official duty to secure the best teachers.

In an effort to refute these charges, Conrad turns the accusation against Batt, who was equally unsuccessful in his campaign against the hiring practices of the city council. When Batt defends his labors in this cause as Herculean, Conrad, an admittedly wavering supporter of *bonae literae*, prevails on Batt to rehearse his refutation of these so-called barbarians so that Conrad can better advocate for educational reform (CWE 23: 38).[10] Reminding Batt and the rest of the assembled company of friends of the charges against the literature of the Greeks and Romans—it is heathen, it is obscure, and it is obscene (CWE 23: 38)—Conrad exhorts Batt to take on the task that directs the remainder of the dialogue. "You are easily the most experienced of all in this field," he tells Batt:

> you must have read and thought many things which would serve to rebut this sort of accusation [*quibus huiusmodi criminationes refelli queant*]; and so really it would be doing something truly great if you would explain this whole controversy from beginning to end, not because your cause seems doubtful to me, but just to make me a more informed defender of it. (CWE 23: 39; ASD I-1, 64 ll. 9–13)

The collective agenda of the *Antibarbarians*, then, is to give a full hearing to Batt's rebuttal or *refellatio* of his opponents' accusations against Greek and Roman literature, the *bonae literae*.

That the assembled company understands their joint undertaking in this way is signaled by Erasmus's account in his own voice of how

10. On the nature of Herculean labors, which bring the laborer no benefit, see *Adages* III.i.1 and Kathy Eden, *Friends Hold All Things in Common: Tradition, Intellectual Property, and the "Adages" of Erasmus* (New Haven, 2001), 158–63.

Batt prepares, on the spur of the moment (and after the fashion of Quintilian's accomplished orator, 12.5.4), to meet the challenge of this daunting oratorical occasion. Visibly summoning his inner resources and communicating to his audience both his stage fright and his resolve to resist intimidation, Batt, according to Erasmus, nervously rehearses the parts of his speech beforehand by counting them out on his fingers (CWE 23: 41). Batt soon confirms Erasmus's account as he resolutely launches into his speech with the assertion that "I am so far from any apprehension of not being able to refute all the objections that the anti-rhetoricians can ever raise [*ut omnia quae ab istis anti-rhetoribus obiici vel soleant, vel queant, refellere me posse diffidam*] that I do not think it necessary in such an easily won cause even to use an introduction" (CWE 23: 41; ASD I-1, 67 ll. 4–7). Countering performance anxiety with bravado, in other words, Batt, at the moment of delivery, dispenses with his traditional arrangement in favor of going immediately on the attack as he refutes the charges laid out by Conrad against *bonae literae*, beginning with the cardinal sin of not having been written by Christians.

Batt's overarching plan to refute this charge is also signposted by one of the dialogue's section headings. "It is absurd," it reads, "to disapprove [*reprehendi*] of anything simply because it was discovered by the ancients" (CWE 23: 55; ASD I-1, 79 ll. 1–2). Like *refellere*, which, as we have seen, figures in the original title and is used by the various interlocutors, *reprehendere* belongs to the cluster of technical terms for the fundamentally forensic procedure of demolishing an adversary's case. In *De inventione* (1.42.78), Cicero calls "that part of an oration in which arguments are used to impair, disprove, or weaken the confirmation or proof in our opponent's speech" the *reprehensio*. Similarly, *Ad Herennium* (2.20.31) distinguishes between those arguments that merit rebuttal or *reprehensio* and those that should be confuted (*confutari*) with a disdainful silence, without drawing any further distinction between the two terms.

In keeping with both these Roman rhetorical manuals and his own advice in *De copia* about diversifying one's word choice, Erasmus shifts back and forth between *refellere, confutare*, and *reprehendere*. Another section heading in the *Antibarbarians* reads "Authorities confuted by authorities" (*Confutat authoritates authoritatibus*, CWE 23: 84; ASD I-1, 105 l. 16), while the dialogue ends with the expectation of yet another refutation, this one, like the open-endedness of the dialogue itself, reaffirming the affiliation of the *Antibarbarians* with *De oratore*.[11] "It remains for us," Batt concludes with an eye to continuing the conversation beyond the confines of this dialogue, "to refute those who say that it is not for a Christian to pay attention to eloquence" (*reliquum est, ut confutemus eos, qui negant eloquentiae dare operam Christianum oportere*, CWE 23: 121; ASD I-1, 137 ll. 8–9). En route to this Ciceronian conclusion coyly linking *eloquentia* to *sapientia*, however, Batt must engage with the arguments of his opponents that *eruditio*, especially the wisdom that is associated with *bonae literae*, is unfitting for a Christian.

Following the advice of the rhetorical manuals, Batt's chief refutative strategy in this effort is to attack his adversary's arguments as inconsistent, contradictory. Chief among the contradictions, as suggested by the section heading noted earlier, is their rejection of the literature of the ancients merely because it was written by Greeks and Romans, even as they embrace the ancient technologies of agriculture, carpentry, weaving, metallurgy, and so on (CWE 23: 56). "Painters, carvers, glaziers, every kind of craftsman, in short," Batt pointedly argues, "must find some other way of earning their living if they can, to avoid defilement of themselves and their families by these heathen arts" (CWE 23: 56). Indeed, the art of writing itself is a "heathen" invention (CWE 23: 57). According to the logic of his opponents, Batt notes, Christians should remain completely illiterate.

Equally illogical is the assumption that piety is of a piece with ignorance—that the more unlearned are more religious. "If a man has a disorderly tongue," Batt asks in an effort to pry false assumptions loose from faulty conclusions, "does it follow that he must have well-ordered morals? . . . Does a man instantly know himself because he does not know geometry? . . . To speak more generally, is the least educated of men to be esteemed forthwith the most religious?" (CWE 23: 76). As part of his refutation of his opponents' case in favor of ignorance, Batt also undertakes to disprove their reading of the proof-texts most often cited. Among these is Paul's declaration at 1 Cor. 8:1 that "Knowledge puffs up; charity builds." In keeping with the hermeneutical principles established in the *Ratio verae theologiae* and elsewhere, Erasmus has Batt insist that when this passage is read in context, taking into account what comes before and after, Paul is

---

11. On the Ciceronian pedigree of this Erasmian dialogue, see chap. 1, n. 64.

far from rejecting the erudition that is everywhere on display in his letters (CWE 23: 71).[12] The most effective advocates for a fledgling Christianity, in fact, are the supremely learned church fathers Jerome and Augustine.[13] Their example, Batt contends, refutes the assertion that the learned are irreligious. "Who could be more pious or more cultured than Jerome or Augustine?" Batt asks (CWE 23: 108; cf. 62–63). He also looks elsewhere in Scripture to corroborate this view, and especially to "that book which, in uncertainty as to its author, is called Wisdom [*Sapientiae*]"; for this scriptural text provides an unambiguous "praise of learning" (*laus eruditionis*, CWE 23: 99; ASD I-1, 119 l. 4).

Finally, Batt's refutation of the arguments of the barbarians includes his personal anecdote of one nameless barbarian in particular, appallingly ignorant and unabashedly self-indulgent, who fully expects to be the one doing the confuting: "Now, said he [to Batt], I will completely confute you" (*Iam, inquit, te confutabo planissime*, CWE 23: 88; ASD I-1, 108 l. 17). Grounding his confutation on the authority of the twelfth-century jurist Gratian, the anonymous acquaintance singles out a number of passages that seem to call into question the usefulness of the liberal arts.[14] Batt, in turn, confutes his confuter not only by countering these apparently disparaging texts with others from the same writer that speak in favor of the liberal arts but by clueing his opponent in to Gratian's signature method of arguing *in utramque partem*, on either side of a question (CWE 23: 89; ASD I-1, 109 ll. 14–15). Those passages taken out of context only seem to condemn

12. On Erasmian hermeneutics, and especially on its attention to historical and textual context, see Eden, *Hermeneutics and the Rhetorical Tradition*, 1–6 and 64–78, and above, chap. 1, p. 57.

13. On Jerome's key role in the *Antibarbari*, see Tracy, *Erasmus of the Low Countries*, 24–26. On the *Antibarbari*'s appropriation of Augustine's *spoliatio Aegyptiorum* and Jerome's *mulier captiva* to make its case for *bonae literae*, see Eden, *Friends Hold All Things in Common*, 15–24.

14. In a preface to volume 2 (part 1) of the 1516 Froben edition of Jerome, Erasmus clarifies that "scholars declare that that collection of Gratian, whoever he was, had never been approved by an official action of the church and had gradually gained its commanding position more by the usurpation of the schoolmen than by synodal decree. Today among the schoolmen themselves, it may be noted, the testimony of that work is not readily accepted; only what has been pertinent to our concerns gains acceptance, and what is at odds with such concerns is rejected as outdated and obsolete" (CWE 61: 81; cf. CWE 61: 93).

learning; they assume a very different meaning when understood as part of Gratian's discussion as a whole. Here as in his approach to the Pauline proof-text, in other words, Batt reveals himself to be a skilled interpreter as well as a first-rate refuter.[15]

Often hailed by modern readers as a manifesto of Renaissance humanism, the *Antibarbarians* finds its place in the Erasmian complete works, projected by the author himself, in the eighth of nine volumes among the *apologiai*.[16] For despite being written as a Ciceronian dialogue, it shares its refutative agenda with all of Erasmus's other defenses. More to the point, Erasmus's placement of this text signals that refutation is no less characteristic of the literary production of Renaissance humanists than dialogue.[17] And the combination can claim the literary pedigree of *De oratore* itself, where the interlocutors not only theorize refutation, as we have seen, but practice it on one another.

In keeping with this practice, Scaevola counters Crassus's arguments, early in the conversation at Tusculum, for the eloquent speaker rather than the legislator as the founder of civilization (1.35–40). Antonius similarly closes the first book by rebutting Crassus's claim that the orator must have broad and deep cultural knowledge—a rebuttal Antonius explains at the beginning of the second book as "my intention to refute you [*te refellissem*] and thus entice these pupils [Sulpicius and Cotta] away from you" (2.40).[18] Whether or not Antonius's argumentative strategy works on his eager young listeners, Cicero's literary strategy of combining dialogue with refutation appealed to writers other than Erasmus, including those featured in chapter 1, Petrarch and Castiglione. Unlike the diplomat from Lombardy, who

15. For Erasmus on the dangers of reading out of context as well as the need to accommodate any partial text to the work as a whole, see Eden, *Hermeneutics and the Rhetorical Tradition*, 1–6, 64–78.

16. On Erasmus's plan for his *opera omnia*, see the letter to Botzheim (Ep. 1341A), *Opus epistolarum*, ed. Allen, 1: 1–46, esp. 41–42; CWE 9: 291–364, esp. 355–56.

17. On humanist dialogue, see David Marsh, *The Quattrocento Dialogue: Classical Tradition and Humanist Innovation* (Cambridge, MA, 1980), and Virginia Cox, *The Renaissance Dialogue: Literary Dialogue in Its Social and Political Contexts, Castiglione to Galileo* (Cambridge, UK, 1992), esp. 9–21.

18. For Cicero's characterization of the general focus of book 1 as distinct from the more technical focus of books 2 and 3, see *Ad Att.* 4.16.3, and Fantham, *Roman World of Cicero's* De Oratore, 76–77 and 267–68.

very likely wrote the *Book of the Courtier* with a complete edition of *De oratore* at his elbow, the so-called "father of humanism" lacked, among other ancient sources, a whole text of this most prized work of Cicero, among whose many lost passages was Antonius's rebuttal of Crassus in book 1.[19] In spite of this and other lacunae, as we will see, Petrarch, like Castiglione, combines the intimacy of dialogue with the antagonism of refutation—a combination he would have found not only in the Ciceronian corpus but in the work of his favorite church father.

CASTIGLIONE AND PETRARCH

Nearly contemporary with Erasmus's *Antibarbarians*, the *Book of the Courtier*, as noted in the previous chapter, stages a friendly conversation thoroughly saturated with the adversarial language of the law courts. In addition to Emilia Pia's closing words marking Gasparo Pallavicino as a potential fugitive from justice (see above), the interlocutors on more than one occasion characterize their exchanges with one another as accusation and defense (1.3, Hoby 14; Meier 77). In one of these exchanges in book 1, Pietro Bembo refutes Ludovico's argument that the courtier's principal occupation should be arms rather than the *bonae literae* defended in the *Antibarbarians*. Ludovico responds with the legal objection that "I would not have you (maister Peter) a judge in this cause, for you would be too partiall to one of the partes" (1.45, Hoby 73, Maier 165).

But Bembo's case against Ludovico is only one of a number of "causes" that structure the first book. Others include Ludovico's case for the courtier's noble birth, countered by Gaspar Pallavicino, Ludovico's case against the superiority of the Tuscan dialect, countered by Federico Fregoso, and Ludovico's case for the superiority of painting over sculpture, countered by sculptor Giancristoforo Romano. So contentious is the wide-ranging conversation of the first book that the interlocutors look back at it from the vantage point of the second as a "disputation" (2.5, Hoby, 91, Maier 195). In this disputatious atmosphere, Ludovico fully expects to be "reprehended"

19. On the so-called *mutili* of *De oratore*, see May and Wisse, in Cicero, *On the Ideal Orator*, 307, and Fantham, *Roman World of Cicero's* De Oratore, 49–50.

by a Tuscan for his Lombard vocabulary (1.39, Hoby 65, Meier 153), as well as refuted by a Frenchman for his insistence that the courtier be well read. "I woulde not now some one of the contrarie parte," he asserts regarding his hypothetical opponent from north of the Alps, "should alledge unto me the contrarie effects to confute [*rifutar*] mine opinion with all: and tell mee how the Italians with their knowledge of letters have shewed small promesse in arms from a certaine time hitherto" (1.43, Hoby 70, Meier 161). Whatever side Ludovico argues, in other words, he is prepared for *reprehension*.

Fully in keeping with this refutative dimension of the dialogue, the interlocutors, as we have seen, invoke the same cluster of specialized terms featured in the rhetorical manuals of Cicero and Quintilian: *reprehendere, confutare, refutare* in their Italian—and English—equivalents. Even those who hope to avoid confutation make use of this terminology. So the Unico Aretino responds to the accusations of Emilia Pia against him as a complacent lover with a *nolo contendere*. "I entend not to attempt to confute [*confuter*] your words," he explains, "because me seemeth it is as well my destinie not to be believed in truth, as it is yours to be believed in untruth" (3.63, Hoby 245, Meier 426). On other occasions, the interlocutors deploy a less overtly forensic lexicon—without abandoning their intentions to refute. With this intention precisely, Gasparo Pallavicino reminds Ludovico and the rest of the company of "the authoritie given us to contrary [*contradire*] you" (1.15, Hoby 33; Meier 106) before refuting the Count's argument in favor of nobility; and Federico begins book 2 with the assurance that he will not "contrarie" (*non gli contradirò*) Ludovico's arguments in book 1 (2.7, Hoby 94, Meier 198). At the end of book 2, Giuliano prepares the company for his defense of women on the following day by reasserting the initial agreement regarding refutation advanced earlier by Gasparo. "Yet if your pleasure be so, that I shall take this burden upon me," Giuliano requests:

> let it be at the least with those conditions that the other have had before me: namely that everie man, where he shall thinke good, may reply against mee [*contradirmi*], and this shall I reckon not overthwarting [*contradizione*], but aide, and perhaps in correcting mine errours [*col correggere gli errori mei*] wee shal finde the perfectiõ of a gentlewomã of the palace which we seeke for. (2.100, Hoby 184; Meier 332)

Unlike some of his fellow courtiers, in other words, the Magnifico is as eager to be refuted (and thereby corrected) as he is to refute.[20]

But the Magnifico is not the only one to acknowledge the benefits of refutation. Castiglione himself opens his prefatory letter to Don Michel de Silva with just such an acknowledgment, for he fully expects that his work will provoke "fault finders" or *riprensori* (Hoby 13, Meier 75). "And if in this behalf," he concedes regarding his portrait of the Duchess, "or in anie other matter worthy reprehention [*riprensione*] (as I know well there want not many in the booke) fault be found in me [*sarò ripreso*], I will not speake against [*non contradirò*] the truth" (Hoby 10–11, Meier 72). On the other hand, he adds with an emphasis on the terminology of the rhetorical manuals lost in Hoby's translation, "men sometime take such delite in finding fault [*riprendere*], that they find fault [*riprendono*] also in that deserveth not reproof [*riprensione*]" (Hoby 11, Meier 72). Given the attention to refutation in the rhetorical handbooks as the orator's most lethal weapon as well as his representation of the conduct of his courtiers at the court of Urbino, it is hardly surprising that Castiglione is alert to the threat posed by his own *riprensori*.

Like the *Book of the Courtier*, Petrarch's *Secret* combines the familiarity of the dialogue with the antagonism of refutation.[21] Petrarch foregrounds the dialogical dimension of Franciscus's exchange with Augustinus by having him refer to it as a *conversatio* (Proem 2.3, p. 4), a *sermo*, and a *colloquium familiare* (Proem 3.5, p. 7). He even goes so far as to identify Plato and Cicero as his literary progenitors in this genre (Proem 4.2, p. 9). But Petrarch also emphasizes the forensic, agonistic dimensions of their conversation, beginning with his recollection of Augustinus's opening words: "What are you doing, wretched man?" (1.1.1, p. 11). Calculated to put Franciscus on the defensive, these words, Petrarch notes at the end of the Proem (4.2, p. 9), signal the aggressiveness with which Augustinus will pursue an agenda that requires him to break a long, blessed silence to engage a fellow mortal. Setting the stage for this aggressive engagement,

20. For this Socratic principle as formulated in the *Gorgias*, see below, pp. 77–78.

21. For Petrarch's success as a writer of invective, see Francesco Petrarca, *Invectives*, trans. David Marsh (Cambridge, MA, 2008), vii–xx, and Pier Giorgio Ricci, "La tradizione dell'invettiva tra il Medioevo e l'Umanesimo," *Lettere Italiane* 26 (1974): 405–14. On the relation of invective to refutation, see above, n. 2.

Petrarch's Proem concludes: *his ille me primum verbis aggressus est* (with these words he assaulted me, 4.2, p. 9). Acknowledging this aggression, Franciscus refers to Augustinus in the course of the dialogue as an *accusator*—one who continually presses him with *accusationes* (2.5.1–3). Their *sermo*, in other words, takes on more than just the trappings of an *altercatio* (1.4.6, p. 23) or even a *lis* (1.8.4, p. 37; 3.18.8, p. 256), a litigation.

In keeping with the litigious nature of their exchange, both Augustinus as prosecutor and Franciscus as defendant call witnesses (1.4.2, p. 21). While Franciscus naïvely expects supporting testimony that is not forthcoming from either Truth or Augustinus, Augustinus is more successful in enlisting Franciscus himself—or rather, Franciscus's conscience—as *his* star witness (1.8.5, p. 37). When Franciscus resists Augustinus's accusation that he only halfheartedly meditates on his mortality, Augustinus responds, "I shall prove it with the greatest of ease, on condition that you set your mind on confessing [*confiteri*] the truth in good faith [*bona fide*]. Here again I'll use a witness who is close at hand" (1.8.5, p. 37). To Franciscus's continued insistence that his conscience testifies otherwise, Augustinus further responds, "When the questioning [*interrogatio*] is confused, the evidence [*testimonium*] of the respondent cannot be conclusive" (1.8.5, p. 37). Having enlisted Franciscus's conscience as a hostile witness, Augustinus adds insult to injury by implying that Franciscus lacks the skill of an effective cross-examiner.

With this exchange, Petrarch clearly establishes that the forensic procedure underway in this dialogue is a refutation: its agenda is to disclose the inconsistencies and contradictions in Franciscus's arguments on his own behalf. That Franciscus also understands the stakes of the exchange in this way is clear from his acknowledgment of the challenge he faces. "You may rest assured," he concedes to Augustinus, "that I will never again believe in myself if you prove to me that in this respect my belief was mistaken" (1.8.4, p. 37). In the course of the lengthy interrogation over three books, Augustinus indeed disabuses Franciscus of a number of his most deeply held assumptions, beginning with his belief that he is immune to self-deception. "It is precisely when you boast that you have never deceived yourself," Augustinus retorts, "that you deceive yourself the most" (1.4.5, p. 23). At this point in the conversation, Franciscus is pressing the unsustainable position featured in the previous chapter: that he *would* shake off his misery if he *could* (see above, p. 28).

But Augustinus also takes aim at other strongholds of Franciscus's self-image, including his fantasy that his love for Laura is entirely spiritual. As Augustinus undertakes to demolish one false opinion after another by exposing their inconsistencies, Franciscus takes notice that he is being refuted—even if he continues to offer resistance. "You have me cornered," he admits, "though I may be able to extract myself" (2.9.7, p. 101). At other moments, the defendant acknowledges the success of the prosecutor's strategy, claiming to "see where you've gradually been leading me" (3.6.4, p. 177). At the end of their encounter, Franciscus thanks Augustinus for refuting him, "for... [wiping] the mist from my eyes and ... [dispelling] the thick surrounding cloud of error" (3.18.2, p. 255). With professions of amity and open-mindedness characteristic of the Renaissance dialogue, Franciscus joins Augustinus in a prayer for his well-being. In the meantime, Petrarch has deployed the literary conventions of the genre to stage not just a refutation but, given the identities of the interlocutors, a self-refutation.

But Petrarch does not restrict his penchant for refuting himself to the genre of the dialogue. In fact, his prose work best known to modern readers, the so-called "Ascent of Mount Ventoux" (*Fam.* 4.1), uses the form of the letter to rehearse this very practice, and it does so, once again, under the influence of Augustine's *Confessions*.[22] Written to his esteemed friend Dionigi da Borgo San Sepolcro, who presented him with his copy of this literary treasure, the "Ascent" offers a personal, highly charged account of a climbing expedition with his brother Gherardo in March of 1336, motivated, Petrarch tells the letter's addressee (as well as us), by a long-standing *cupiditas videndi*— an Augustinian "lust of the eyes" to see an unfamiliar wonder, the

22. In *The Quattrocento Dialogue*, Marsh argues that the influence of the Ciceronian dialogue wanes between the fourth century, with the Augustinian dialogues in ascendance, and the *Secretum*, hailed as the first modern dialogue (4): "Nearly a thousand years after Augustine's conversion and his condemnation of the Ciceronian dialogue, the spirit, if not the form, of ancient dialogue was revived by Petrarch in his *Secretum* (1347–53), a soliloquy-like interchange between the author's literary self and his Augustinian conscience. The return to the classical model evidently could not bypass the Church Father who had previously barred the way, and Petrarch openly confronts the obstacles posed by the figure of Augustine." For the centrality of this Augustinian text, see also Brian Cummings, "Autobiography and the History of Reading," in *Cultural Reformations: Medieval and Renaissance in Literary History*, ed. Brian Cummings and James Simpson (Oxford, 2010), 635–57.

highest mountain in his region.[23] The more immediate provocation, he also tells us, was reading Livy's account of Philip of Macedon's ascent of a mountain in Thessaly from whose great height the Macedonian king believed he could see two seas simultaneously. At stake for Petrarch as reader, then, is the veracity of Philip's belief, which the ancient Roman historian denies and which Petrarch insists he could either confirm or refute if only he could see it for himself.[24]

The well-known climax of this famous letter, once Petrarch has reached the summit, also entails a reading experience—not this time an ancient historian but his favorite saintly author. In an episode conspicuously modeled on Augustine's encounter in the garden with a passage from Paul's letter to the Romans, Petrarch "randomly" opens his *Confessions* to a passage in book 10 that negates not only the opening question of the letter about a mountain in Thessaly that motivated this particular expedition but the very quest itself for worldly experience. For Augustine sharply reproaches those, like Petrarch, who "go to admire the summits of mountains and the vast billows of the sea" and "overlook themselves" (1.178, quoting *Confessions* 10.8.15). Deeply stung by this reproach, Petrarch registers the radical change of perspective it effects. "How often, do you think, upon returning home that day," he asks in a rhetorical question designed to communicate his thoroughly altered frame of mind, "when I turned back to look at the summit of the mountain, it seemed to me scarcely a cubit high in comparison with the loftiness of human meditation, if only it were not plunged into the mire of earthly filthiness" (1.179). Bookending the mountain-climbing adventure with two episodes of reading, Petrarch not only establishes the shift in preoccupation from physical to spiritual matters but stages the second reading episode as a refutation of the first. Whereas Petrarch opens his letter intending to refute Livy, he structures its climax as his being refuted by Augustine.

23. On Augustinian *cupiditas oculorum* or "lust of the eyes"—Petrarch's *cupiditas videndi*—see, in response to 1 John 2:16, *De vera religione* 38.69 and *Confessions* 10.35.54.

24. *Letters on Familiar Matters*, 1: 172; *Le Familiari*, ed. Vittorio Rossi, 4 vols. (Florence, 1933–42), 1: 153–61. On this letter, see, for instance, Michael O'Connell, "Authority and the Truth of Experience in Petrarch's 'Ascent of Mount Ventoux,'" *Philological Quarterly* 62 (1983): 507–19; Robert Durling, "The Ascent of Mont Ventoux and the Crisis of Allegory," *Italian Quarterly* 18 (1974): 7–28; Quillen, *Rereading the Renaissance*, 137–47.

But Petrarch has prepared for this climactic, Augustinian moment with a carefully constructed *gradatio* of refutations that punctuates the stages of the climb. Both times he stops for rest before reaching the summit, he converses with himself; and both inner dialogues offer an opportunity for self-accusation. The first, he tells us with an eye on the allegory, occurs after he has lost his way up the mountain three or four times and taken refuge in a valley. This internal self-address is introduced with the words *his aut talibus me ipsum compellabam verbis*, "I reproached [or better, "arraigned," "indicted"] myself with these or similar words" (1.174; Rossi 1: 155 ll. 91–92).[25] In his self-indictment, Petrarch includes not only the "crime" of failing to perform a spiritual ascent but the punishment of "perpetual torments" awaiting him if he persists in failing (1.175). The second inner dialogue, after scaling the highest peak, is considerably more dramatic as Petrarch pits his mind against itself in adversarial fashion. "What I used to love I no longer love," he attests:

> I am wrong, I do love it but too little. There, I am wrong again. I love it but I am too ashamed of it and too sad over it. Now indeed I have said it right. For that is the way it is; I love, but something I would like not to love, and would like to hate.

> [Quod amare solebam, iam non amo; mentior: amo, sed parcius; iterum ecce mentitus sum: amo, sed verecundius, sed tristius, iantandem verum dixi. Sic est enim; amo, sed quod non amare amem, quod odisse cupiam.] (1.176; Rossi 1: 157 ll. 154–59)

Simulating ever so briefly the inner cross-examination that convicts him, Petrarch feels compelled to relinquish his false beliefs and admit the truth.

In his efforts at self-refutation, as already noted, Petrarch takes as his literary model Augustine; and Augustine often relies on the terminology of the rhetorical handbooks, and especially *refellere* and *reprehendere*, to characterize some of the many agonistic encounters that propel his own journey to God. Among them are the Manichees' efforts to refute (*reprehenderant*) the Hebrew Scriptures—efforts that

25. For the legal sense of *compellare*, see C. T. Lewis and C. Short, eds., *A New Latin Dictionary* (New York, 1879), s.v., IIB.

the young Augustine admits to having found persuasive for a time (*Confessions* 5.11.21). "In my blindness," he recalls in regard to the Hebrew prophets, "I reprehended [*reprehendebam*] [them] not only for acting at the time as God commanded them, but also for predicting the future as God revealed it to them" (3.7.14); and he remembers his pleasure in refuting through ridicule (*inrisis refellere*) the astrologers who misled his more gullible acquaintances (7.6.10).

Augustine also recalls not just being refuted but imploring refutation. From the outset, this refutation, in keeping with its fundamentally legal pedigree, goes hand in hand with confession. "Let no critics shout against me (I am not afraid of them now)," he proclaims, "while I confess [*Confiteor*] to you the longing of my soul, my God, and when I accept rebuke [*adquiesco in reprehensione*] for my evil ways and wish to love your good ways" (*Confessions* 1.13.22)[26] On one decisive occasion, Augustine further recalls, a wise priest refuses Monica's urgent request to "make time to talk to me and refute my errors [*refellere errores meos*]" (3.12.21), trusting that Augustine would discover his mistakes independently through his reading—that, in other words, he would eventually refute himself.

In keeping with his willingness to be refuted, moreover, Augustine confesses that as an infant he "must have acted reprehensibly" (*tunc ergo reprehendenda faciebam*) even though he neither remembers his earliest sins nor understood "the person who admonished [*reprehendentem*] me," since at the time "neither custom nor reason allowed me to be reprehended [*reprehendi*]" (1.7.1). Once drawn to the teachings of Ambrose, however, Augustine experiences the more relentless stirrings of a conflicted will. Wavering between belief and disbelief, he, like Franciscus in the *Secret*, confronts a despair (*desperatio*) that can begin to be overcome only through a powerful process of self-refutation (*iam reprehendebam desperationem meam illam dumtaxat*, 5.14.24).

But if Petrarchan self-refutation openly shares its agenda with Augustinian confession, the *Secret*, by its own account, belongs to a dialogical tradition that looks back not only to Cicero but to Plato. Plato's early dialogues, in fact, are all arguably refutative; and one in partic-

---

26. In *Ecclesiastes*, his manual for the preacher, Erasmus highlights the similarities between legal and spiritual confession, even though he claims to be stressing the differences (CWE 68: 705).

ular, the *Gorgias*, both practices and preaches refutation, including self-refutation.[27] It is not likely, however, that Petrarch knew of its arguments in any detail. The medieval Latin Plato he owned contained the *Timaeus* in a partial translation by Calcidius and the *Phaedo* and possibly the *Meno* translated by Henricus Aristippus, while the Greek manuscript in his possession, which included the *Clitophon*, the *Republic*, the *Timaeus*, the *Critias*, the *Minos*, the *Laws*, the *Phaedrus*, and the *Letters*, and which he could not read, lacked the *Gorgias*.[28] Unavailable to Petrarch in the middle of the fourteenth century, this elenchic dialogue, on the other hand, provided a model of refutation that sixteenth-century writers from Erasmus to Montaigne could readily find in printed editions not only in the original Greek but in Latin in Ficino's widely acclaimed translation.[29]

27. On the Socratic *elenchos* on display in Plato's early dialogues, which has received renewed attention since the 1983 article by Gregory Vlastos, see Robinson, *Plato's Earlier Dialectic*, 7–32, and Don Adams, "Elenchos and Evidence," *Ancient Philosophy* 18 (1998): 287–307. On the conversion-like experience occasioned by Socratic *elenchus*, see Charles Kahn, "Drama and Dialectic in Plato's *Gorgias*," *Oxford Studies in Ancient Philosophy* 1 (1983): 115, and James King, "Elenchus, Self-Blame and the Socratic Paradox," *Review of Metaphysics* 41 (1987): 105. The self-refutation discussed in this chapter should not be confused with the so-called self-refuting argument or *peritropē*, which also looks back to Socrates, on which see M. F. Burnyeat, "Protagoras and Self-Refutation in Later Greek Philosophy," *Philosophical Review* 85 (1976): 44–69, and Barbara Herrnstein Smith, "Unloading the Self-Refutation Charge," in *Self and Deception: A Cross-Cultural Philosophical Enquiry*, ed. Roger T. Ames and Wimal Dissanayake (Albany, 1996), 143–59.

28. For Petrarch's acquaintance with Plato's dialogues, see Trinkaus, *Poet as Philosopher*, 7–8. For translations of Plato before Ficino, see James Hankins, *Plato in the Italian Renaissance*, 2 vols. (Leiden, 1990), who characterizes Ficino's Socrates as well as his interlocutors as more polite than aggressive: "Hence, like Bruni, Ficino reads the rancorous interchanges among Socrates, Gorgias, and Callicles as playful sparring concealing an underpurpose of serious inquiry" (327). Without knowing the dialogue itself, Petrarch would have known Quintilian's discussion at 2.15.18–29.

29. For Montaigne's knowledge of the *Gorgias*, see below. For a more general awareness earlier in the century on the part of Erasmus and his contemporaries, see Jacques Chomarat, "Érasme et Platon," *Bulletin de l'Association Guillaume Budé* 1 (1987): 25–48. In a letter from one of these contemporaries, Rutgerus Sycamber, Erasmus is reminded of the lesson of the *Gorgias*: "Has anything new or unusual happened to you, reverend Father, if some false or cunning man has deluded you? Are we not deceived, and do we not deceive others, every day? It would have been grievous matter for sorrow, very bitter sorrow, if you yourself had deceived someone else; as it is, we may rejoice that you were not the doer

PLATO'S *GORGIAS* AND MONTAIGNE'S
ART OF CONVERSATION

In both original and translation, sixteenth-century readers of the *Gorgias*, including Montaigne, would discover a Socrates eager to take on not one but three adversaries over the course of an increasingly aggressive exchange. With all three of these sparring partners, moreover, Socrates adheres to a double agenda: examining their claims for inconsistencies and contradictions and being examined in turn by them.[30] With the first of his opponents, he even takes the time to lay out the ground rules and to make sure they are understood and accepted before launching into his examination. "Now I am afraid to refute you [*delenchein se*]," he tells a complacently confidant Gorgias whose opening remarks are already raising contradictions:

> lest you imagine I am contentiously neglecting the point and its elucidation, and merely attacking you. I therefore, if you are a person of the same sort as myself, should be glad to continue questioning you: if not, I can let it drop. Of what sort am I? One of those who would be glad to be refuted [*elengthentōn*] if I say anything untrue, and glad to refute [*elenxantōn*] anyone else who might speak untruly; but just as glad, mind you, to be refuted [*elengthentōn*] as to refute [*elenxantōn*], since I regard the former as the greater benefit, in proportion as it is a greater benefit for oneself to be delivered from the greatest evil than to deliver someone else.[31]

---

but the victim of the injury. Or do you count happy one who wrongs another, and the wronged person pitiable and unhappy? Plato himself did not think so, gentile and pagan though he was, but on the contrary declared a man who suffers wrong less to be pitied than him who inflicts it. And you, a Christian and vowed to a religious life, do you not feel something that was evident to a pagan and a gentile?" (Ep. 65A, CWE 1: 139–40). In *The School of Montaigne in Early Modern Europe*, 2 vols. (Oxford, 2017), 2: 192–93, Warren Boutcher notes that Montaigne's translator Florio placed the *Essais* in the tradition of *De oratore* as a work dedicated to the formation of the educated statesman.

30. For a skeptical view of Socrates' willingness to be refuted, see Robinson, *Plato's Earlier Dialectic*, 9.

31. *Gorgias*, trans. W. R. M. Lamb (Cambridge, MA, 1925; rpt. 1983), 457E–458B. All further references are to this edition and cited in the text. For the Greek I have used the edition by E. R. Dodds (Oxford, 1959). On Socratic refutation as reduction to contradiction, see Robinson, *Plato's Earlier Dialectic*, 29–30.

Having just identified rhetoric as an agonistic activity designed to engage large crowds (456CD; cf. 457A, 458E, 459A) and himself as a master rhetorician poised to answer any question, Gorgias is not about to shy away from this *agōn*, although he certainly does not endorse Socrates' preference for being refuted over refuting.

Both the formulation of the preference and its paradoxical nature, however, are key; for they parallel the Socratic core value that both Polus and Callicles, Socrates' next two interlocutors, will find utterly repugnant and do their very best to refute: namely, that it is better to suffer wrongdoing than to commit it.[32] As the conversation winds down, a Socrates trying hard not to gloat over his victory takes a moment not only to make the parallels explicit but to effect their intersection. "But among the many statements we have made," he recapitulates, "while all the rest are refuted [*elenchomenōn*] this one alone is unshaken—that doing wrong [*to adikein*] is to be more carefully shunned than suffering it [*to adikeisthai*]" (527B). Fully committed to this position, Socrates is no less committed to the refutative procedure that validates it.

But refutation in the *Gorgias* takes a number of forms, and Socrates does not value them all equally. In fact, he summarily dismisses Polus's attempt to refute him with ridicule: "What is that I see, Polus? You are laughing? Here we have yet another [*allo au*] form of refutation [*eidos elenchou*]—when a statement is made, to laugh it down, instead of disproving it [*elenchein de mē*]" (473E).[33] With his "yet another" Socrates alludes to the refutative procedure he rejected moments earlier, although less summarily: the rhetorical procedure of the law courts outlined earlier in this chapter.[34] "For there, one party is supposed to refute [*elenchein*] the other," he explains:

> when they bring forward a number of reputable witnesses to any statements they may make, whilst their opponent produces only

32. For the conventional view that it is indeed better to commit wrongdoing than to suffer it, see Isocrates, *Panathenaicus* 117–18; Gerard Watson, "Plato's *Gorgias* and Aristotle," 66n23; and C. H. Kahn, "Drama and Dialectic in Plato's *Gorgias*," 85–97.

33. For Erasmus's association of the irony identified with Socrates with mockery and refutation, see *Ecclesiastes*, CWE 68: 834–37.

34. On Socrates' distinction between his own and legal refutation, see Robinson, *Plato's Earlier Dialectic*, 15–16.

one, or none. But this sort of refutation [*elenchos*] is quite worthless for getting at the truth; since occasionally a man may actually
be crushed by the number and reputation of the false witnesses
brought against him. (471E)

Like the art of rhetoric Gorgias envisioned earlier in the dialogue, in
other words, Polus's procedure depends on large numbers, a crowd—
here the number of witnesses—whereas Socrates drastically reduces
the number to one. Only his interlocutor matters, Socrates insists; and
the same holds for Polus as far as Socrates is concerned. If Socrates
is unpersuaded by Polus's argument, then no number of witnesses in
its favor will count for anything:

> But I, alone here before you, do not admit it, for you fail to con-
> vince me: you only attempt, by producing a number of false wit-
> nesses against me, to oust me from my reality, the truth. But if on
> my part I fail to produce yourself as my one witness to confirm
> what I say, I consider I have achieved nothing of any account to-
> wards the matter of our discussion, whatever it may be; nor have
> you either, I conceive, unless I act alone as your one witness, and
> you have nothing to do with all these others. Well now, this is one
> mode of refutation [*tropos elenchou*], as you and many other people
> conceive it; but there is also another which I on my side conceive.
> Let us therefore compare them with each other and consider if we
> find a difference between them. (472BC)

Precisely because Socratic dialogue shares its deepest structures with
forensic rhetoric, as both Aristotle and Quintilian have noted, it is
a matter of the greatest importance to differentiate legal refutation
from Socratic refutation.

At this point in the dialogue, however, Socrates offers as the single
most important differentiating factor the number of witnesses, one
in place of many. This factor is so decisive that Socrates reaffirms it
moments later when dismissing Polus's attempt to refute him by calling on the testimony of those assembled (473E), since that is decid-
edly not the kind of refutation Socrates has in mind. "For I know how
to produce one witness in support of my statements," Socrates tells
Polus, "and that is the man himself with whom I find myself arguing;
the many I dismiss: there is also one whose vote I know how to take,

whilst to the multitude I have not a word to say" (474AB). But even this drastic reduction in both number of witnesses and audience size eventually proves insufficient. For Socratic refutation can and should be practiced not on one's adversaries at all but on one's loved ones and ultimately on oneself. Instead of defending ourselves against the accusations of others, Socrates insists contrary to common belief, we should become our own most ardent accusers (480CD). The kind of refutation Socrates values most, in other words, is self-refutation.[35]

While Polus remarks on the absurdity of this position, the real measure of its outlandishness is that it draws the recalcitrant Callicles into the conversation, allowing Socrates to cast his third and final interlocutor as someone who pays a price for holding inconsistent and contradictory positions because he cannot refute either himself or those he loves, including Demos and his Athenian counterpart, the crowd (481BE).[36] Socrates' beloved, in contrast, is Philosophy, and she is always ready for the give-and-take of refutation:

> So you must either refute [Philosophy], as I said just now, by proving that wrongdoing and impunity for wrong done is not the uttermost evil; or, if you leave that unproved, by the Dog, god of the Egyptians, there will be no agreement between you, Callicles, and Callicles, but you will be in discord with him all your life. (482B)

Unprepared as yet for self-refutation, Callicles, whether he likes it or not, will have to rely on Socrates to do the job. In light of Callicles' continued resistance, the final part of the dialogue features a chipping

---

35. In contrast to my reading, Dodds (*Gorgias*, 257) reads Socrates' position about refuting our loved ones and ourselves as ironic and warns against taking it literally, although he does notice the "theme of self-reform," if not self-refutation, in this dialogue as in the *Phaedo* and *Republic* (384). For the inconsistency at the heart of Polus's conventional beliefs, see C. H. Kahn, "Drama and Dialectic in Plato's *Gorgias*," 95.

36. On the identity of Demos, see Dodds, *Gorgias*, 261. On the Calliclean position being refuted, including its contradictions and inconsistencies, see George Klosko, "The Refutation of Callicles in Plato's 'Gorgias,'" *Greece and Rome* 31 (1984): 126–39, and C. H. Kahn, "Drama and Dialectic in Plato's *Gorgias*," 102–10. On the role of Demos in these inconsistencies, Kahn writes: "As an ambitious politician in a democracy, [Callicles] is obliged to be a lover of the demos and an endorser of popular views . . . But he is himself an aristocrat . . . and has nothing but contempt for the egalitarian principles of democracy" (100).

away at his inconsistencies and contradictions. Like most if not all of the parties to an Athenian legal dispute (but unlike Castiglione's Magnifico), Callicles to the bitter end would rather refute than be refuted.

When Petrarch turns in the middle of the fourteenth century to staging his own most sustained self-refutation in the *Secret*, as we have seen, he openly pays homage to Plato by structuring it as a dialogue as well as to the *Confessions* by making the self-accusing (and Platonizing) Augustine his interlocutor. Even without direct access to the *Gorgias*, Petrarch appreciates the refutative dimension of dialogue as practiced by other favorite ancient authors, including Cicero, whose *Tusculan Disputations,* a founding text for Renaissance humanists, not only grounds the quest for philosophical truth in the ability "to refute without obstinacy [*et refellere sine pertinacia*] and be refuted without anger [*refelli sine iracundia*]" (*Tusc. Disp.* 2.2.5) but attributes this procedure to Socrates, whose model Cicero himself claims to be following as he opposes (*contra dicere*) the arguments put forward by his own interlocutor (*Tusc. Disp.* 1.4.8).[37]

Like Petrarch in drawing attention in his writing to his own inconsistencies and contradictions, Montaigne is unlike Petrarch in two important ways: on the one hand, as noted above, he has direct access to Plato's dialogues in Ficino's Latin translations; on the other, he snubs the genre in which Plato stages Socrates' refutations of his opponents, preferring his own innovation of the essay.[38] Explicitly fashioning this innovative form to be supple enough to follow his thoughts wherever they lead, even if they collide with one another en route to a dead end, Montaigne writes one essay in particular as a tribute not only to the common cause of dialogue and refutation but to the self-refutation advocated—if not actually enacted—in Plato's *Gorgias*.

"De l'art de conferer"—"Of the Art of conferring" in Florio's 1603

37. On the privileged place of the *Tusculan Disputations,* see Martin McLaughlin, "Petrarch and Cicero: Adulation and Critical Distance," in *Brill's Companion to the Reception of Cicero,* ed. William H. F. Altman (Leiden, 2015), 19–38, esp. 36–37.

38. For Montaigne's familiarity with not only the figure of Socrates but the Platonic dialogues themselves, evident throughout the *Essais,* see, for instance, I.26, which references the *Symposium, Republic,* and *Laws,* and John O'Brien, "Montaigne and Antiquity: Fancies and Grotesques," in *The Cambridge Companion to Montaigne,* ed. Ullrich Langer (Cambridge, UK, 2005), 53–77, esp. 59. For Montaigne's appraisal of his chosen genre as an innovation, see, for instance, II.6, Fl 2: 58, and II.8, Fl 2: 66.

translation—opens with a brief but pointed reference to Plato on judicial correction and self-accusation (*Gorgias* 525BC, 527BC) before turning to the topic announced in its title.[39] After characterizing *conference* as the "most fruitfull and natural exercise of our spirit . . . more delightsome, then any other action of our life" (Fl 3: 159), Montaigne pivots to its agonistic, adversarial nature, comparing it to wrestling and jousting.[40] The discursive activity he has in mind, in other words, is not casual conversation (*sermo*) but disputation (*disputatio*); and he invokes Cicero's authority to back up his fundamentally Socratic claim that "Disputation cannot be held without reprehension"— Florio's (actually, Matthew Gwinne's) translation of Cicero's *De finibus* 1.8: *Neque enim disputari sine reprehensione potest.*[41] There is no discussion or disputation or *conference* without refutation, what Montaigne, following the rhetorical manuals, sometimes calls *reprehension* and at other times *correction*, recalling the opening of the essay with its reference to Plato on judicial punishment. Whereas others go to great lengths to avoid being refuted or corrected—"We commonly shunne correction whereas we should rather seeke and present ourselves unto it, chiefly when it commeth by way of conference" (Fl 3: 161, V 2: 924)—Montaigne himself claims to welcome the opportunity to be shown the inconsistencies and contradictions in the positions he takes. "When I am impugned or contraried," he admits, "then is mine attention and not mine anger, stirred up: I advance my selfe toward

---

39. For Plato on judicial correction, see Mary Margaret Mackenzie, *Plato on Punishment* (Berkeley, 1981).

40. For the text of Montaigne, I have used *Les Essais de Michel de Montaigne*, ed. Pierre Villey and V.-L. Saulnier, 2 vols. (Paris, 1924; rpt. 1978), cited here and hereafter as V with volume and page number in the text, and for the English translation, *The Essays of Montaigne*, trans. John Florio, 3 vols. (1603; London, 1892; rpt. New York, 1967), here and hereafter Fl with volume and page number in the text. On this translation, see Warren Boutcher, "The Origins of Florio's Montaigne: 'Of the Institution and Education of Children, to Madame Lucy Russell, Countess of Bedford,'" *Montaigne Studies* 24 (2012): 7–32, and *School of Montaigne*, 2: 189–215. On the agonistic as well as the legal dimensions of conversational style as discussed in this essay, see Eden, *Renaissance Rediscovery of Intimacy*, 106–9.

41. For Gwinne as the translator of the Latin quotations in the Florio translation, see Boutcher, *School of Montaigne*, 2: 200–202. On the Ciceronian elements of Montaigne's style, despite his avowed anti-Ciceronianism, see Kathy Eden, "Cicero's Portion of Montaigne's Acclaim," *Brill's Companion to the Reception of Cicero*, 39–55.

him, that doth gainsay and instruct me. The cause of truth, ought to be the common cause, both to one and other" (Fl 3: 161, V 2: 924). Like Socrates, Montaigne claims to advance the cause of truth even if it means losing his argument.

Also like Socrates, Montaigne claims to place a higher premium on being refuted than on refuting (Fl 3: 162, V 2: 925), on bending "under the power of my adversaries reason" than on obtaining the victory over him. And not only does Montaigne, like Socrates, consider the size of the audience a decisive factor—"I love to contest and discourse, but not with many, and onely for my selfe" (Fl 3: 160, V 2: 923)—but he looks to Socrates as the model for this behavior. For Socrates "ever smiling, made a collection of such contradictions as were opposed to his discourse" (Fl 3: 162, V 2: 925). Also like Socrates, Montaigne admits to being "well pleased to be reproved" (Fl 3: 162, V 2: 924): *je preste l'espaule aux reprehensions.* And while this eagerness to be *reprehended* or *refuted* makes him like Socrates, it also makes him unlike his contemporaries, who "have not the courage to correct, because they want the heart to endure correction" (Fl 3: 162, V 2: 924). Even Montaigne's paradoxical elevation of the passive over the active—suffering correction over doing the correcting—echoes the formulation of his ancient model. So does Montaigne's stated aim in conferring or disputing with others. "I love to have them entangle and bemire themselves more then they are," Montaigne admits in Florio's translation, "and if it be possible, to wade so deepe into the gulphe of error, that in the end they may recall and advise themselves" (Fl 3.177–78). What Montaigne actually writes is "qu'en fin ils se recoignoissent" (V 2: 937)—echoing the Delphic and Socratic *gnōthi seauton.* His stated aim is to bring his interlocutors to a better understanding of themselves, to self-knowledge. So far, then, this essay seems to present a Montaigne who is more preacher than practitioner of self-refutation; for there is arguably more than a little self-commendation, in contrast to self-correction, in his effort to align himself with the wisest man in Athens.

But Montaigne opens the essay, as mentioned earlier, by claiming that he "reape[s] more honor by accusing, then by commending myself" (Fl 3: 158, V 2: 921); and the essay tries to make good on this claim as Montaigne turns almost immediately to refuting himself for his impatience with stupidity—an imperfection that is only slightly less worthy of condemnation than stupidity itself:

Sottishness is an ill quality, but not to be able to endure it, and to fret and vex at it, as it hapneth to me, is another kinde of imperfection, which in opportunity is not much behind sottishness: and that's it I will now accuse in myself (Fl 3: 160, V 2: 923)

Before long, however, Montaigne revises his self-accusation from mere impatience with stupidity to the more reprehensible imperfection of stupidity itself. For only a sot, he counters, is vexed by human folly. "Now, what if I take things otherwise then they are?" he asks:

So it may bee: And therefore I accuse my impatience . . . since there is not a greater fondnesse, a more constant gullishnesse, or more heteroclite insipidity then for one to move or vex himselfe at the fondnesse, at the gullishnesse, or insipidity of the world. (Fl 3: 166–67, V 2: 928–29)

Hastening to expose this inconsistency in his position, Montaigne not only turns his refutation of stupidity on himself but once again singles out Socrates—or in this case, Plato—as his model in doing so:

Let us ever have the saying of Plato in our mouthes: 'What I finde unwholesome, is it not to be unhealthy my selfe? Am not I in fault my selfe? May not mine owne advertisement be retorted against my selfe?' Oh wise and divine restraint, that curbeth the most universell and common error of men. (Fl 3: 167, V 2: 929)

Despite the reflexive refrain and the self-accusation it underwrites, Montaigne is here refuting, as he says, a common or universal folly rather than an idiosyncratic fault.

Not just daily but a hundred times a day, Montaigne maintains, we all unwittingly and stupidly refute ourselves when we laugh at our neighbors, that is, when we practice the very kind of refutation that Polus tries to pull on Socrates (and Augustine recalls practicing on the astrologers) only to have Socrates summarily dismiss it (Fl 3: 168, V 2: 929). Admittedly, Montaigne does not openly connect our refutative laughter with Socrates' rejection of it in the *Gorgias*; but he does explicitly align this essay not only with the Platonic dialogue most obviously focused on refutation but also with its core valuation of refuting oneself over refuting others:

And Socrates is of opinion, that he, who should find himselfe, and his son, and a stranger guilty of any violence or injury, ought first begin by himselfe, and present himselfe to the sentence and condemnation of the law, and for his owne discharge and acquittal implore the assistance of the executioners hand: secondly for his son, and lastly for the stranger: If this precept take his tone somewhat too high: it should at lest be first presented to the punishment of one's owne conscience. (Fl 3: 168–169, V 2: 930)

At once embracing the Socratic value and keeping it at arm's length on account of its high-mindedness (presumably in its Brutus-like willingness to condemn one's own children), Montaigne nevertheless holds fast to the so-called internal forum of the mind, the conscience, as our most pressing and powerful advocate against our own wrongdoing.

As Montaigne affirms in his essay that bears its name ("Of conscience," II.5, Fl 2: 44–45, V 1: 366–69), our consciences are ever ready to refute us. "[F]or want of other evidences," Montaigne declares, "shee produceth our selves against our selves" (Fl 2: 45, V 1: 367). No small part of the first essayist's agenda, in fact, is to follow Socrates' advice in the *Gorgias* to produce himself against himself. In so doing, Socrates provides one high-profile example for early modern readers and writers of how refutation shapes literary production. For the *Gorgias*, like *De oratore*, not only models refutative practice but theorizes it.

SOCRATIC *EPAGŌGĒ* AND ERASMUS'S *CICERONIANUS*

As we have seen, the Ciceronian dialogue structures this adversarial procedure as arguments offered at length on both sides of the question (*in utramque partem*), a procedure Cicero identifies with Aristotle (*more Aristotelio*). The *Gorgias*, in contrast, showcases Socrates' technique of dismantling an opponent's argument through a series of brief questions and answers.[42] In the *Rhetoric* (1.2.8–9, 2.20.2–4),

---

42. For the Aristotelian procedure of *disputatio in utramque partem*, see *De oratore* 3.80. Whereas I am stressing in Socrates and Cicero a common refutative

Aristotle calls this technique *epagōgē* and characterizes it as proof by means of aggregating comparable particulars to support a general conclusion.[43] In *De inventione*, Cicero prefers the Latin *inductio* but concedes singular mastery in the art to Socrates. Cicero also stresses the element of similarity or likeness (*propter similitudinem*) in this Socratic method of interrogation (*ratio rogandi*), which establishes the certainty of a disputed claim by revealing how it resembles claims that are undisputed (1.51–54). Writing more succinctly to the lawyer Trebatius later in the *Topica*, Cicero reaffirms that "this form of argument which attains the desired proof by citing several parallels is called induction [*inductio*], in Greek ἐπαγωγή [*epagōgē*]; Socrates frequently used this in his dialogues" (*Topica* 42). Following Aristotle and Cicero, Quintilian explains to his readers that these *interrogationes Socratis* (5.11.27) work by inferring "the conclusion of the problem under discussion from its resemblance [*ut simile*] to the points already conceded" (5.11.3). As illustration he offers a Socratic line of questioning:

> "What is the finest form of fruit? Is it not that which is best?" This will be admitted. "What of the horse? What is the finest? Is it not that which is best?" Several more questions of the same kind follow. Last comes the question for the sake of which all the others were put: "What of man? Is not he the finest type who is best?" The answer can only be in the affirmative. (5.11.4)

Like his predecessors in identifying this technique with Socrates (5.11.3), Quintilian also suggests how Socratic *epagōgē* joins forces with Socratic *elenchus*.

This suggestion is not lost on Erasmus. In *De copia*, he both features Socrates as the master practitioner of induction and, like Quintilian, offers his readers an illustration—one that takes its direction

---

agenda aimed at exposing inconsistencies and contradictions, one recognized by Aristotle and Quintilian, Fantham reminds us that "the most important features of Plato's dialogues, the Socratic *elenchus*, would be inconceivable in Roman society, whether in Cicero's generation or after" (*Roman World of Cicero's* De Oratore, 53).

43. On *epagōgē*, see Robinson, *Plato's Earlier Dialectic*, 33–48; Ausland, "Forensic Characteristics of Socratic Argumentation," 59, and Kathy Eden, "Plato's Poetics and the Erasmian *Parabola*," *Poetics before Modernity*, ed. Micha Lazarus and Vladimir Brljak (Oxford, forthcoming), and chap. 3, below.

from Socrates' refutation of the eponymous sophist in the *Gorgias*.
"Do you expect a sailor to talk more knowledgeably about sailing than
a doctor?" Erasmus asks,

> and a doctor more authoritatively about medicine than a painter?
> and a painter better about the techniques of colour and light and
> shade and perspective than a cobbler? Will not a charioteer be
> better at discussing the art of driving a chariot than a sailor? . . .
> But what will the orator discuss best, when he professes to be
> able to talk on any topic? (CWE 24: 624; ASD I-6, 247 l. 234–248
> l. 241)

With this series of parallel cases regarding the nature of an art or
technē, Erasmus models for the beginner how to structure an inductive argument intended to disclose the weakness of an opponent's position. In *De conscribendis epistolis*, Erasmus's wildly popular manual
of letter writing, the master letter writer turns this technique on his
own opponents.[44]

Defending himself against those "classicizing" theorists who take
a rigid view of epistolary style, Erasmus compares their "one size fits
all" attitude regarding the familiar letter to that of "a cobbler who
would insist on stitching a shoe of the same shape for every foot, or a
painter who tried to depict every animal with the same colours and
outline, or a tailor set on making identical clothes fit both a midget
and a giant" (CWE 24: 12; cf. 24: 42–43). And this same antipathy to a
"classicizing" rigidity fuels the satire of the *Ciceronianus*, where Erasmus, as we will see, has his *porte-parole* Bulephorus strike an unmistakably Socratic pose as he refutes the Cicero-worshiping Nosoponus.

In the *Antibarbarians*, as we have already seen at the beginning of
this chapter, Erasmus stages a Ciceronian-style dialogue in which the
principal interlocutor mounts a refutation of the arguments against
the *bonae literae* bequeathed to early modern Europe by ancient

44. On the widespread popularity of *De conscribendis epistolis*, see Mack,
History of Renaissance Rhetoric, 91–96 and 245–46, who labels it the "second
most printed renaissance letter-writing manual with ninety-two editions" (245);
A. Gerlo, "The *Opus de Conscribendis Epistolis* of Erasmus and the Tradition of the
Ars Epistolica," in *Classical Influences on European Culture, A.D. 500–1500*, ed. R. R.
Bolgar (Cambridge, UK, 1971), 107 and 112–13, and Eden, *Renaissance Rediscovery
of Intimacy*, 77n6.

Greece and Rome. While published only eight years later, the satiric *Ciceronianus* (1528) is written after this literary bequest has been fully acknowledged on both sides of the Alps. Marking this sea change, the imitators of Cicero it satirizes cast those, like Erasmus himself, who appreciate the ancient legacy without turning their backs on Christianity, as the barbarians. Not even acclaimed Ciceronian Christophe de Longueil, whose early death is briefly commemorated in the dialogue, is spared censure by his Italian supporters because he dared, as "a barbarian praising fellow barbarians" (CWE 28: 432), to admire Erasmus and countryman Guillaume Budé.

Signaling a radical shift in attitude toward the literature of so-called classical antiquity, the *Ciceronianus* is also unlike the *Antibarbarians* in the genre of dialogue it imitates and therefore the kind of refutation it stages. Whereas Batt and the others assembled, including Erasmus, represent a real circle of friends like those who regularly gather in Cicero's garden settings, Bulephorus and his interlocutors, whose fictional names rely on Greek derivations, recall Lucianic dialogue as well as some of Erasmus's own colloquies.[45] More to the point, the chance encounter with Nosoponus that gets the conversation rolling follows a convention that looks back to the openings of such Platonic favorites as the *Phaedrus* and the *Republic*. Indeed, Erasmus's satiric dialogue begins on a Platonic note as Bulephorus first diagnoses the *zelodulea* or "style-addiction" plaguing Nosoponus (CWE 28: 342; ASD I-2, 606 l. 19) and then pretends to be in love with the same nymph (*nympholēptos*), Peithō or Persuasion (CWE 28: 344; ASD I-2, 607 l. 21), in order to minister to his friend's lovesickness.[46] As Bulephorus introduces the method of his ministrations, moreover, its pedigree is hard to miss; for his apology for his inexperience is dripping with Socratic irony. "You must forgive me, Nosoponus, if I make my points in a rather labored and clumsy fashion," Bulephorus

45. On the differences between Ciceronian, Lucianic, and Platonic dialogue, including setting, the role of history, and the use of names, see Cox, *Renaissance Dialogue*, 9–21. For an Erasmian colloquy that, like the *Ciceronianus*, uses fictional names derived from Greek, consider "The Religious Feast" (CWE 39: 171–243). For the close association of the *Ciceronianus* with the *Colloquies*, see CWE 28: 335 and ASD I-2, 584, 593–94.

46. At ASD I-2, 606 and 607, Pierre Mesnard flags the Platonic allusions to *Rep.* 584A, 553A, and *Phaedrus* 238D, even though he concludes his introduction by noting that in the *Ciceronianus* Erasmus has coupled "très heureusement l'imitation de Lucien à celle de Marcus Tullius" (596).

requests, "as I am not experienced in dialectic" (CWE 28: 357; ASD I-2, 616 ll. 28–29).[47]

At the end of the dialogue, Bulephorus similarly shows his Platonic colors when he invokes Dr. Word (Medicus ὅ λόγος), who, having saved him from perishing from unrequited love of Peithō, stands ready with logotherapy to treat any recurrence of Nosoponus's affliction.[48] Reminiscent of Plato's two dialogues about erotic love, the *Ciceronianus* leverages the deep connection between *erōs* and *logos*; and while Bulephorus's mention of the *pharmakon* echoes the *Phaedrus* (229C, 230D, 274E), his offer early in the dialogue to play the role for Nosoponus that Dr. Word played for him draws an obvious link to the *Symposium* (201E), where Socrates rehearses to the assembled company at Agathon's house what he learned from the Mantinean prophetess Diotima (CWE 28: 408; ASD I-2, 656 ll. 26–29).

Compounding these well-known allusions to Socrates' conversations about love, Bulephorus's refutative practice imitates Plato's elenchic dialogues, like the *Gorgias*—a practice described, as we have seen, in the manuals of the Roman rhetoricians. For Bulephorus interrogates Nosoponus with the aim of disclosing the inconsistencies and contradictions in his most closely guarded assumptions. Among these assumptions is Nosoponus's view that the best way to imitate Cicero is to be as like him as possible, right down to the rigid reproduction of his words, phrases, figures, and rhythms. To dismantle this misguided position, Bulephorus brings *epagōgē* to the aid of *elenchus*.[49]

Unaware as yet that he is falling victim to Bulephorus's refutation, Nosoponus grows impatient almost immediately with his interrogator's inductive method. Advancing the position that imitating Cicero's rhetorical virtues will lead instead to imitating his faults, Bulephorus pursues an unmistakably Socratic line of questioning:

BULEPHORUS: It's inevitable that imitation falls short when it tries only to follow a model, not surpass it. Consequently, the more determinedly you aim to copy Cicero, the nearer you come to a fault.

---

47. For an early appreciation of Socrates' feigned humility known as *eironeia*, see Quintilian 9.2.46.

48. On *logotherapy*, see Marjorie O'Rourke Boyle, "Erasmus' Prescription for Henry VIII: Logotherapy," *Renaissance Quarterly* 31 (1978): 161–72.

49. On the reliance of Socratic *elenchos* on Socratic *epagōgē*, see Robinson, *Plato's Earlier Dialectic*, 38–42.

NOSOPONUS: I don't quite see what you mean.

BULEPHORUS: I'll explain. Don't doctors hold the theory that the best state of health is the least secure, because it's closest to sickness?

NOSOPONUS: So I've heard. What then?

BULEPHORUS: And isn't supreme monarchy very close to tyranny?

NOSOPONUS: So they say.

BULEPHORUS: Yet nothing is better than supreme monarchy, provided there is no sign of tyranny. And supreme generosity is very close to the fault of extravagance, isn't it, and extreme severity to positive brutality?

NOSOPONUS: Certainly.

BULEPHORUS: And great gaiety and wit come very near to frivolity and scurrility?

NOSOPONUS: You needn't go through the list. Take it that I've said yes to all of them. (CWE 28: 377; ASD I-2, 632 ll. 2–14)

Nosoponus responds to Bulephorus's Socratic-style *epagōgē*, in other words, by trying to short-circuit the procedure. But Nosoponus's effort does not discourage Bulephorus; in spite of Nosoponus's impatience, Bulephorus returns to the same strategy, which his friend eventually calls out by name. Finding himself being trotted once again through a number of particular instances—these having to do with conventions regulating dress, painting, and sculpture (see chapter 4, below)—Nosoponus asks his examiner, "What's all this Socratic introduction [*Socraticae* εἰσαγωγαί] of yours leading up to?" (CWE 28: 382; ASD I-2, 636 ll. 15–16). Famously unwilling to revise or even proofread his own writing, the Dutch "scribbler" has inadvertently written *eisagōgē* for *epagōgē*.[50] Editorial errors notwithstanding, it is this *epagogic* questioning that brings Nosoponus to the *aporia* or logical impasse that marks the success of the refutation or *elenchus*.[51]

50. In the *Antibarbari*, Batt refers to Erasmus's habit of indiscriminate writing with the accusation that "Whatever he dreams at night he blackens his paper with in the daytime" (CWE 23: 40; ASD I-1, 66 ll. 13). while in the *Ciceronianus* Nosoponus laments that the so-called *Batavus orator* "throws everything off in a hurry" and lacks "sufficient mental discipline to reread what he has written even once" (CWE 28: 425; ASD I-2, 681 ll. 11–13).

51. For Socratic *epagōgē* in the service of *elenchos*, see *Republic* 332C–333E.

In the course of their conversation, that is, Bulephorus discloses a number of inconsistencies and contradictions in Nosoponus's positions. These include the incoherence of considering only those Ciceronian stylistic elements found in his extant works when so much of his corpus is missing; the related unwillingness to use vocabulary not found in Cicero, when Cicero himself thought nothing of coining new words; and, above all, the agenda of imitating only Cicero when Cicero himself chose rather to follow multiple models. Countering one by one the mandates of these strict Ciceronians, Bulephorus leads Nosoponus step by step to the paradoxical position that in order to be *like* Cicero, one must be *unlike* him. "This view, quite the opposite of yours," Bulephorus tells Nosoponus,

> is the one to which our discussion has led, as it seems to me. You say no one can speak well unless he reproduces Cicero; but the very facts of the matter cry out that no one can speak well unless he deliberately and with full awareness abandons the example of Cicero. (CWE 28: 383; ASD I-2, 636 l. 35–637 l. 3)

And this paradox proves true not only for Nosoponus but for other Ciceronians as well, including Paolo Cortesi, who famously took the strict Ciceronian position against Angelo Poliziano. Weighing in at the end of the *Ciceronianus* on this high-profile debate of the 1480s, Bulephorus refutes Cortesi on the grounds of his practice rather than his theory.[52] That is to say, Bulephorus offers in evidence Cortesi's failed refutation of Poliziano, which entirely lacks the point and precision of a Ciceronian rebuttal. "If [Cortesi] agrees with [Poliziano]," Bulephorus asks,

> why does he reply as if he disagrees? If he disagrees, he should have refuted [*refellenda*] Poliziano's points. It is a particularly Ciceronian characteristic to recognize what is in dispute and where one is in agreement with one's adversary, to identify the real point at issue in the case [*et in quo sit causae status*], and not to say anything that has no bearing on it. (CWE 28: 444; ASD I-2, 707 ll. 10–13)

---

52. On the epistolary debate between Poliziano and Cortesi, see McLaughlin, *Literary Imitation in the Italian Renaissance*, 187–227.

Caring little for the words, phrases, and figures recorded in Nosoponus's indexes, the accomplished imitator of Cicero, Erasmus has
Bulephorus insist, understands not only how and why Cicero mas-
tered the art of refutation but how to put into practice in his own
refutations what he has understood. Chief among the rhetorical elements requiring understanding, as both the passage above and the
first chapter of this book illustrate, is the *status causae*—the "real point
at issue in the case." No less important, as Erasmus himself will insist
and we will see in the next chapter, is an indispensable strategy closely
aligned with Socratic refutation as practiced in the *Ciceronianus*: the
similitude.

✳ 3 ✳

Similitude

In *Ecclesiastes*, his manual for the preacher, Erasmus returns on multiple occasions to the many rhetorical uses of similarity and dissimilarity, even weaponizing them in the service of refuting those in the congregation dissenting silently (CWE 68: 590). "A line of argument that is made through likenesses [*per similia*]," Erasmus instructs the writer of sermons, "is refuted through unlikenesses [*per dissimilia*] . . . for resemblance [*similitudo*] is often deceptive" (CWE 68: 667; ASD V-4, 418 ll. 285–86). As an illustration of this refutative practice, Erasmus imagines adversaries offering dueling similitudes. When one argues that "Just as [*Quemadmodum*] old silver is to be preferred to new, so [*ita*] old and established friends are more to be valued than new ones," Erasmus informs his readers, "that is a likeness [*simile*]." An opponent then responds with an unlikeness (*dissimile*): "No, just as [*ut*] a new house and new clothing is better than old, so [*ita*] a new friend should be preferred to an old" (CWE 68: 667; ASD V-4, 418 l. 286–419 l. 289). One way to marshal similarity against an adversary, then, is to counter his similitude with one that contradicts it—in this case with an example of something new being of greater value than something old.

Another way to refute an adversary is to press his similitude *ad absurdum* (CWE 68: 878; ASD V-5, 162 ll. 183–85). To an Arian who reasons that because the Father creates willingly rather than unwillingly (for otherwise He would not be God), the Word must be His Son not by nature but by will,[1] the preacher should respond with a

---

1. On the Arian heresy, see CWE 61: 100, and F. L. Cross and E. A. Livingstone, eds., *Oxford Dictionary of the Christian Church*, 2nd ed. (London, 1974).

simile that renders this reasoning absurd: "Did your father create you willingly or unwillingly? Willingly of course. Therefore you are a son not of nature but of will, but this contains a manifest absurdity" (CWE 68: 878; ASD V-5, 162 ll. 186–90). Clearly refutative in this case, the *similitudo*—which, we're told, Cicero calls a *collatio*—differs, Erasmus points out, from other closely related figures such as the *imago* (CWE 68: 878; ASD V-5, 162 ll. 183–84).

In addition to providing a straightforward illustration of how the subject of the previous chapter, refutation, aligns with the focus of this one, Erasmus's treatment of the similitude in his last rhetorical textbook locates a number of concerns central to the pages that follow. First of all, it raises the vexed question of terminology, as Erasmus toggles between *similitudo*, *simile*, and *collatio*. (More to the point, as we will see shortly, his last rhetorical *technē* steers clear of the very term he favors in earlier manuals, including *De copia* and *De conscribendis epistolis*). It also raises the question of Erasmus's sources. While Cicero is featured in the passages cited above, he is far from the only or even the most authoritative source for the early modern similitude. Then there is the complicated relationship between this figure and others that resemble it. Sometimes Erasmus includes a whole array of strategies like the *imago* under the umbrella of the similitude, while at other times, as suggested above, he applies the term to a comparison rendered more formulaically.[2] And finally, there is the unmistakable affinity between the similitude and deception—an affinity that brings us back to the question of sources.[3]

THE SOCRATIC SIMILITUDE AND
RHETORICAL THEORY

In book 2 of *Ecclesiastes*, Erasmus, following Quintilian, sets out a reading list for the preacher. Among the preferred authors is Plato, as

2. For Erasmus's formulaic construction, discussed in greater detail below, see ASD I-5, 39 and Carol Clark, "Erasmus and the Four-Part Simile in Sixteenth-Century Vernacular Writing," in *Neo-Latin and the Vernacular in Renaissance France*, ed. Grahame Castor and Terence Cave (Oxford, 1984), 216–26. For a similar list including *collatio, imago, abusio, aenigma, allegoria, proverbium*, and *apologus*, see CWE 68: 930; ASD V-5, 218 ll. 404–6.

3. On the deceptiveness of similitudes, see also CWE 68: 705.

noted in the introduction (p. 11), who is "free-flowing and agreeable, and through comparisons [*per similitudines*] . . . lends one a sort of guiding hand towards knowledge of the truth" (CWE 68: 489; ASD V-4, 264 ll. 420–22).[4] At this point in his exposition Erasmus offers no illustration of the Platonic passages he has in mind. In the earlier *Ratio verae theologiae*, again without illustration, he labels these comparisons *similitudines Socraticae* (CWE 41: 633; H260); and elsewhere in his writings he singles out such well-known favorites as the ship of state and the cave from the *Republic* (488A–489A, 514A) and the charioteer and pair of horses from the *Phaedrus* (246A). In the *Republic*, in fact, Socrates admits to Adeimantus how dependent he is on similitudes to get his points across (487E–488A). On this particular occasion, Socrates refers to his comparisons as *eikones*. When referencing the most elaborately constructed of these, he also calls them *mythoi*, presumably in recognition of their elaborate narrative dimension.[5]

But not all *similitudines Socraticae* are so elaborate. Many, on the contrary, are only long enough to feature one significant commonality. Still in conversation with Adeimantus in the *Republic*, Socrates compares the fate of the philosophical soul in Athenian politics to the seedling that struggles to survive in an inhospitable environment:

[J]ust as [*hōsper*] a foreign seed sown in alien ground, is likely to be overcome by the native species and to fade away among them, so [*houtō*] the philosophic nature fails to develop its full power and declines into a different character. (497B)

---

4. For Erasmus's appreciation of Plato's similitudes, see Chomarat, "Érasme et Platon," 34–45, and Erasmus Bartholin and Lynda Gregorian Christian, "The Figure of Socrates in Erasmus' Works," *Sixteenth Century Journal* 3 (1972): 1–10. That readers continue to appreciate Plato's use of images is demonstrated by many current scholarly books and articles, including P. Destree and R. G. Edmonds III, eds., *Plato and the Power of Images* (Leiden, 2017).

5. For Plato's use of the *eikōn* as well as other terms for comparison, including *parabolē* and *homoiōsis*, see Marsh H. McCall, *Ancient Rhetorical Theories of Simile and Comparison* (Cambridge, MA, 1969), 12–23. On the narrative dimension of the *eikōn*, see Kathryn Morgan, "Plato's Goat-Stags and the Uses of Comparison," in *Plato and the Power of Images*, 179–98.

Like the Erasmian *similitudo* deployed above for the purposes of refutation, this one effects its comparison by pairing together two clauses: the first is introduced with some version of "just as" (Gr. *hōsper*; Lat. *quemadmodum, ut*); the second responds with "so" (Gr. *houtō*; Lat. *ita*).[6] Socrates deploys the same strategy when detailing how carefully young philosophical souls must be educated for political life. "Like [*hōsper*] those who lead colts into noise and tumult to see if they're afraid," Socrates explains, "[so] [*houtō*] we must expose our young people to fears and pleasures, testing them more thoroughly than gold is tested by fire" (413DE). As Erasmus would know from his close and continuous reading of Plato's dialogues, the many *similitudines Socraticae* run the gamut from single sets of paired clauses conforming to a "just as . . . so" construction to lengthy stories about liberated prisoners and deaf and blind sea captains.

Erasmus would also know from his close encounters with these same dialogues that Plato was no less worried about the deceptiveness of these similitudes. On the so-called divided line of the *Republic*, itself an *analogia* akin to a similitude, the cognitive process for both making and apprehending *eikones*, the *eikasia*, is relegated to the very bottom of the line (509D–511E).[7] Meanwhile, misusing the commonality that underwrites the similitude unmasks the speaker as a mere debater, not a philosopher (*Republic* 454AD). In the *Phaedrus*, Socrates makes every effort to impress upon his young interlocutor the full import of this distinction, driving home his point with the help of an *eikōn* that compares horses not to human beings, as in the comparison mentioned earlier between colts and children, but

6. In his *Encomium of Helen*, trans. D. M. MacDowell (Bristol, 1982), 14, Gorgias uses the same construction: "Just as [*hōsper*] different drugs expel different humours from the body, and some stop it from being ill but others stop it from living, so [*houtō*] too some speeches cause sorrow, some cause fear, some give the hearers confidence, some drug and bewitch the mind with an evil persuasion." Very much in passing and without any attention to its afterlife, Robinson does put his finger on the Socratic formulation: "What the middle dialogues really rely upon, in order to persuade us and apparently also in order to intuit the truth, is analogy and imagery. Analogy is extremely frequent in the dialogues of Plato. 'As this, so that' is his refrain" (*Plato's Earlier Dialectic*, 204–5).

7. For Erasmus on *analogia* and *similitudo*, see CWE 68: 662, and for Quintilian, see *Inst. orat.* 5.11.34. And see Jean-Claude Margolin, "L'analogie dans la pensée d'Erasme," *Archiv für Reformationsgeschichte* 69 (1978): 24–49.

to asses or mules. Whereas the philosopher is defined as one who knows how to perform the complementary operations of dividing and collecting—operations rooted in the apprehension of similarity and dissimilarity—the mere debater, whether rhetorician or sophist, takes advantage of not only irrelevant and captious similarities (here between the horse and the ass) but the audience's inexperience in detecting the differences that would disclose the deception. By means of these sleight-of-hand likenesses, Socrates warns Phaedrus, the debater can destroy the *polis*, persuading its citizens not only to ride their pack-mules into battle (260BC) but, even more dangerously, to pursue expediency instead of its look-alike, justice. One crucial mark of Plato's philosopher, then, is the soundness of his similitudes.[8]

According to this standard, Socrates is preeminently philosophical; and his mastery of the *similitudo* goes hand in hand with the argumentative strategy singularly associated with his name. As we saw in the previous chapter, that strategy is routinely called *epagōgē* in Greek, *inductio* in Latin—although the *Ciceronianus* mistakenly identifies it with *eisagōgē*.[9] In *Ecclesiastes*, written over many years but ultimately rushed into print, Erasmus also gets it wrong. Calling it in this case *paragōgē*, he nevertheless both describes it in recognizable terms as "elicit[ing] the assent of the person with whom [one] is dealing by adducing many likenesses, either true or invented [*multis similibus sive veris sive confictis*], and then infer[ring] that which most resembles what has been granted," and associates it with Socrates (CWE 68: 663–64; ASD V-4, 416 ll. 201–4).[10] This association, as

---

8. For Aristotle on the fundamental role of similarity and difference in philosophical argument, see *Topica* 1.13, and for the deceptions, 8.2, 157a 26–29.

9. On the long-standing association of Socrates with *epagōgē* or *inductio*, see Hayden W. Ausland, "Socratic Induction in Plato and Aristotle," in *The Development of Dialectic from Plato to Aristotle*, ed. J. L. Fink (Cambridge, UK, 2012), 224–50, and Mark L. McPherran, "Socratic Epagōgē and Socratic Induction," *Journal of the History of Philosophy* 45 (2007): 347–64. In *Plato's Earlier Dialectic*, Robinson addresses the important relation between what Socrates calls an *eikōn* and *epagōgē*: "There is no brief description that successfully conveys a general idea of this feature [of the early dialogues]; but it is something like 'the use of cases' or 'analogy'. It ranges without a break from the clear use of cases in what we should naturally call epagoge to something that we should say is not a use of cases but a use of images or icons. At one end it is epagoge and at the other imagery" (41–42).

10. For *paragōgē* see also CWE 24: 338.

Erasmus knows full well, looks back to Aristotle's *Topica* and *Rhetoric*, singled out in *Ecclesiastes* as required reading for preachers.[11]

In the first book of the *Rhetoric*, Aristotle references his *Topica* in defining *epagōgē* as "show[ing] on the basis of many similar things [*homoiōn*] that something is so" (1.2.9); he then identifies this procedure with the *paradeigma* or example. In the *Rhetoric*'s second book, Aristotle further divides *paradeigmata* into those that are true and those that are constructed or made; and among those "made" he locates what he calls the *parabolē*, a form of argumentation identified with Socrates.[12] "Socratic sayings" (*Ta Sōkratika*), Aristotle explains,

> are an instance of comparison [*parabolē*], for example, if someone were to say that officials should not be chosen by lot (for that would be as if someone chose athletes randomly—not those able to contest, but those on whom the lot fell); or [as if] choosing by lot any one of the sailors to act as pilot rather than the one who knew how. (*Rhetoric* 2.20.4)

A speaker making the case against strict democratic procedure, in other words, is advised to draw a comparison to athletics and sailing as similar activities on the grounds that their best practitioners are those with the most skill. In its first and second books on proof, then, Aristotle's *Rhetoric* features the affiliation of the *parabolē* with both the example or *paradeigma* and *epagōgē*—an affiliation that remains a prominent feature of rhetorical theory, early modern as well as ancient.

The third book of the *Rhetoric*, which, as previously noted, turns from matters of proof to matters of style, complicates the specialized terminology underwriting the early modern similitude. There Aristotle treats the *eikōn* as a kind of metaphor, illustrated by a number of those in the *Republic*, including the disabled sea captain (3.4.1–4). In

---

11. On the greater helpfulness of these texts in place of the *Organon*, see CWE 68: 612. And see *Rhetoric* 2.23.11 on *epagōgē*, esp. Theodectes' Socratic-sounding argument based on similarity.

12. For the Aristotelian *parabolē*, see also *Topica* 8.1 and Samuel McCormick, "Argument by Comparison: An Ancient Typology," *Rhetorica* 32 (2014): 150–53, and McCall, *Ancient Rhetorical Theories of Simile and Comparison*, who notes that "identifying features of παραβολή do not, in Aristotle's mind, seem to include a particular form" (27).

all cases, the *eikōn* expands the more compressed metaphor by adding some term that highlights the comparison. Whereas "he rushed on like a lion [*hōs de leōn*]" is an *eikōn* according to Aristotle, "a lion [he] rushed on" is a metaphor (3.4.1). Like Plato's Socrates, Aristotle considers the astute apprehension of similarity not only the foundation of a sound metaphor but the mark of a philosophical nature (2.20.7). Here deployed in the service of a stylistic strategy, similarity also underwrites the probative power of *epagōgē* and *parabolē*.

Like Aristotle, the young Cicero speaks to this probative power of comparisons in his early work on the invention of arguments, *De inventione*. Addressing the force of similarity or *similitudo* in making one's case, Cicero both acknowledges a strategy referred to as *ex paribus* (1.30.46–47) and distinguishes three kinds of arguments rooted in "a certain principle of similarity running through diverse material" (*in rebus diversis similem aliquem rationem*): *imago, collatio, exemplum* (1.30.49). Although mentioned very much in passing, the argument *ex pari*, as Cicero illustrates it, conforms to the "just as . . . so" pair of clauses discussed above. "For as [*ut*] a place without a harbor cannot be safe for ships," Cicero fashions his illustration, "so [*sic*] a mind without integrity cannot be relied on by friends" (1.30.47). (As Quintilian will be quick to point out, the oratorical Cicero relies heavily on this kind of argument.) Meanwhile, the Ciceronian triad of strategies, not easily distinguishable from one another according to his vague descriptions, nevertheless does at once not only strengthen the alliance between the similitude, the example (Lat. *exemplum*, Gr. *paradeigma*), and the *imago* but also launch *collatio* as the term routinely identified with the Ciceronian similitude, defined as "a passage [*oratio*] putting one thing beside another on the basis of their resemblances [*ex similitudine*]" (1.30.49). For Cicero, then, *similitudo* remains the general quality informing a number of argumentative strategies, while *collatio* emerges as a particular strategy—one that will eventually come to include the argument *ex paribus*.[13] Seemingly aware that his discussion raises more questions than it answers, the teenage Cicero begs his reader's patience until he returns to these matters as part of a forthcoming treatise on style (1.30.49). Although Cicero never fulfills this promise even when he finally revisits style

---

13. For Cicero on comparison, see McCall, *Ancient Rhetorical Theories of Simile and Comparison*, 87–129.

much later in life (see chapter 4), the promise itself presses the point that the similitude crosses the boundary reinforced by the architecture of the rhetorical manuals beginning with Aristotle between proof and style.[14] The probative value of the similitude, on the other hand, is taken up again in Cicero's *Topica*, where it is aligned not only with *collationes* and *exempla* but with the *epagōgē* or *inductio* associated with Socrates (*Topica* 10.41–44).[15]

This dual identity receives even more attention from Quintilian, who not only addresses the similitude first in book 5 on proof and then again in book 8 on style but in both cases refers his reader to the complementary discussion in the other book (5.11.5–6, 8.3.72).[16] With both Aristotle's *Rhetoric* and Cicero's *De inventione* in mind, Quintilian begins his treatment in book 5 by sorting out two sets of relations causing confusion: one between what the Greeks call *paradeigma* and *parabolē*; the other between this Greek terminology and its Latin equivalents. As we have seen, Aristotle unequivocally considers the *parabolē* a kind of *paradeigma*, authorizing Quintilian to elevate the *exemplum*, the Latin equivalent of *paradeigma*, to the more generic category (*Instit. orat.* 5.11.1–2)—despite the dissent of Cicero, who, in contrast, "separated comparison [*collationem*] from example [*ex exemplo*]" (5.11.2). And whereas Cicero prefers to call the Greek *parabolē* a *collatio*, as Erasmus has already alerted us, Quintilian, in solidarity with the majority of Roman writers, renders it instead as *similitudo* (5.11.1).[17] Like Aristotle, moreover, Quintilian associates the *parabolic* (which he cites almost exclusively in Greek) with the *epagogic* and both with Socrates (5.11.1–3).

When later in book 5 Quintilian turns his attention more single-mindedly to the *similitudo* (*Instit. orat.* 5.11.22–26), he makes a point of distinguishing Ciceronian theory from practice. After repeating his Roman predecessor's unapproved choice of *collatio* for παραβολή

---

14. At *Orator* 138, Cicero includes the *similitudo* among his thirty-nine figures.

15. For the identification in *De inventione* of epagogic argumentation with Aspasia, see 1.31.51–52 and McCormick, "Argument by Comparison," 153–57.

16. In *Ancient Rhetorical Theories of Simile and Comparison*, McCall singles Quintilian out as "the first critic to distinguish these two purposes of comparison and yet to see that they are facets of a central idea of comparison and, while he is treating one of them, to show that he is aware of the other" (192).

17. On Quintilian's *similitudo*, which occupies a "liminal zone between sameness and difference" (160), see McCormick, "Argument by Comparison," 158–63.

(5.11.23), Quintilian illustrates the strategy he has in mind with a number of passages from this same prince of eloquence's oratory, including *Pro Cluentio* 53,146, where Cicero argues that "As [*Ut*] our bodies can make no use of their members without a mind to direct them, so [*ita*] the state can make no use of its component parts, which may be compared to the sinews, blood and limbs, unless it is directed by law" (5.11.25). Quintilian then follows this illustration with reference to two other Ciceronian similitudes constructed according to the same "just as . . . so" formula, one from the lost *Pro Cornelio*, the other from *Pro Archia* (8.19). Following these illustrations, Quintilian offers one of his own similitudes to reinforce this "ready-to-use" argumentative strategy: "As [*ut*] oarsmen are useless without a steersman, so [*sic*] soldiers are useless without a general" (5.11.26).

But Quintilian does not restrict his lessons on the similitude to theory about the similitude reinforced by illustration. When addressing, for instance, the foundational role of theory (*ars*) itself, as one of the three elements, along with practice (*exercitatio*) and nature (*natura, ingenium*), that combine to make the accomplished speaker, Quintilian reaches for a similitude to make his case.[18] "But it is only by constant practice (*exercitatione*) that we can secure that," he argues:

> Just as [*quemadmodum*] the hands of the musician, even though his eyes be turned elsewhere, produce bass, treble or intermediate notes by force of habit, so [*sic*] the thought of the orator should suffer no delay owing to the variety and number of possible arguments, but the latter should present themselves uncalled and, just as [*ut*] letters and syllables require no thought on the part of the writer, so [*sic*] arguments should spontaneously follow the thought of the orator. (*Instit. orat.* 5.10.125)[19]

As he lovingly details the kinds of proof available to the orator-in-training, in other words, Quintilian deploys one of them, the similitude, to persuade the young man that if he perseveres, he will eventually find his arguments with the same facility that the skilled musician

18. On these three ingredients for accomplished oratory, see Shorey, "Phusis, Melete, Episteme," and above, pp. 42–43.

19. For the fully elaborated similitude, see *Inst. orat.* 5.10.124–25 and cf. 10.3.2–4.

finds his notes and the skilled writer the letters that make up his words. Given the intrinsic difficulty of the topic (not to mention the topics) of invention, the Roman schoolmaster understandably holds out hope that hard work over time can be transformed into habit.[20]

In book 8 of his *Institutio oratoria*, Quintilian returns to similitudes, focusing on those that "make our pictures yet more vivid" (*ad exprimendam rerum imaginem*) instead of those that "help our proof" (*probationis gratia*, 8.3.72). Among them, Quintilian includes the metaphor (*metaphora*), defined as a shorter similitude (*brevior similitudo*) and illustrated by Aristotle's rushing lion (8.6.8–9). "It is a comparison [*comparatio*] when I say that a man did something *like a lion* [*ut leonem*]," Quintilian explains (8.6.9), but "it is a metaphor [*translatio*] when I say of him, *He is a lion* [*leo est*]." Shifting terminology (from *similitudo* to *comparatio* and from *metaphora* to *translatio*) from one sentence to the next, Quintilian sets in high relief the problem of terminology that Erasmus and his fellow early moderns inherit. Whereas Quintilian recycles Aristotle's illustration of the relation between the two figures, moreover, he reverses the Aristotelian taxonomy: Aristotle's master trope is the metaphor, which can be expanded into a simile, while Quintilian favors the similitude, which can be compressed into a metaphor.[21] And when Quintilian takes note very much in passing of "what the Greeks call εἰκών" (5.11.24), he recommends it be used very sparingly in oratory, unlike the similitude—a recommendation he bolsters with a Socratic-sounding comparison between young minds and carefully cultivated soil (5.11.24).

Finally, Quintilian, like Socrates before him and Erasmus after him, worries about how deceptive similarity and the similitudes it generates can be. "For though a new ship is more useful than one that is old," Quintilian warns, "this simile will not apply to friendship" (*Instit. orat.* 5.11.26). In *Ecclesiastes*, as we have seen, Erasmus challenges the apprenticing preacher to hone his skill in constructing similitudes in the service of refutation by leveraging both sides of the question on the relative merits of old and new friendships.[22]

20. For the key role of habit or *hexis* in Quintilian's theory of imitation, see Burrow, *Imitating Authors*, 91–93.

21. On this reversal, see McCall, *Ancient Rhetorical Theories of Simile and Comparison*, 230.

22. On old and new friendship, see also CWE 24: 623.

ERASMUS ON SIMILITUDES

Fully in keeping with Quintilian's double treatment of the similitude in the *Institutio oratoria*, in fact, Erasmus's *De copia* addresses this crossover figure in its first book on *verba* as well as in its second on *res*, having reversed the customary order of treating proof before style.[23] In an early section that openly cites Quintilian's book 8 on metaphor, Erasmus explains to his sixteenth-century readers that a *similitudo* is a *metaphora* "made explicit and specifically related to the subject" (CWE 24: 337; ASD I-6, 66 l. 854). Reminding them that Cicero prefers the term *collatio*, Erasmus uses Ciceronian practice to illustrate the complementary processes of expansion and compression at the heart of his most popular textbook. "'He was white-hot with anger' is a metaphor," Erasmus notes with a nod to the *Tusculan Disputations* (4.43), while "'just as [*non aliter quam*] iron glows in the fire, so [*ita*] his whole face was suffused with rage' is a simile [*collatio*]" (CWE 24: 337; ASD I-6, 66 ll. 855–57).[24] It is a *similitudo*, moreover, "when Cicero compares [*comparat*] the tides of a narrow sea-strait with the uncertainty of elections" (CWE 24: 337; ASD I-6, 66 ll. 857–58). The first book of *De copia*, in other words, reinforces the "just as . . . so" structure of this figure, whether it is called by its Ciceronian name (*collatio*) or the term favored by Quintilian (*similitudo*).[25] For more on this crossover figure that bridges proof and style, Erasmus sends his readers to book 2.

Even more to the point, Erasmus revisits the similitude in the section of book 2 specifically dedicated to *probationes* and *argumenta* (Gr. *pisteis*) (CWE 24, 605; ASD I-6, 230 l. 802), among which, like Aristotle and Quintilian before him, Erasmus considers the *paradeigma* or *exemplum*; and it is within this category or *genus* that he includes the similitude, albeit called by yet another name: "We include under 'examples,'" Erasmus contends, "stories, fables, proverbs, opinions, parallels or comparisons, similitudes, analogies [*fabulam, et apo-*

23. On the original title of *De copia*, where *res* and *verba* are reversed, see CWE 24: 280, and see Chomarat, *Grammaire et rhétorique*, 2: 712–61.

24. I have altered the translation to clarify the Latin. For a similar explanation of how metaphors become similitudes and vice versa, see *Desiderii Erasmi Roterdami opera omnia*, ed. J. Leclerc, 10 vols. (Leiden, 1703–6), vol. 5, 1010C, and Clark, "Erasmus and the Four-Part Simile," 218.

25. On the formula, see Chomarat, *Grammaire et rhétorique*, 2: 788–89.

logum, proverbium, iudicia, parabolam seu collationem, imaginem, et analogiam], and anything else of the same sort" (CWE 24, 607; ASD I-6, 232 ll. 843–45).[26] In place of Quintilian's *similitudo* as stand-in for Cicero's *collatio*, Erasmus here offers *parabola*, Latinizing Aristotle's Greek *parabolē*—although Erasmus continues to think of the *parabola* not only as a kind of *similitudo* but as one that conforms more often than not to a "just as . . . so" construction (CWE 24: 616; ASD I-6, 240 ll. 56–61). This conformity, as we will see, serves to differentiate the similitude from other closely related probative strategies and stylistic figures.

In a subsection of the part of the second book of *De copia* that treats the example as a kind of proof—a subsection entitled *De parabola*—Erasmus awkwardly distinguishes genus from species. Whereas an example takes something as "definitely done by someone" (a *certa res gesta*), a *parabola* is a *similitudo* "found in events in general, or natural or chance accompaniments of events" (CWE 24: 621; ASD I-6, 244 ll. 145–47). The famous story from Cicero's *De officiis* (3.99) of Atilius returning to his death at the hands of his enemy in order to keep his word is an *example* of fidelity, while a ship raising and lowering sail to accommodate a changing wind compared to the actions of a prudent man who takes circumstances into account (CWE 24: 621) is a *parabola*. In *A Treatise of Schemes and Tropes* (1550), Richard Sherry offers these same illustrations to his English-speaking audience without attribution to his Latin source.[27]

In the next subsection of book 2 of *De copia*, the *eikōn* (Gr.) or *imago* (Lat.) is distinguished from the *collatio* by its greater compression. As an illustration of the more expansive *collatio*, Erasmus offers "Just as [*Ut*] an ass will not be driven by blows from the pasture until it has had its fill, even so [*ita*] a warrior will not cease from slaughter until he has sated his soul" (CWE 24: 623; ASD I-6, 246 ll. 214–16). Achilles "glowing like fire," Erasmus goes on to say, is an *imago* rather than a *similitudo*, adding to this section a fourth term, alongside *sim-*

26. For a similar list, see CWE 24: 635, ASD I-6, 258 ll. 507–9, and CWE 25: 27, 85. For the inclusion of the *parabola* among *exempla*, see Chomarat, *Grammaire et rhétorique*, 2: 745–52.

27. "As Attilius retournyng agayne to hys enemies is an example of kepynge faythe and promise: But a shyp in the which the sayles be hoysed vp, or taken down after blowing of the winde, is a parable whiche teacheth a wyse man to geue place to tyme, and applye himselfe to the world that is presente." *A Treatise of Schemes and Tropes* (1550), ed. Herbert W. Hildebrandt (Gainesville, FL, 1961), 91.

ile, collatio, and *parabola* to designate one and the same strategy. With these shifts from one specialized term to another, Erasmus may be modeling the lexical variety (*varietas*) he recommends to his readers as one of the most basic resources of *copia*. But he also runs the risk of distracting and even confusing them. Seemingly aware of the potential distraction, Erasmus follows Quintilian in downplaying the role of technical vocabulary, dismissing those who worry about it as unnecessarily pedantic (*superstitiosi*) (CWE 24: 621; ASD I-6, 244 l. 145).[28] Instead, Erasmus features the key functions these strategies serve and the benefits they bring to one's writing and speaking. Whereas the *eikōn* or *imago* contributes primarily to "stylistic attractiveness," the similitude, in contrast, enriches style while "help[ing] considerably in generating consent in our hearers"—especially when combined with induction, for which the Greek, Erasmus reminds us yet again, is *epagōgē*. "Plato's Socrates," he adds somewhat predictably, "makes great use of this" (CWE 24: 623; ASD I-6, 246 ll. 222–24).[29]

The frequently mentioned Socratic pedigree of both the similitude and its logical cousin, the inductive argument or *epagōgē*, is also on display, as demonstrated by a passage quoted earlier (p. 87), when Erasmus illustrates "induction combined with a parallel [*simile*]." Showcasing how to use a Socratic technique to make a Socratic point (in this case that rhetoric is not an art), Erasmus demonstrates the figure's versatility as he expands its "just as . . . so" structure to the dimensions of a refutative argument:

Do you not expect a sailor to talk more knowledgeably about sailing than a doctor? And a doctor more authoritatively about medicine than a painter? and a painter better about the techniques of colour and light and shade and perspective than a cobbler? Will not a charioteer be better at discussing the art of driving a chariot than a sailor? (A number of comparisons like this will make everyone prepared to accept the idea that each person will speak best about the thing he knows best. Then one brings in one's parallel case [*similitudo*]). But what will the orator discuss best, when he professes to be able to talk on any topic? (CWE 24: 624; ASD I-6, 247 l. 234–248 l. 241)

28. See *Instit. orat.* 5.10.75, 5.11.30–31.

29. On the overlap of *epagōgē* and similitude, see also CWE 68: 702, and see Chomarat, *Grammaire et rhétorique*, 2: 748.

With the help of the sailors, charioteers, and cobblers of the Platonic dialogues, Erasmus's similitude effectively serves his textbook's principal agenda. For it makes its contribution to copiousness by adjusting itself as needed to the compression of the metaphor at one extreme as well as to the amplification of the full-fledged argument or narrative at the other—or anywhere in between. Socrates' most famous fiction (*ficta narratio*) in the *Republic*, Erasmus asserts, is nothing other than an expanded *parabola* based on a comparison of those unaware of any reality beyond their sensory experience to prisoners in a cave (CWE 24: 634–35; ASD I-6, 257 l. 491–258 l. 493). By the time Erasmus's protégé has learned the lessons of *De copia* (even if he still lacks Plato's skill in storytelling and argumentation), he will know how to make his own adjustments to the similitudes that enrich his compositions along a wide spectrum from compression to expansion.

In the interest of helping his reader hone this skill (and showing off his own), Erasmus offers at the end of *De copia* a virtuoso display of a dozen or so similitudes, introduced as *parabolae* and *similia*, derived from ships and sailing and rivaling the copious treatment in book 1 of the notorious line "Your letter pleased me mightily" (CWE 24: 348–54). Each similitude offers some variation on the "just as . . . so" construction, opening with "Just as [*Ut*] storms demonstrate the good helmsman, so [*ita*] reverses reveal the good general" and ending with "As [*Ut*] sailors drop the sheet anchor only in the most violent tempests, so [*ita*] one should not resort to the final remedy unless in the gravest peril when hope is practically gone" (CWE 24: 641–42; ASD I-6, 263 l. 674–264 l. 704). Despite the seemingly endless variety on display, Erasmus assures his readers in closing that thousands more *similitudines* are possible on this topic (CWE 24: 642; ASD I-6, 264 ll. 705–6). By this point in his textbook, these same readers are used to not only Erasmus's personal indulgences in what he calls the *suppellex copiae* but this master strategy called by a cluster of names, including *similitudo*, *parabola*, *collatio*, and *simile*. And just in case they feel they need further illustrations, they can turn to Erasmus's collection of similitudes from Plutarch, Seneca, and others, the *Parabolae sive similia*, often published with *De copia* and *De conscribendis epistolis*.[30]

---

30. On this popular collection of similitudes, see Chomarat, *Grammaire et rhétorique*, 2: 782–803, and Clark, "Erasmus and the Four-Part Simile," who re-

When Erasmus turns his attention from the rules for expanding and contracting literary composition in general to the more particularized task of composing letters, he continues to feature the similitude, which, as we have seen, belongs to the larger category of example and operates as an effective instrument of expansion and contraction. Echoing *De copia* on compression and expansion, *De conscribendis epistolis*, Erasmus's wildly popular textbook on letter writing, opens with a reformulation of this fundamental lesson in the form of a similitude. "For just as [*quemadmodum*] in Plato Socrates concludes that the best forger of lies is also the best teller of the truth," Erasmus argues *parabolically*, "similarly [*ita*] no one will earn credit for brevity who cannot also express himself in a more ample style [*copiosissime*]" (CWE 25: 13; ASD I-2, 212 l. 17–213 l. 3).[31] Like *De copia*, moreover, *De conscribendis epistolis* couples the *parabolic* with the *epagogic*, once again identified with Socrates. With its very first words, it refutes those who would impose rigid requirements on epistolary writing (along the lines of the strict Ciceronians profiled in the previous chapter) with an inductive argument that could easily be restated in *parabolic* form. "Indeed I find this attitude no less absurd," Erasmus admits regarding the rigidity of his opponents,

> than that of a cobbler who would insist on stitching a shoe of the same shape for every foot, or a painter who tried to depict every animal with the same colours and outline, or a tailor set on making identical clothes fit both a midget and a giant. (CWE 25: 12; ASD I-2, 209 ll. 8–11)

As an advocate for flexibility in letter writing, in other words, Erasmus invokes the cobblers, painters, and tailors of the Platonic dialogues to help him make his case.

But the *parabola* or similitude should figure no less in the instruc-

---

minds her readers that by the mid-sixteenth century the *Parabolae sive similia* was a regular school text (217).

31. As this and subsequent quotations from Erasmus's works suggest, Clark is perhaps too hasty in concluding that "The complete four-part form . . . is not one of which Erasmus makes great use in his own finished writing" ("Erasmus and the Four-Part Simile," 219).

tions to the aspiring letter writer than in the defense of a reasonable
epistolary theory. Accordingly, Erasmus recommends that instruc-
tors teach their students when and how to incorporate such similitudes into their letters. In one advising a friend to adapt his actions
to shifting circumstances, for instance, the *parabola* of the prudent
helmsman who adjusts to tides and wind, borrowed from Cicero, may
be in order (CWE 25: 28; ASD I-2, 237 ll. 18–24). Similarly, an epistolary theme featuring a repentant youth name Lucius laboring to persuade his profligate friend Antonius to give up his reprobate life could,
in addition to relying on maxims, examples, and other proofs (CWE
25: 30), strengthen its argument for moral reform with any number
of *parabolae*, also called *similitudines*, in the customary "just as . . .
so" structure, including those that compare the cultivation of young
minds in Socratic fashion to the arduous work of agriculture and hor-
ticulture: "[J]ust as [*Ut*] when the oat degenerates into tares through
the deficiency of the soil or when wheat goes into spelt it loses the
name of its genus, so [*ita*] a man begins to be a brute when he neglects
good learning and begins to care only for his appetites and his lusts . . .
just as [*ut*] it is quite natural for an implanted graft to retain the taste of
the tree from which it was taken, so [*ita*] the mind of man, which has
a heavenly origin, should not degenerate from its kind" (CWE 25: 33;
ASD I-2, 245 l. 9–246 l. 9). Exercises such as these, Erasmus assures
his readers, are more worthwhile than those provided by Aphthonius,
who, Erasmus neglects to tell these same readers, features a *parabolē*
in his *Progymnasmata* very much like those cited above.[32]

In the *Ratio verae theologiae*, on the other hand, Erasmus initi-
ates young readers rather than young writers, and especially young
readers of Scripture, into the complex workings of the similitude.
Without this initiation, understanding *sacrae literae* is impossible because Christ himself "clothed almost all his teachings in comparisons"
(*Parabolis omnia paene convestivit*, CWE 41: 511, H 190). By *parabola*

---

32. On this particular *parabolē*, see *Progymnasmata*, trans. Kennedy, 99;
Rhetores Graeci, ed. Spengel, 3.24: "Just as [*Hōsper*] those who work the earth cast
the seeds in the ground with toil but reap the fruits with greater pleasure, in the
same way [*ton auton*] those exchanging toil for education have by toil acquired
future renown." See also Kathy Eden, "Erasmus on Dogs and Baths and Other
Odious Comparisons," *Erasmus Studies* 38 (2018): 12.

here Erasmus means not only the so-called "parables" of the Gospels but the flexible strategy at once probative and stylistic that is known under a cluster of names, including *similitudo, collatio,* and *simile* as well as *parabola.*[33] As *De copia* suggests, moreover, the fuller narrative dimension of some of Jesus's more elaborate parables does not distinguish them generically from his briefer comparisons between the kingdom of heaven and a mustard seed or a pearl of great price (CWE 41: 641, H264). Without in any way diminishing the sanctity of Jesus's words, Erasmus affirms that all of Jesus's *parabolae* or *similitudines* fall somewhere on the spectrum between compression and expansion that informs the compositions of young schoolboys. Even Jesus's controversial words spoken at the Last Supper (John 6:53–54), Erasmus contends on the authority of Augustine, are better understood by those practiced in "drawing comparisons [*similibus*] from any kind of thing" (CWE 41: 667, H278). Like Socrates, in fact, Jesus tends to take his comparisons from those things "best known to the common crowd" (CWE 41: 633, H260)—things like the sowing of seed, the casting of fishing nets, and the cutting off of dry branches (CWE 41: 676, H283).[34]

Erasmus also clarifies in the *Ratio* why Jesus relies so heavily on similitudes. "No mode of teaching," Jesus understood, "is more familiar or more effective than teaching by means of the comparison of similar things [*per similium collationem*]" (CWE 41: 676, H283). The similitude goes beyond mere instruction, however, to a persuasion rooted in moving the emotions, thereby planting its lessons deeply in the listeners' or readers' minds (CWE 41: 632–33, H259–60). Accordingly,

---

33. On this cluster of figures, see Chomarat, *Grammaire et rhétorique,* 1: 568–70; Kathy Eden, "The Parable of Sincere and Sophistical Discourse in the *Ratio,*" in *Erasmus on Literature,* ed. Vessey, 93–107, and CWE 41: 183–90. On the rhetorical orientation of Erasmus's hermeneutics, see Eden, *Hermeneutics and the Rhetorical Tradition,* 64–78.

34. On Socrates' inductive or epagogic method as rooted in comparison to familiar things, see Ausland, "Socratic Induction in Plato and Aristotle." In *The Religious Feast* (CWE 39: 185; ASD I-3, 243 ll. 368–72), Eusebius notes that God uses a *similitudo* to explain Proverbs 21: 1–3: "There's a comparison [*similitudo*] at hand to explain it. A king's mind, when aroused, is violent and unrestrained; it cannot be led this way or that but is driven by its own force, as if excited by a divine frenzy, just as [*quemadmodum*] the sea spreads itself over the land and frequently changes course, heedless of fields, buildings, and whatever stands in its way."

readers of Scripture must learn how to recognize the *summa sententia* or "main point" of a *parabola*—the basis, that is, for the comparison—so that they can avoid the "flat and trivial comments" that come from reading *superstitiose*: that is, reading to find correspondences to each and every detail (CWE 41: 672–73, H281–82).[35] As an illustration of this wrong way of reading, Erasmus turns to the so-called "Parable of the False Steward" (Luke 16), where "the analogy [*collatio*]," Erasmus warns, "does not in every respect correspond" (CWE 41: 672, H281).[36]

But Jesus is not the only one in Scripture to wield his similitudes to great effect. In keeping with his thoroughgoing *imitatio Christi* throughout his apostolic letters, Paul too relies on this strategy, often (though not always) in its most compressed, metaphorical form. In his Letter to the Romans, for instance, Paul returns to Jesus's similitude of the vines, which he refashions, Erasmus informs his young readers, into a *comparatio* "of the olive tree and the wild olive grafted into it" (CWE 41: 591, H234). Elsewhere the apostle to the gentiles figures the faithful metaphorically as the "unleavened," the repentant as "awakened," their bodies as earthen vessels, garments, and tabernacles (CWE 41: 637–39, H262). Given Paul's characteristic forms of expression, Erasmus concludes, "it would be superfluous to recount the number of times he introduces a similitude [*similitudinem*] from athletes and soldiers, from stadiums, boxers, wars" (CWE 41: 639, H263). In the ninth chapter of 1 Corinthians (9:7), Erasmus records, Paul drives home his *summa sententia* that "thanks is owed for a kindness" by drawing his similitudes from soldiering, winemaking, and shepherding:

Who serves as a soldier at any time at his own charge? Who plants a vineyard and does not eat of the fruit thereof? Who feeds a flock and does not take the flock's milk? (CWE 41: 639, H263)

35. Like the *scopus*, the *summa sententia* in interpretation corresponds to the *status* in constructing a case. On the relation of these terms, see chap. 1, p. 18, and Stillman, *Philip Sidney and the Poetics of Renaissance Cosmopolitanism*, 74–75, 91–92.

36. In *Ecclesiastes*, Erasmus reinforces this point: "But a similitude or an analogy does not have to fit in every respect; it is enough for it to agree in the area where it is being applied" (CWE 68: 705).

Like Socrates, in other words, Paul alternately compresses and expands his arguments, sometimes making his case metaphorically, at other times inductively, asking, in this case, a series of parallel questions about the mode of compensating those who practice a trade.

An appreciative reader of both the Athenian philosopher and the apostle, Erasmus follows them in the *Ratio* in relying on similitudes to make his own case on a number of issues. Among them is the vexed question of the conflicting creeds espoused by Christians at different times and in different places. In addressing this issue, Erasmus compares Jesus's extraordinary ability to forge a community of believers out of a multitude of disparate followers to a musical composition. "[J]ust as [*sicut*] in song the sweetest harmony arises from different voices aptly ordered," Erasmus argues *parabolically*, "so [*ita*] the diversity [*varietas*] of Christ produces a fuller harmony" (CWE 41: 552, H211). In *De copia*, this same *varietas* is considered the source of the best literary compositions. And in *Ecclesiastes*, this consideration is extended to sermonizing.

Like the schoolboy, the preacher must learn how to vary his compositions along the axis of compression and expansion. In the schoolroom as in church, as we have seen, the similitude proves to be an especially effective instrument of this variety, encompassing a full range of figurative expression from metaphor to full-fledged narrative in the form of fable and allegory. In *Ecclesiastes*, in fact, Erasmus sends the preacher-in-training back to *De copia* (as well as to Quintilian) for further instruction on this key figure, adding only that

> One should take care that the simile [*similitudo*] square with that to which it is being applied; that it not be tawdry or obscene; that it not be taken from subjects unfamiliar to the people we are addressing unless the nature of the thing is so important that it is worthwhile for them to learn it; that it not be difficult and far-fetched, that it not be readily twisted another way. (CWE 68: 877; ASD V-5, 162 ll. 175–79)

Whereas *De copia* looks to ancient and especially Ciceronian examples, *Ecclesiastes* reminds its readers that *scriptura divina* "everywhere abounds with this figure [*hoc schemate*]," which, among the early church fathers, was a special favorite of John Chrysostom (CWE 68: 877; ASD V-5, 162 ll. 179–82).

AFTER ERASMUS

Rhetorical theory after Erasmus, in Latin and in the vernacular, pays particular attention not only to the similitude but to the Dutch humanist's treatments in both *De copia* and *Ecclesiastes*. Even those theorists who cite other authorities often take their directions from the Dutchman. In his widely read *Epitome troporum ac schematum*, for instance, Joannes Susenbrotus openly attributes his division of the *similitudo* (Gr. *homoiōsis*) into *icon, parabola,* and *paradeigma* to his Velletrian predecessor Antonio Mancinelli, while without attribution he repeats more or less verbatim Erasmus's instructions to preachers quoted above, including the reference to Chrysostom:

> Care must be taken that the comparison [*similitudo*] corresponds to that for which it is used, that it not be sordid or obscene or derived from things unknown to the listener, that it not be unfavorable and affected or of such a kind, finally, that it may be twisted immediately to different meanings. Divine scripture everywhere abounds in this scheme. Among the doctors of the Church no one uses this figure more extensively than St. John Chrysostom.[37]

In keeping with this unacknowledged borrowing, Susenbrotus also repeats for his readers that the similitude serves the aims of both proof and style. "It lends to discourse much brilliance and dignity [*lucis ac dignitatis*]," he notes in terms echoing Erasmus, "but it also contributes much to demonstration [*probationem*]."[38]

Erasmus's introduction of the similitude in *Ecclesiastes*, for which he, like Susenbrotus, provides the Greek *homoiōsis*, similarly and somewhat suspiciously singles out the same two qualities, *lux* and *dig-*

---

37. Joseph X. Brennan, "The *Epitome Troporum ac Schematum of Joannes Susenbrotus*: Text, Translation and Commentary," PhD diss., University of Illinois, 1953, p. 95. On Susenbrotus's reliance on Erasmus, see Joseph X. Brennan, "The *Epitome Troporum ac Schematum*: The Genesis of a Renaissance Text," *Quarterly Journal of Speech* 46 (1960): 59–71, and Mack, *History of Renaissance Rhetoric*, 218–21. Susenbrotus's reluctance to cite Erasmus as his source, as one of the readers of my manuscript reminds me, may be rooted in the former's Catholicism. On a similar tripartite division of *homoiōsis* in the third book of Donatus's *Ars maior*, the so-called *Barbarismus*, see Murphy, *Rhetoric in the Middle Ages*, 37.

38. Brennan, "*Epitome Troporum ac Schematum of Joannes Susenbrotus*," 95.

nitas, as stylistic virtues.[39] Whereas Susenbrotus, by his own account, follows Mancinelli in limiting the kinds of similitude to *icon, parabola*, and *paradeigma*, Erasmus's fuller list includes *fictio* and *unulogia* (CWE 68: 662; ASD V-4, 414 l. 167), alongside *exemplum* and *imago*. The omission of *parabola* is hardly surprising since, as we have seen in *De copia*, Erasmus considers it more or less a synonym for *similitudo*. In *Ecclesiastes*, in contrast, he seems, like Quintilian, to favor the more authentically Latin term, leaving the Latinized Greek term *parabola* to its more Christian setting. Finally, when Susenbrotus offers two illustrations of the similitude, they not only conform to the "just as . . . so" construction but reproduce almost word for word those from the Erasmian manual, first comparing a badly advised prince to a poisoned well and then a government run by the wealthy rather than the wise to a ship navigated by a rich but unskilled pilot.[40]

Among the many vernacular treatments indebted to Erasmus, directly or indirectly, George Puttenham's *The Art of English Poesy* (1589) makes no bones about the importance of his topic when he claims, as we have seen earlier (p. 10), that "no one thing more prevaileth with all ordinary judgments than persuasion by similitude."[41] Like Erasmus and Susenbrotus, Puttenham provides the Greek equivalent—in this case transliterated as *homoeosis* and set alongside the English "resemblance." Also like Erasmus and Susenbrotus, Puttenham foregrounds its stylistic as well as its probative functions. For both poets and persuaders use similitudes not only to "beautify [their] tale but also very much enforce and enlarge it."[42] And like Susenbrotus, Puttenham makes a "triple division" of the figure into *icon* (or *resemblance by imagery*), *parabola* (or *resemblance mystical*), and *paradeigma* (or *resemblance by example*), insisting all the while that the "general similitude" is the "common ancestor" of all three.[43] Like Erasmus and Susenbrotus, Puttenham associates *parabola* with Scripture insofar as "[s]uch parables were all the preachings of Christ in the Gospel," although Puttenham too extends this figure to "fables and other apologues."[44]

39. See ibid., 95, and cf. CWE 68: 662.
40. Brennan, "*Epitome Troporum ac Schematum of Joannes Susenbrotus*," 95.
41. Puttenham, *Art of English Poesy*, 326.
42. Ibid.
43. Ibid.
44. Ibid., 330.

Unlike Erasmus and Susenbrotus, however, Puttenham illustrates what he also calls the "bare similitude" with instances of vernacular poetry. Most, if not all, of these illustrations preserve the "just as . . . so" construction characteristic of their prose counterparts. The first two quote a verse of Henry Howard, Earl of Surrey:

> But as the wat'ry showers delay the raging wind,
> So doth good hope clean put away despair out of my mind.

followed by

> Then as the stricken deer withdraws himself alone,
> So do I seek some secret place where I may make my moan.[45]

With yet another illustration, Puttenham offers his own translation of Petrarch, signaling the conclusion of the poem's argument with "then" and reminding his readers of the alliance between the similitude and a more expanded *epagōgē*:

> After ill crop the soyle must eft be sowen
> And fro shipwracke we sayle to seas againe,
> Then God forbid whose fault hath once bene knowen
> Should for ever a spotted wight remaine.[46]

It is only when he turns from "general similitudes" to *icons* or *resemblance by imagery* that Puttenham invokes revered contemporary poet Philip Sidney. For Sidney outspokenly discredits the similitude in his *Defence of Poesy*, not only reducing it to a stylistic strategy incapable of proving anything to "a contrary disputer" or unpersuaded listener (50) but also rejecting the overuse of "all herbarists, all stories of beasts, fowls and fishes," thinking presumably about collections like Erasmus's *Parabolae sive similia* as "a surfeit to the ears" and "a most tedious prattling" (50).

45. Ibid., 326.
46. Ibid., 328. For Puttenham's use of Erasmus's *Parabolae* in crafting this and other translations, see notes to this edition, pp. 326–29; and see Clark, "Erasmus and the Four-Part Simile" for the influence of the *Parabolae*, especially in the "utilitarian edition" of Conrad Lycosthenes, on literature in England, France, and Italy.

This disdain for similitudes notwithstanding, Sidney demonstrates his mastery of *epagogic* argument in his *Defence* when he sets out to make the case that the great danger poetry allegedly poses speaks to the correspondingly great benefits it can provide:

> Do we not see skill of physic, the best rampire to our often assaulted bodies, being abused, teach poison, the most violent destroyer? Doth not knowledge of law, whose end is to even and right all things, being abused, grow the crooked fosterer of horrible injuries? Doth not (to go to the highest) God's word abused breed heresy, and His name abused become blasphemy? Truly, a needle cannot do much hurt, and as truly (with leave of ladies be it spoken) it cannot do much good. With a sword thou mayst kill thy father, and with a sword thou mayst defend thy prince and country. So that, as in their calling poets fathers of lies they said nothing, so in this their argument of abuse they prove the commendation. (36)

Marshaled here in keeping with a refutative agenda as discussed in the previous chapter, Sidney's inductive argument proceeds in three stages: first it establishes the parallel between medicine, law, and divinity regarding their commensurate power for both great good and great evil; then it briefly contrasts these disciplines with the more or less innocuous activity of sewing (metonymically identified with the needle), which, while admittedly doing no great harm, does no great good either, in contrast to military activity (identified metonymically with the sword), which has the power to protect as well as destroy; finally, it concludes—with its "so that"—that his opponents' charge of poetry's outsized harm entails, against their claim, that poetry is equally capable of outsized good, thereby deserving commendation (as well as condemnation). In spite of his rejection of the similitude as an instrument of proof, Sidney deploys with considerable skill its probative power in the service of a refutative agenda in the form of an *epagōgē*.

LYLY'S *EUPHUES* AND MONTAIGNE'S *ESSAYS*

Sidney's outspoken rejection of similitudes is often taken as a criticism of the literary style called Euphuism, identified most closely with the work of John Lyly, whose singularly popular novel in two parts, *Euphues: The Anatomy of Wit* (1578) and *Euphues & His England* (1580), supplies much of the material for *The Second Part of Wit's Commonwealth* (1598), a collection of "over seven hundred octavo pages of euphuistic similitudes," designed, like Erasmus's *Parabolae sive similia*, to enrich its readers' written compositions.[47] A generation before Sidney voices his disdain for this stylistic figure and its euphuistic associations, famed schoolmaster Roger Ascham praises the quality embodied in Lyly's hero with his own elaborate similitude. "And even as a fair stone requireth to be set in the finest gold with the best workmanship or else it loseth much of the grace and price," Ascham notes about the comeliness of mind and body that defines euphuism, "even so excellency in learning, and namely divinity, joined with a comely personage, is a marvelous jewel for the world."[48]

Lyly himself both generously litters his prose, including that of his fictional protagonists, with this figure and has them call one another out for its overuse. So, for instance, Euphues' reprobate companion Philautus refutes in a letter the arguments of his sexual target Camilla for keeping her virtue; and he does so by discrediting her chief probative strategy. "Many similitudes thou bringest in to excuse youth," he charges against her, "thy twig, thy corn, thy fruit, thy

47. On Sidney's opposition to Euphuism, associated with Lyly, see Alexander, *Sidney's 'The Defence of Poesy' and Selected Renaissance Literary Criticism*, 365n265 and 293–94, which describes how Michael Drayton, in his poem "To Henry Reynolds, of Poets and Poesy," commends the "noble Sidney" for ridding the language of Lyly's "idle similes" (ll. 85–92), and G. K. Hunter, *John Lyly: The Humanist as Courtier* (London, 1962), 280–88, who also makes the case for *Euphues* as a "success without parallel in its age" (72). On the collection of similitudes in "over seven hundred octavo pages," many in the "just as . . . so" form, see Morris Palmer Tilley, *Elizabethan Proverb Lore in Lyly's "Euphues" and in Pettie's "Petite Palace"* (New York, 1926), 384. And see William Ringler, "The Immediate Source of Euphuism," *PMLA* 53 (1938): 678–86, who, in arguing for John Rainolds's style as Lyly's model, places in evidence a number of passages from Rainolds's Latin lectures that showcase the "just as . . . so" structure featured in this chapter (680). For Socrates on Pericles as *euphuēs*, see *Phaedrus* 270A, and for Pericles' singular rhetorical abilities, see the introduction, p. 6.

48. Roger Ascham, *The Schoolmaster*, ed. Lawrence Ryan (Charlottesville, 1967), 28. For Lyly's *Euphues* as the "bastard child" of Ascham's *Schoolmaster*, see Burrow, *Imitating Authors*, 231–34. And see Boutcher, *School of Montaigne*, 2: 214–15.

grape, and I know not what; which are as easily refelled as they are to be repeated"—although he immediately adds that he is "unwilling to confute anything," she says.[49] His suspect unwillingness to refute her is part and parcel of a suspect faithfulness he expresses, despite his refutation, by means of a similitude: "For as the loadstone what wind soever blow turneth always to the north, or as Aristotle's Quadratus which way soever you turn it is always to the north; so the faith of Philautus is ever more applied to the love of Camilla, neither to be removed with any wind or rolled with any force."[50] Like his equivocating characters, moreover, Lyly himself is a master at both advancing and refuting any argument with the aid of a similitude.

In his own voice in his dedicatory epistle to *The Anatomy of Wit*, Lyly refutes his would-be adversaries by confessing to their accusation of folly by means of a cleverly devised inductive proof:

> It may be that fine wits will descant upon him that, having no wit, goeth about to make the Anatomy of Wit; and certainly their jesting in my mind is tolerable. For if the butcher should take upon him to cut the anatomy of a man because he hath skill in opening an ox, he would prove himself a calf; or if the horse-leech would adventure to minister a potion to a sick patient in that he hath knowledge to give a drench to a diseased horse, he would prove himself an ass. The shoe maker must not go above his latchet, nor the hedger meddle with anything but his bill. It is unseemly for the painter to feather a shaft, or the fletcher to handle the pencil. All which things make most against me in that a fool hath intruded himself to discourse of wit.[51]

49. John Lyly, *Euphues: The Anatomy of Wit and Euphues & His England*, ed. Morris Croll and Henry Clemons (New York, 1916; rpt. 1964), 352. Exercising an Erasmian *varietas*, Philautus helps himself to the cluster of terms associated with refutation as discussed in chapter 2.

50. Lyly, *Euphues*, 351.

51. Lyly, *Euphues*, 5. On the "string of similes" as the signature feature of Lyly's style, characterized as anti-Ciceronian although it looks back to Cicero and Erasmus, see Hunter, *John Lyly*, 257–78. In her recent edition of the two-part novel (Manchester, 2003), Leah Scragg traces Lyly's "exemplary analogies which form such a distinctive feature of [his] style" (11) to Pliny's *Historia naturalis* and Erasmus's *Similia* and *Adagia*. See also Jonas Barish, "The Prose Style of John Lyly," *English Literary History* 23 (1956): 14–35, esp. 23.

Echoing not only Socrates' fondness for the commonplace practices of cobblers, carters, and tailors but also his preoccupation with
technē's proper purview, Lyly assembles an intentionally copious
supply of parallel cases to effect the fundamentally Socratic aim featured in chapter 2: self-refutation. Without mentioning the Athenian
philosopher by name in this passage, Lyly disarms his opposition by
arguing *epagogically* for his Socratic-style knowledge of his own ignorance.

Lyly's Socratic posture as well as his affection for similitudes is
characteristic of another work first published in 1580, the same year as
the second installment of *Euphues*. Throughout the *Essais*, Montaigne
singles Socrates out as "the worthiest man to be knowne, and for a
patterne presented to the world" (III.12, Fl 3: 291)—a model for how
to conduct not only one's life but one's conversation or discourse; and
the signature features of this discourse, Montaigne reminds his readers, are "the inductions and similitudes, drawen from the most vul-
gar and knowen actions of men"—those of "Coach-makers, Joyners,
Coblers, and Masons" (III.12, Fl 3: 290).[52] An outspoken admirer of
the man who "erected not onely the most regular, but the highest and
most vigorous opinions, actions and customes, that ever were" (Fl 3:
291), Montaigne, as we will see, enriches his own discourse with Socratic inductions and similitudes. He does so, moreover, fully aware of
the dangers that lurk in similarity—dangers highlighted, as we have
seen, by Socrates himself in Plato's dialogues and by Erasmus in his
textbooks and *Ciceronianus*.

In the final, culminating chapter of the three-book collection of
essays, Montaigne famously addresses these dangers head-on. For the
long, last essay opens with a warning about the ruling quality of dissimilitude not only endorsed but engineered by nature despite the
efforts of art. "Dissimilitude doth of it selfe insinuate into our works,"

52. In "Erasmus and the Four-Part Simile," Clark addresses the role of similitudes in sixteenth-century French vernacular writing, including that of Montaigne
and Jean Talpin, who was a teacher at the Collège de Guyenne during the training
of its most well-known student. On this essay (III.12, "De la phisionomie"), see
Terence Cave, *The Cornucopian Text: Problems of Writing in the French Renaissance*
(Oxford, 1979), 302–12. On the similarities between Euphuistic style and that of
Montaigne as understood by his English translator Florio, see Boutcher, *School
of Montaigne*, 2: 190–91. For the efforts late in his career of Florio's publisher,
Edward Blount, to revive Lyly's work, see Boutcher, *School of Montaigne*, 2: 204.

Montaigne contends, "no arte can come neere unto similitude . . . Nature hath bound herselfe to make nothing that may not be dissemblable" (Fl 3: 322). In light of this reigning quality of diversity or difference and its consequences for discourse, Montaigne further warns that "All things hold by some similitude [*per quelque similitude*]: every example limpeth . . . Comparisons [*les comparaisons*] are neverthelesse joined together by some end [*coin*] (Fl. 3: 328, V 2: 1070)." Like Erasmus and the ancient rhetoricians he follows in worrying about how similitudes mislead, Montaigne is also like them in lumping similitudes together with examples and other kinds of comparisons.

Open in his admission that his writing is "too full of figures" (III.5, Fl 3: 103) and even more hostile to the intimidating names of these figures found in the rhetorical handbooks, Montaigne nevertheless relies on the whole range of strategies rooted in similarity, from metaphor at the extreme of compression to fable at the extreme of expansion. More to the point, his use of similitudes forms an identifying feature of his style.[53] Often these similitudes conform to the standard "just as . . . so" structure employed by Socrates, as we have seen, in conversation with his interlocutors in the *Republic*. On many occasions, Montaigne even echoes Socrates' comparison between the educational curriculum that cultivates a young mind and the soil that nurtures a new shoot:

> For as [*Tout ainsi qu'*] in matters of husbandrie, the labor that must be used before sowing, setting, and planting, yea in planting it selfe, is most certaine and easie. But when that which was sowen, set and planted, commeth to take life; before it come to ripenesse, much adoe, and great varietie of proceeding belongeth to it. So in men [*pareillement aux hommes*], it is no great matter to get them, but being borne, what continuall cares, what diligent attendance,

53. While I agree with Clark's conclusion that "like Erasmus, Montaigne varies the wording of his comparisons," I believe her claim that the essayist "only very rarely" uses the "schematic form of the four-part simile" (223) is overstated. On other aspects of Montaigne's style, see Carol Clark, *The Web of Metaphor: Studies in the Imagery of Montaigne's "Essais"* (Lexington, KY, 1978); R. A. Sayce, "The Style of Montaigne: Word-Pairs and Word-Groups," in *Literary Style: A Symposium*, ed. Seymour Chatman (London, 1971), 383–405; Kathy Eden, "Montaigne on Style," in *Oxford Handbook of Montaigne*, ed. Philippe Desan (Oxford, 2016), 384–96, and "Cicero's Portion of Montaigne's Acclaim."

what doubts and feares, doe daily wait on their parents and tutors, before they can be nurtured and brought to any good? (I.26 [25], Fl 1: 173, V 1: 149)

While preserving the broad outlines of the structure of a Socratic similitude, Montaigne here complicates it considerably; and he does so by dividing or enumerating the various stages of activity involved—a logical (topical) move that allows him to comment discreetly but pointedly on the potentially quick and casual sexual act as the cause in stark contrast to the responsibility-laden long-term effects.

Montaigne opens "On idleness" with a similar complication:

> As [*comme*] we see some idle-fallow grounds, if they be fat and fertile, to bring foorth store and sundrie roots of wilde and unprofitable weeds, and that to keepe them in ure we must subject and imploy them with certaine seeds for our use and service. And as [*comme*] wee see some women, though single and alone, often to bring foorth lumps of shapelesse flesh, whereas to produce a perfect and natural generation, they must be manured with another kinde of seed: So [*ainsin*] is it of mindes, which except they be busied about some subject, that may bridle and keepe them under, they will here and there wildely scatter themselves through the vaste field of imaginations. (I.8, Fl 1: 33, V 1: 32)[54]

Once again barely accommodating the constraints of the "just as . . . so" structure, Montaigne analogizes agricultural production, human procreation, and intellectual (perhaps literary) creation, in this case adding a Plutarchan dimension to his Socratically inflected comparison, without explicitly identifying either author.[55]

Elsewhere Montaigne is more explicit. In "Of vanity," for instance, he signals the Socratic source of his similitude of the seedling that

---

54. On I.21, where Montaigne turns "comme" into a verb ("Si je ne comme bien, qu'un autre comme pour moy"), see Clark, "Erasmus and the Four-Part Simile," 223–24. On Montaigne's "comparison words" and the source of his "comparaisons prolongées" in Seneca and Plutarch, see Yves Délègue, "Les comparaisons dans les *Essais* de Montaigne," *Revue d'Histoire Littéraire de la France* 66 (1966): 593–618, which does not align Montaigne's similitude with its rhetorical counterpart.

55. On Montaigne's sources, see Villey, ed., *Les Essais*, 1226, and Diotima's speech at *Symposium* 205B–212A.

struggles in an inhospitable environment, quoted above (p. 95), even while contracting its structure to feature the "just as" portion as something of an afterthought:

> Plato saith, that *who escapes untainted and cleane-handed from the managing of the world; escapeth by some wonder.* He says also, that when he instituteth his Philosopher as chiefe over a Commonwealth, he meanes not a corrupted or law broken commonwealth, as that of *Athens*; and much lesse, as ours, with which wisedome herselfe would be brought to a *nonplus* or put to her shifts. And [*Comme*] a good hearb, transplanted into a soile very diverse from her nature, doth much sooner conforme it selfe to the soile, then it reformeth the same to it selfe. (III.9, Fl 3: 240–41, V 2: 992)

In "Of books," Montaigne similarly punctuates with half a similitude— the first half—his preference for works of literature, mostly ancient, that avoid "fantasticall, new fangled" flourishes. As it builds on a series of parallel cases to drive home its point, this demisimilitude approaches an *epagōgē*:

> Even as [*Tout ainsi qui'*] in our dances, those base conditioned men that keepe dancing-schooles, because they are unfit to represent the port and decencie of our nobilitie, endevour to get commendation by dangerous lofty trickes, and other strange tumbler-like friskes and motions. And some Ladies make a better shew of their countenances in those dances, wherein are divers changes, cuttings, turnings, and agitations of the body, than in some dances of state and gravety, where they need but simply to tread a natural measure, represent an unaffected carriage, and their ordinary grace; And as [*Comme*] I have also seene some excellent Lourdans, or Clownes attired in their ordinary worky-day clothes, and with a common homely countenance, afford us all the pleasure that may be had from their art: Prentises and learners that are not of so high a forme, to besmeare their faces, to disguise themselves, and in motions to counterfeit strange visages, and antickes to enduce us to laughter. (II.10, Fl 2: 98, V 1: 412)

Amplifying a key similarity between the most skilled writers, the most skilled dancers, and the most skilled clowns, in other words, Montaigne fleshes out his analogy in the "just as" portion of the similitude—a structure that could easily be rephrased as a Socratic induction.

But the content of Montaigne's similitude is no less Socratic than the form. For Montaigne, like Socrates, is preoccupied with the reaches as well as the limits of *technē* or skill. In the final essay of book 2, the essay that closes the 1580 edition, Montaigne turns to his preoccupation with medicine, the *technē* that Socrates invokes more than any other in his considerations of what constitutes a skill. Anticipating his treatment of the art in "Of experience," the essay that will eventually end the three-book volume of the *Essais*, and giving his own slant to the genre of the humanist invective against physicians, Montaigne amplifies his censure at one point by comparing doctors in his own time and place to those of ancient Egypt. Conforming to the conventional structure of a similitude, the comparison nevertheless takes on the contours of a Socratic induction complete with tailors, tanners, and cooks:

> As [*Comme*] we have doublet and hose-makers to make our cloths, and are so much the better fitted, in as much as each medleth with his owne trade, and such have their occupation more strictly limited, then a Tailer that will make all. And as for [*comme*] our necessary foode, some of our great Lords, for their more commodity and ease have severall cookes, as some only to dresse boyled meates, and some to roste, others to bake, whereas if one Cooke alone would supply all three in general he could never doe it so exactly. In like sort [*de mesmes*] for the curing of all diseases, the AEgyptians had reason to reject this general mysterie of Physitians, and to sunder this profession for every malady, allotting each part of the body his distinct workman. (II.37, Fl 2: 509, V 1: 774)

Varying Lyly's sentiment, perhaps based on the common source of an Erasmian adage, that "the shoemaker must not go above his latchet," Montaigne prescribes that "each medleth with his owne trade."[56] Like Lyly, in other words, Montaigne gives copious treatment to a Socratic

---

56. Although the origin of this adage, I.vi.16 (CWE 32: 14), according to Erasmus, is Pliny, Erasmus aligns it with Socrates by linking it in a threesome with I.vi.14 and I.vi.15, both of which feature Socrates as the origin of this sentiment. See also IV.iii.93 (CWE 36: 56–57) for a similar idea.

principle regarding the artist or technician, whether painter, potter, or physician; and like Lyly, he does so in a variation of a Socratic strategy: showcasing the similarity between this and that—a strategy that includes the similitude and its close cousin, *epagōgē*.

In *Ecclesiastes*, to return briefly to the work that opened this chapter, Erasmus reinforces the stylistic dimension of similitudes by identifying it according to a slightly modified version of the traditional *tria genera dicendi*, the three levels of style: grand, middle, and plain.[57] "The character of the language [*orationis character*] will vary according to the nature of the comparison [*qualitate similitudinis*]," Erasmus explains: "it will be pleasant if it is drawn from something pleasant, grand if from something lofty, harsh if from something frightening, moderate if from something moderate, humble if from something humble" (CWE 68: 879; ASD V-5, 262 ll. 209–12). But even this modification, fully illustrated with examples following a "just as . . . so" construction, soon proves too restrictive as Erasmus concludes the section on "those three types of speaking" (*tres orationis characteres*) applied to similitudes (CWE 68: 880; ASD V-5, 164 l. 234) with a recommendation, endorsed by Quintilian (12.10.66–67), to mix them as needed: the harsh with the gentle, the fiery with the calm, and so on. And while designed for the preacher, Erasmus's recommendations regarding the stylistic dimension of the similitude find their way to a broader audience through Susenbrotus's nearly *verbatim* discussion of this figure in his widely read *Epitome*, here as elsewhere borrowed without attribution from his Dutch predecessor.[58]

Despite reliance here and there on the long tradition of stylistic levels, however, Erasmus's most innovative and far-reaching stylistic theory, like Cicero's (and, following Cicero, like Quintilian's), acknowledges the individuality and particularity of style.[59] This acknowledgment, taking hold in the Renaissance, reaches beyond

57. On the three levels of style, see *Ad Herennium* 4.8.11–4.10.14; Cicero, *Orator* 75–99; Quintilian 1.10.24, 11.1.6, 12.10.58–65; and A. D. Leeman, *Orationis ratio: The Stylistic Theories and Practice of the Roman Orators, Historians, and Philosophers* (Amsterdam, 1986).

58. Brennan, "*Epitome Troporum ac Schematum of Joannes Susenbrotus*," 96–97.

59. On individuality in style, see Chomarat, *Grammaire et rhétorique*, 2: 815–40; Jean Lecointe, *L'idéal et la différence: la perception de la personnalité littéraire à la Renaissance* (Geneva, 1993); and Eden, *Renaissance Rediscovery of Intimacy*.

the *personal* to the *temporal* and *local*. For how we speak and write, according to not only Cicero but some of the most prominent anti-Ciceronians, depends on our time and place as well as our natural talents. As conditioned by these factors, style is the focus of the fourth and final chapter.

Style

Recalling himself from a brief digression at the start of *De copia*, Erasmus restates its central theme by means of a similitude. "But to return to my main point," he reprises,

> style [*elocutio*] is to thought as clothes [*vestis*] are to the body. Just as [*Neque enim aliter quam*] dress [*cultu*] and outward appearance can enhance and disfigure the beauty and dignity of the body, so [*itidem*] words [*verbis*] can enhance or disfigure thought. (CWE 24: 306; ASD I-6, 36 ll. 225–27; cf. *De orat.* 3.155)

In the *Ciceronianus*, Erasmus rehearses this similarity between words and clothing, often formulated by the metaphorical shorthand of the "garment of style."[1] Having secured Nosoponus's agreement through his Socratic-style interrogation that "language is a sort of dress" (*orationem quasi vestem*, CWE 28: 381; ASD I-2, 635 l. 5), Bulephorus presses two further points: first, that clothing suitable for a wedding is out of place at a funeral and, second, what was acceptable, even fashionable, a hundred years ago would not be so now.[2]

Eager to get in on the act, Hypologus underscores Bulephorus's (and Erasmus's) points with a vivid tableau of garishly dressed and

1. On the so-called "garment of style," see Rosemond Tuve, *Elizabethan and Metaphysical Imagery* (Chicago, 1947), 61–78.

2. On Socrates' epagogic method of questioning and its relation to the similitude, see chap. 3, p. 105.

plucked matrons alongside men with bizarrely shaved heads and tunics that barely cover their private parts—all in the interest of getting from Nosoponus the relativizing concession that "people of those days [*illis temporibus*] would have found the clothes [*cultus*] we think perfectly respectable just as monstrous as we find theirs." To which Nosoponus unforcedly answers, "We're of one mind on the subject of clothes" (*De veste convenit*, CWE 28: 381; ASD I-2, 635 ll. 20–21). There is no disagreement among the interlocutors of this dialogue, in other words, that styles of dress, or what we would call "fashion," are conditioned by time and place, the regular coordinates of not only rhetoric but history.[3]

But what about literary or rhetorical style, especially Ciceronian style? Bulephorus and Hypologus have a much harder time persuading Nosoponus to consider *its* historical dimensions. In their efforts to do so, this chapter will argue, they, like other Renaissance champions of a historicizing attitude to style, will look back for support to Ciceronian stylistic theory, and especially to Cicero's newly recovered *Brutus*, arguably the first history of style. Among the supports they will find there is the metaphor of style as a garment (*Brutus* 274), which, in the first century BCE as in the sixteenth, should not only respond to the local and temporal demands of fashion but fit the speaker to a tee. Another is the corresponding history of the arts of painting and sculpture, which Cicero combines with this metaphor to characterize the highly accomplished style of his rhetorical (and political) other, Julius Caesar, whose orations resemble beautifully sculpted statues, "bare, straightforward, alluring, with all rhetorical elaboration stripped away, like a garment" (*omni ornatu orationis tamquam veste detracta*, *Brutus* 262). Cicero's *Brutus,* as we will see, is at the very center of some of the most high-profile Renaissance debates regarding style.[4] It also informs other Roman treatments of style simi-

3. On these shared coordinates, see Nancy Struever, *The Language of History in the Renaissance: Rhetoric and Historical Consciousness in Florentine Humanism* (Princeton, 1970), esp. 5–39.

4. For the centrality of *Brutus* in the discourse of Renaissance art history, see E. H. Gombrich, "The Debate on Primitivism in Ancient Rhetoric," *Journal of the Warburg and Courtauld Institutes* 29 (1966): 24–30, and "Vasari's *Lives* and Cicero's *Brutus,*" *Journal of the Warburg and Courtauld Institutes* 23 (1960): 309–11. For its centrality in Renaissance literary history, see Martin McLaughlin, "Histo-

larly recovered in the course of the fifteenth century, all of which take as their point of departure Aristotle's *Rhetoric*. Like these others in gradually entering the rhetorical mainstream in the fifteenth century, this earliest full-fledged rhetorical manual not only acknowledges the historical dimension of style but theorizes the very rhetorical principle whose hermeneutic counterpart, as we will also see, underwrites Renaissance historicism.[5]

ARISTOTELIAN STYLISTIC THEORY

After treating the sources of proof in the first two books of his *Rhetoric*, as detailed in earlier chapters, Aristotle addresses style (*lexis*) in the third. In contrast to the later rhetorical tradition (and maybe even to nameless rhetoricians of his own day), Aristotle insists on two and only two excellences or virtues (Gr. *aretai*) of style, namely, clarity and appropriateness: *saphēneia* and *to prepon* (3.2.1).[6] By assigning style qualities or virtues, Aristotle tethers his stylistic theory to his ethical theory. Indeed, Aristotle begins his treatment of style by asserting that stylistic excellence, like moral excellence, is strictly a qualitative matter. "[F]or it is not enough to have a supply of things to say," he warns, "but it is also necessary to say it in the right way [*hōs*

---

ries of Literature in the Quattrocento," in *The Languages of Literature in Renaissance Italy*, ed. Peter Hainsworth et al. (Oxford, 1988), 63–80, and "*Renascens ad superos Cicero.*"

5. On Renaissance historicism, see George Huppert, "The Renaissance Background of Historicism," *History and Theory* 5 (1966): 48–60; Donald H. Kelley, "Hermes, Clio, Themis: Historical Interpretation and Legal Hermeneutics," *Journal of Modern History* 55 (1983): 644–68; Zachary Sayre Schiffman, "Renaissance Historicism Reconsidered," *History and Theory* 24 (1985): 170–82. See also Georg G. Iggers, "Historicism: The History and Meaning of the Term," *Journal of the History of Ideas* 56 (1995): 129–52, and Dwight E. Lee and Robert N. Beck, "The Meaning of Historicism," *American Historical Review* 59 (1954): 568–77.

6. On the virtues of style, see George A. Kennedy, "The Evolution of a Theory of Artistic Prose," in *The Cambridge History of Literary Criticism: Classical Criticism*, ed. Kennedy (Cambridge, UK, 1989), 193–95, and D. C. Innes, "Theophrastus and the Theory of Style," *Rutgers University Studies* 2 (1985): 251–67. Following Quintilian (*Institutio oratoria* 4.2.63), Kennedy (Aristotle, *On Rhetoric* 3.12.6, p. 257) suggests Theodectes or perhaps Isocrates as among those left unnamed.

dei eipein], and this contributes much toward the speech seeming to have a certain quality [*poion tina*]" (*Rhetoric* 3.1.2, p. 217).

In the *Nicomachean Ethics*, Aristotle painstakingly theorizes *quality* as distinct from *quantity* as part of his well-known discussion of virtue as a choiceworthy mean or midpoint (*to meson*) between extremes. Whereas the *quantitative* midpoint is measured in terms of the thing itself (*kat'auto to pragma*) and is therefore fixed and inflexible—six is the midpoint between ten and two in all cases—the *qualitative* midpoint or mean is measured in terms relative to us (*pros hēmas*) and so will change according to circumstances (2.6, 1106a26–36).[7] Like the quality of a speech, as Aristotle warned above, the quality of an action depends on its being performed "in the right way" (*hōs dei*, 2.6, 1106b22); and this rightness will depend on the particularities of the situation, including the time, the place, and the persons involved. In an effort to clarify his concept of a qualitative or relative mean in ethics, Aristotle draws an explicit analogy to the arts, with the discursive arts like rhetoric chief among them. "Thus a master of any art," he concludes, "avoids excess and defect, but seeks the intermediate [*meson*] and chooses [*haireitai*] this—the intermediate not in the object [*to tou pragmatos*] but relatively to us [*to pros hēmas*]" (*Nic. Ethics* 2.6, 1106b5–7). As a qualitative matter, then, artistic style, like ethical action, must meet two conditions in order to qualify as excellent: it must strike a relative mean by accommodating particular circumstances, and it must strike this mean on purpose, by choice.

In both the *Nicomachean Ethics* (5.10.3–7) and the *Rhetoric* (1.13.17–19), Aristotle further aligns this qualitative, choiceworthy midpoint

---

7. On the distinction between *quality* and *quantity* and their relation to two forms of intelligibility—what is known to us (*hēmin* or *pros hēmas*) and what is known in itself (*haplōs* or *kat'auto to pragma*)—see Trimpi, *Muses of One Mind*, 116–29. See also *Nicomachean Ethics* 1.4, 1095b2–3: "For, while we must begin with what is evident, things are evident in two ways—some to us, some without qualification" (trans. David Ross [Oxford, 1980]). Unless otherwise indicated, I have used this translation throughout. See also *Posterior Analytics* 1.2, 71b31–72a6: "Things are prior and more familiar in two ways; for it is not the same to be prior by nature and prior in relation to us, nor to be more familiar and more familiar to us. I call prior and more familiar in relation to us what is nearer to perception, prior and more familiar *simpliciter* what is further away. What is most universal is furthest away, and the particulars are nearest; and these are opposite to each other" (trans. Jonathan Barnes [Oxford, 1975]).

with the concept of equity or *epieikeia* as a corrective to legal justice.[8] Whenever the law, because of its universality formulated as an absolute statement, is unable to deal with the details of a particular case, equity functions, like the flexible rule used by the builders of Lesbos, to adapt itself to these particulars and to decide as the lawgiver himself would have decided if he had been able to foresee present circumstances. With his fictional hypothesis of a revivified lawgiver, Aristotle inaugurates a legal principle destined to play a leading role not only in Western ethical and legal theory but, as we will see later in this chapter, in stylistic theory as well.

In the meantime, Aristotle applies the term *prepon* to this qualitative, choiceworthy mean designed to accommodate the style of the speech to the particular circumstances.[9] And he not only begins and ends his discussion of style with this principle (3.2.1, 3.12.6) but integrates it into the rhetorical art as a whole by insisting that among the circumstances needing accommodation are the subject matter under consideration (*logos*) and the character of both the speaker (*ēthos*) and the audience (*pathos*) (3.7.1), the three sources of proof treated in detail in the previous two books of his manual.[10] A faulty or frigid style, in contrast, is one that misses this mean (3.3.3). Even clarity itself, as the other of the two Aristotelian stylistic excellences, has a hard time maintaining its independence from *to prepon* insofar as Aristotle defines clear style as a midpoint between luxuriance (*adoleschia*) and concision (*syntomia*) (3.12.6).

On the other hand, Aristotle sets his treatment of style in book 3 of the *Rhetoric* apart from his treatment of the sources of proof in

8. On Aristotelian equity as a qualitative measure, see Trimpi, *Muses of One Mind*, 266–75, and Kathy Eden, *Poetic and Legal Fiction in the Aristotelian Tradition* (Princeton, 1986; rpt. 2014), 32–54. See also Struever, *Language of History in the Renaissance*, 14.

9. On Aristotelian *to prepon*, see Max Pohlenz, "To Prepon: Ein Beitrag zur Geschichte des griechischen Geistes," *Philologisch-historische Klasse* 1 (1933): 57–62, and Stephen J. McKenna, *Adam Smith: The Rhetoric of Propriety* (Albany, 2006), 36–44. On the relation between *to prepon* and equity, see Wesley Trimpi, "Reason and the Classical Premises of Literary Decorum," *Independent Journal of Philosophy* 5/6 (1988): 103–11, esp. 103–5.

10. On the centrality to the rhetorical tradition of this Aristotelian triad— *logos, ēthos, pathos*—see Solmsen, "Aristotelian Tradition in Ancient Rhetoric," and James M. May, *Trials of Character: The Eloquence of Ciceronian Ethos* (Chapel Hill, 1988), 3.

books 1 and 2 not only because style, like delivery, only belatedly becomes a part of the art of rhetoric (3.1.5) but also because rhetorical
or prose style, like poetic style, changes over time. While its lexicon
has become more conversational (3.1.9), Aristotle notes, its rhythms
have become more natural (3.8.4) and its syntax more structured or
periodic (3.9.2). Unlike such inventional strategies as the enthymeme
and the example, in other words, stylistic elements, as Aristotle understands them, appear to be subject to historical development.[11]

CICERONIAN STYLISTIC THEORY

Both Aristotle's *to prepon* and his recognition of a historical dimension to style find Roman footing in Cicero's mature rhetorical theory.
Whereas the *Rhetoric* couples appropriateness and clarity as the only
two excellences, however, Cicero's Crassus in the third book of *De oratore*, the book on style, assumes the by-now-traditional four virtues
of style.[12] He also aligns speaking clearly (*plane dicere*) with speaking
correctly (*latine dicere*) as the pair of virtues that can be more or less
taken for granted (*De orat.* 3.48–49), while speaking ornately (*ornate
dicere*) and speaking appropriately (*apte dicere*), because they garner
oratorical acclaim, are worthy of more attention (3.52). But Crassus
does not attend to *apte dicere* in the same detail as *ornate dicere*—and
for good reason. Because "no single style [*genus orationis*] is fitting for
every case or every audience or every person involved on every occasion," Crassus admits, "there is really no rule that I could give you at
this point, except that when choosing [*deligamus*] a type of speech—a
fuller [*figuram orationis plenioris*] or more slender one [*tenuioris*], or
indeed the middle type [*mediocris*]—, we should see to it that it is
adapted [*accommodatam*] to the problem at hand" (*De orat.* 3.210–

11. In *Poetic and Legal Fiction*, 12–18, I suggest that proof, like style, evolves, in
this case from an emphasis on *atechnoi* to one on *entechnoi pisteis*, as demonstrated
by Attic tragedy and oratory, but Aristotle himself does not indicate such an evolution in either the *Rhetoric* or the *Poetics*. At *Orator* 192–96 Cicero comments on
Aristotle's treatment of prose rhythm.

12. On Cicero's familiarity with Aristotle's *Rhetoric*, see May and Wisse, in Cicero, *On the Ideal Orator*, 39; and on *De oratore*'s handling of the Theophrastan
virtues of style, see May and Wisse, 35–36.

12).[13] Without much fanfare or elaboration, then, appropriateness in *De oratore* preserves the two Aristotelian conditions of choiceworthiness and accommodation, applied in this case to the post-Aristotelian three levels of style. For Cicero as for Aristotle, moreover, the cardinal rule of accommodating circumstances in the qualitative matter of style trumps all other hard and fast rules.

In the *Orator*, written roughly a decade after *De oratore*, Cicero once again treats appropriateness as one of the four virtues of style, only he does so in considerably more detail.[14] Building on Crassus's well-known argument throughout *De oratore* that eloquence requires knowledge or wisdom—that *eloquentia* requires *sapientia*—Cicero in the *Orator* identifies appropriateness itself with a kind of knowing (*Orator* 70, 123; cf. *Brutus* 23). Some knowledge pertains to what is right under all circumstances and in all times and places. Cicero contrasts this unconditional right or *rectum* (*Orator* 72) with a circumstantially sensitive aptness, and he reinforces the contrast with a distinction presumed to be familiar to philosophers between *oportere*, applicable to duties "that should be performed always and by everyone," and *decere,* applicable to "what suits a circumstance and character [*tempori et personae*]" (73–74).[15] On the basis of this distinction, moreover, Cicero famously settles on *decorum*, derived from *decere*, as the best equivalent of Aristotle's *to prepon* (70). Whereas Aristotle restricted the term to stylistic matters, however, Cicero overrides this restriction, not only reintroducing *decorum* back into the ethical

13. On Cicero's allusion here to the *tria genera dicendi*, see A. E. Douglas, "A Ciceronian Contribution to Rhetorical Theory," *Eranos* 55 (1957): 18–26; Elaine Fantham, "*Orator* 69–74," *Central States Speech Journal* 35 (1984): 123–25, and "On the Use of *Genus*-Terminology in Cicero's Rhetorical Works," *Hermes* 107 (1979): 441–59.

14. In the *Orator*, Cicero refers to the stylistic *aretai* (Gr.), which *Ad Herennium* calls somewhat vaguely the *res* of style (4.7.10), as *laudes* (79, 231) and *quasi virtutes* (139). In *Brutus* (66), however, he refers to the many *oratoriae virtutes* in Cato's speeches.

15. *Orator*, trans. Robert Kaster (Oxford, 2020). For the Latin, I have used the edition by Rolf Westman (Leipzig, 1980). Unless otherwise indicated, all references are to this edition and noted parenthetically in the text. On the analogous distinction for both Cicero and Augustine between *facinus* and *flagitium*, see Carlo Ginzburg, "The Letter Kills: On Some Implications of 2 Corinthians 3:6," *History and Theory* 49 (2010): 71–89, esp. 73–77. On the combined requirements of *apte* and *decere* in Ciceronian *decorum*, see Fantham, "*Orator* 69–74."

arena, where Aristotle, as we have seen, first formulated a qualitative or relative (as opposed to an absolute) mean, but also designating it the universal rule both in oratory and in life (71).[16]

Following Aristotle, Cicero also specifically aligns stylistic *decorum* with the three sources of proof established in the *Rhetoric*, claiming that it depends on "the matter dealt with and on the character of both speakers and listeners" (*Orator* 71)—dependent, that is, on *logos*, *ēthos*, and *pathos*. When Cicero returns to the subject of *decorum* later in the treatise as part of his portrait of the consummate speaker or *eloquens*, he begins by repeating his insistence that this speaker must know *quid deceat*—what is fitting or appropriate—and then features the two singularly important quiddities of *tempus* and *persona*. "This wisdom [*sapientia*] is an eloquent speaker's most important tool," Cicero asserts,

> for I do not believe all orators should speak in the same way at all times, before all audiences, against all opponents, for all defendants. The eloquent speaker will be the one who aligns his speech with the standard of appropriateness [*Is erit ergo eloquens, qui ad id quodcumque decebit poterit accommodare orationem*]. (*Orator* 123)

In the *Orator*, then, Cicero both builds on his treatment of *apte dicere* in *De oratore* and aligns it more closely with *apte facere*—a realignment of stylistics and ethics. He also renames it. But he does not change it—at least not essentially. Like Aristotelian *to prepon*, Ciceronian *decorum* remains an indispensable quality of style because it responds to circumstances, especially to times and persons. *Temporal* and *personal* considerations, above all, should inform oratorical production. More to the point, no oration can be successful without this responsiveness.[17]

---

16. See McKenna, *Adam Smith*, 47–51 (where the *Orator* is mistakenly identified as Cicero's first mature work on rhetoric), and Victoria Kahn, *Rhetoric, Prudence, and Skepticism* (Ithaca, 1985), 30–36.

17. In an appendix at the end of *Truth and Method*, trans. Joel Weinsheimer and Donald Marshall (New York, 1975; rpt. 1992), Hans-Georg Gadamer first presses the challenging point that "the concept of style is one of the undiscussed assumptions on which historical consciousness lives" (493) and then locates three dimensions of this concept: the *normative*, the *personal*, and the *historical*. Both the deep affiliation of style to historical consciousness and the three dimensions

Written shortly after the *Orator*, Cicero's *De officiis* (*On Duties*) re-affirms not only the designation of Latin *decorum* for Aristotle's *to prepon* (1.93) but the central role of *decorum* in ethics as in art—a re-affirmation that underscores in turn the centrality of times and persons.[18] Like the best poets, who accommodate the verses they write and the actions they emplot to the characters or *(dramatis) personae* fashioned to perform them (1.97–98), Nature, an artist in her own right, creates humans with *personae* that similarly require accommodation. More precisely, she endows individuals with two of their four *personae*, the first of which, a *communis persona*, they share with all other human beings by virtue of the rationality (*ratio*) that distinguishes them from beasts. In keeping with this *persona*, in other words, we are all more or less alike. The second *persona*, in contrast, renders us different from one another (1.107); and it is this *persona* that *De oratore* and the *Orator* refer to as the *natura* (or *ingenium*) of the orator. It is this *persona*, moreover, that Cicero tells his son Marcus in *De officiis* requires the greatest accommodation. "Each person should hold on to what is his," father advises son,

> so that the seemliness [*decorum*] that we are seeking might more easily be maintained . . . let us follow our own nature [*propriam nostram (naturam)*], so that even if other pursuits be weightier and better, we should measure our own by the rule of our own nature [*naturae*]. For it is appropriate neither to fight against nature [*naturae*] nor to pursue anything that you cannot attain. (1.110)[19]

---

of style proposed by Gadamer figure prominently in the argument of this chapter, which, noting the subordination of the traditional rules (that is, the *normative* element), charts the shift from *personal* to *temporal* (or *historical*) difference not only in Cicero's mature rhetorical works but in discussions of style in the early sixteenth century after these Ciceronian works in their entirety entered the theoretical mainstream. For a different reading of Gadamer's generative appendix, see Willibald Sauerländer, "From Stilus to Style: Reflections on the Fate of a Notion," *Art History* 6 (1983): 253–70.

18. For the difficulty of Cicero's treatment of *decorum* in this late philosophical treatise, see Andrew R. Dyck, *A Commentary on Cicero, "De Officiis"* (Ann Arbor, 1996), 241. For its centrality to Cicero's notion of an individual or personal style, see Eden, *Renaissance Rediscovery of Intimacy*, 25–28.

19. Cicero, *On Duties*, ed. M. T. Griffin and E. M. Atkins (Cambridge, UK, 1991). On Cicero's four-*personae* theory, see Christopher Gill, "Personhood and Personality: The Four-*Personae* Theory in Cicero, *De officiis* I," *Oxford Studies in*

In this late work, then, Cicero understands our natures (that is, our second, personal *natura*) to constrain our activities, determining not only what we can but, more pointedly, what we cannot achieve. And this limitation on our achievement is further marked by the third *persona*, which is subject to the forces of chance (*casus*) and time (*tempus*) (1.115). In *De officiis*, as in his later rhetorical works, in other words, *temporal* and *personal* factors condition our efforts. Only the last of the four *personae*, through an exercise of the will (*voluntas*), enjoys freedom of choice, whether in selecting a profession or pursuing a virtue. Whereas Aristotle endows his ethical agent, like his orator, with an almost unhampered agency, Cicero warns his son about the inevitable, seemingly overwhelming constraints on his—constraints, as we will see in more detail, that afflict the Ciceronian stylist as well.

Some years after *De oratore* and shortly before the *Orator*, Cicero writes *Brutus*.[20] In contrast to their idealizing approach to the concept of style, *Brutus* features the very same variables of times and persons but from a *historical* point of view.[21] Arguably the oldest surviving his-

---

Ancient Philosophy 6 (1988): 169–99. See also Michèle Lowrie, "Cicero on Caesar or Exemplum and Inability in the *Brutus*," in *Notions of the Self in Antiquity and Beyond*, ed. Alexander Arweiler and Melanie Möller (Berlin, 2008), 131–54, who, in regard to the performative aspect of the Roman self, concludes: "Although this is not specified, style presumably permeates every *persona* and results from a combination of the givens of our individual personalities with our choices, subjected to the constraints of the circumstances governing our lives" (140). In *Making a New Man: Ciceronian Self-Fashioning in the Rhetorical Works* (Oxford, 2005), John Dugan argues for a Ciceronian stylist who exercises more control: "The *Brutus* thus presents the formation of the self as a conscious choice to fashion one's identity according to exemplary individuals. One's self is therefore the product of the deliberate decision to internalize the examples of other figures" (200).

20. On the date of *Brutus*, see the edition by A. E. Douglas, *M. Tulli Ciceronis Brutus* (Oxford, 1966), ix–x, and Edward A. Robinson, "The Date of Cicero's *Brutus*," *Harvard Studies in Classical Philology* 60 (1951): 137–46.

21. On the historical agenda of *Brutus*, see C. E. W. Steel, "Cicero's *Brutus*: The End of Oratory and the Beginning of History?" *Bulletin of the Institute of Classical Studies of the University of London* 46 (2002–3): 195–211; Dugan, *Making a New Man*, 172–250; and Elizabeth Rawson, "Cicero the Historian and Cicero the Antiquarian," *Journal of Roman Studies* 62 (1972): 33–45, who considers *Brutus* "among other things, Cicero's most sustained, sensitive and successful historical achievement. Here he could combine both his interest in cultural history, including his interest in comparing Greek and Roman developments, with his interest in distinguished individuals; for once basing himself on documentary knowledge of a

tory of style, *Brutus* also shifts the focus from one pairing of stylistic excellences to another. Whereas *De oratore* and the *Orator* couple the two more demanding virtues of *ornate dicere* and *apte dicere* (or *decorum*), *Brutus*, in contrast, features *ornate dicere* and *Latine dicere* as part of a carefully orchestrated comparison of the styles (and politics) of Cicero and Caesar.[22] It also adds to these featured virtues, as we will soon see, a fifth virtue of style that challenges the stylistic purity of Cicero's detractors.

From the opening words of his conversation with friends Atticus and Brutus at his house in Rome, Cicero establishes both the dialogue's historical agenda and its corresponding preoccupation with temporality. Inspired by Atticus's *Liber Annalis* (*Brutus* 72, 74; cf. *Orator* 120), characterized by Cicero as "all of history set out comprehensively in chronological order [*ordinibus temporum*]" (15), Cicero's *historia*, as Atticus calls it (292), undertakes to chart (*persequi*) the *aetates* and *tempora* of famous speakers (74)—a task Brutus describes as "distinguish[ing] types of orators across successive generations" (*oratorum genera distinguere aetatibus*, 74).[23] Encouraging his host

---

scope probably unrivalled in his day" (41). For a distinction between the approach of *De oratore* (and *Brutus*) and that of the *Orator*, see G. L. Hendrickson, "Cicero de optimo genere oratorum," *American Journal of Philology* 47 (1926): 109–23.

22. On the status of *Latinitas* in *Brutus*, see G. L. Hendrickson, "Cicero's Correspondence with Brutus and Calvus on Oratorical Style," *American Journal of Philology* 47 (1926): 234–58; Dugan, *Making a New Man*, 177–89; and Lowrie, "Cicero on Caesar or Exemplum and Inability in the *Brutus*," 141–42. For the contrast between Ciceronian and Caesarian *virtus*, see William H. F. Altman, "Womanly Humanism in Cicero's *Tusculan Disputations*," *Transactions of the American Philological Association* 139 (2009): 407–41 esp. 422–23. For the analogy between painting and rhetoric in relation to both style and politics, see Tonio Hölscher, "Greek Styles and Greek Art in Augustan Rome: Issues of the Present versus Records of the Past," in *Classical Pasts: The Classical Traditions of Greece and Rome*, ed. James I. Porter (Princeton, 2006), 237–59, esp. 249: "In very similar ways, Roman Rhetoric adopted stylistic forms from the Greek classical and Hellenistic periods and employed them next to one another. For one, Hellenistic pathos and classical discipline were taught as antithetical stylistic forms and were polemically played off against each other under the rubrics of Asianism and Atticism. In the struggle between Antony and Octavian, they could even be elevated to political styles. Contrasting forms of rhetoric were simultaneously contrasts in political *habitus*."

23. On Cicero's two interlocutors in the dialogue, see Douglas, *M. Tulli Ciceronis Brutus*, xvii–xxii. For Cicero on his use of interlocutors in dialogue, see *Ad Att.* 13.19.3–5. On Atticus's *Liber Annalis*, see Douglas, *M. Tulli Ciceronis Brutus*,

to share with his guests his survey of Roman oratory, Brutus gives this sort of chronological treatment (*quasi notatio temporum*, 74) his wholehearted approval. Fully responsive to this approbation, Cicero not only credits the chronology or *ordo aetatum* with moving the conversation along (232) but expresses the need both to apologize for disrupting it briefly with an orator out of temporal sequence (223) and to defend it as something more than a mere *enumeratio oratorum*, a straightforward catalogue of speakers (319). But such a defense is really unnecessary. For Cicero has modeled his history of oratory on a history of the visual and plastic arts that moves well beyond a simple enumeration of artists. More than just another version of the *ut pictura rhetorica* familiar to readers of Cicero's earliest rhetorical theory, stylistic history in *Brutus* purposefully and tellingly reworks the lesson from "art history" offered in *De oratore*.[24]

In the third book of this earlier dialogue (*De oratore* 3.25–31), Crassus outspokenly counters a claim upheld by manuals like *Ad Herennium*, which favor a single best oratorical style that epitomizes the art and should, to the exclusion of all others, be imitated. On the contrary, Crassus argues here as elsewhere in opposition to these manuals, there are many excellent rhetorical styles, all different, just as

---

lii; Steel, "Cicero's *Brutus*," 196–97. And on this and other sources of Cicero's history, see Douglas, *M. Tulli Ciceronis Brutus*, xxii and xliv–liv; Rawson, "Cicero the Historian and Cicero the Antiquarian," 34–35, and Alain Gowing, "Memory and Silence in Cicero's *Brutus*," *Eranos* 98 (2000): 39–64, who, surveying the scholarship, concludes that there is no "specific work prior to the *Brutus*, Latin or Greek, which may be said directly to inspire it. Rather the *Brutus* was evidently an unusual work written to fulfill an unusual purpose" (39). On Cicero's aim to distinguish the *genera oratorum* according to the *aetates* of the orators, see A. E. Douglas, "Oratorum Aetates," *American Journal of Philology* 87 (1966): 290–306.

24. For the young Cicero's analogy between his own method of composing an *ars dicendi* and Zeuxis's method of composition in painting the Helen of Croton, see *De inventione* 2.1–5. For the subsequent influence, *mutatis mutandis*, of Cicero's late rhetorical theory on early modern theories of the visual arts, see Gombrich, "Vasari's *Lives* and Cicero's *Brutus*," 309–11, and "The Renaissance Conception of Artistic Progress and Its Consequences," in *Norm and Form*, 1–10; Baxandall, *Giotto and the Orators*, 51–78; Sauerländer, "From Stilus to Style"; Martin Kemp, "'Equal excellences': Lomazzo and the Explanation of Individual Style in the Visual Arts," *Renaissance Studies* 1 (1987): 1–26; Philip Sohm, "Ordering History with Style: Giorgio Vasari on the Art of History," in *Antiquity and Its Interpreters*, ed. Alina Payne, Ann Kuttner, Rebekah Smick (Cambridge, UK, 1999), 40–54.

there are many different painterly and sculptural styles—a diversity that does not preclude an art of painting or sculpture:

> There is one art of sculpture; among its most outstanding practitioners were Myron, Polyclitus and Lysippus, all of whom were different [*dissimiles*] from one another, but still in such a way that you could not wish any of them different [*dissimilem*] from what he was. There is one systematic art of painting, yet Zeuxis, Aglaophon and Apelles are entirely different from one another; but there is not one among them whose art seems deficient in any respect. And if this is surprising but still true in the case of these so-called silent arts, it is certainly much more surprising in the case of speech, that is, language. (*De orat.* 3.26)[25]

Among the practitioners of equal oratorical excellence in Greece, Crassus applauds Isocrates for grace, Lysias for precision, Aeschines for sonorousness, and Demosthenes for force. Their Roman counterparts include Scipio for weight, Laelius for smoothness, Galba for harshness, and Carbo for flow and melody (*De orat.* 3.28). Crassus's point is that no one among Greek or Roman contemporaries, whether artists or orators, excludes the others. Each excels in his own way, according to his own natural talent, his *natura* or *ingenium*. To set in high relief the determining factor of individual talent, Crassus relates an anecdote regarding Isocrates' pedagogical method of using the spur with Ephorus and the bridle with Theopompus to "reinforce in each what his natural abilities [*natura*] allowed" (3.36). Crassus's invocation of the pantheon of artists in *De oratore*, in other words, foregrounds the *personal* dimension of style.

Like *De oratore* but more pointedly, *Brutus* addresses this *personal* dimension of style. It even repeats the anecdote about Isocrates' attention to the distinguishing *ingenia* of his two pupils, Theopompus and Ephorus, invoked on this occasion to provide context for the very different but equally accomplished styles of two contemporaneous Roman orators, Sulpicius and Cotta (*Brutus* 204). Throughout the later dialogue, however, Cicero takes stock of the constraints, personal and otherwise, that condition style. These constraints restrict

25. For Crassus's rejection of the lessons from the rhetorical handbooks, see chap. 1, p. 16.

an orator's ability, granted, as we have seen, to both Aristotle's ethical agent and his rhetorical stylist, to freely choose his manner of speaking, writing, and acting. So Cicero wonders why Marcus Calidius's style was able to teach and to delight but not to move—whether the failure was the consequence of choice (*consilium*), nature (*natura*), habit (*non consuesset*), or some disability (*non posset, Brutus* 276); and he raises a similar question about the florid style of Demetrius of Phaleron (285): was it natural bent (*natura*) or deliberate choice (*voluntas*)? Complicating Socrates' famous triad in the *Phaedrus* (269CD), which locates *physis* as the site of rhetorical potential, Ciceronian *natura* factors into the equation for oratorical success the personal limitations of the orator.[26]

Inevitably constrained (as well as fostered) by natural ability, Cicero suggests in *Brutus*, style is also conditioned by place—a point he drives home in his treatment of the almost indefinable quality of *urbanitas*. For there are speakers, Cicero warns, who are betrayed by some ineradicable *sapor vernaculum*—something like a regional dialect— that affects not only their word choice but their pronunciation and even their intonation (*vox* or *sonus*). Such was the case with Theophrastus, who was considered the consummate speaker of his day but was nevertheless outed as a foreigner by an old woman in the marketplace when she detected his ever-so-slight accent (*Brutus* 170–72).

Locality also prevails in *Brutus* as the traditional *tria genera dicendi* are reimagined and even reevaluated in terms of a place of origin: Attica for a narrowly conceived plain style, Asia for a belated and arguably degenerate version of the grand style, and Rhodes for something in between (*Brutus* 51). In keeping with this reevaluation rooted in place, Cicero refutes the so-called Atticists who exclude him from their cohort not only by reprising the argument for dissimilarity used to great effect, as we have seen, in *De oratore* but by reformulating their judgment that only those who speak in an Attic style speak well.[27] On the contrary, Cicero insists in a reversal of this

26. On the Platonic triad of natural talent, knowledge, and exercise or practice, see above, p. 101. On *potestas* or ability as one of the two factors in agency as well as one of the two topics, with *voluntas*, of the *conjectural status*, see chap. 1 above.

27. On the controversy over Atticism, including its opposition to Asianism, see J. Wisse, "Greeks, Romans, and the Rise of Atticism," in *Greek Literary Theory after Aristotle*, ed. J. G. J. Abbenes, S. R. Slings, and I. Sluiter (Amsterdam, 1995),

judgment that broadens the category to include himself, all who speak well (*bene dicere*) speak in Attic style (*Attice dicere*). To the traditional four virtues of style, in other words, Cicero adds a fifth. *Attice dicere*. While factoring in such circumstances as person and place, however, *Brutus* features the determining condition of time: *tempus* or *aetas*. In contrast to *De oratore*, in fact, the main agenda of *Brutus* is to set style in a *historical* rather than a *personal* light.

This contrast between the two dialogues is especially evident when Cicero introduces into *Brutus* some of the same painters and sculptors who appear in *De oratore*. "For among those who attend to the lesser arts," Cicero asks,

> who does not recognize that Canachus' statues are too inflexible to represent real bodies? Those of Calamis are stiff, to be sure, but still more supple than Canachus's; Myron's are not yet realistic, yet they're the sort you'd readily call beautiful; those of Polyclitus are more beautiful, in fact quite perfect, at least to my eye. A similar pattern [*ratio*] obtains in painting: we praise Zeuxis and Polygnotus and Timanthes, and the shapes and lines [*formas et liniamenta*] of those who used no more than four colors; but in the work of Aetion, Nicomachus, Protogenes, Apelles, all the elements have already been perfected. And the same would probably turn out to be true in all other areas, for nothing has been both discovered and perfected all at once [*nihil est enim simul et inventum et perfectum*]. (*Brutus* 70–71)

Whereas Zeuxis and Apelles, like Myron and Polyclitus, exemplify *personal* stylistic difference in *De oratore*, in *Brutus* that difference speaks more directly to changes over time, to *historical* difference.[28]

65–82, and Emanuele Narducci, "*Brutus*: The History of Roman Eloquence," in *Brill's Companion to Cicero*, ed. May, 404–19.

28. In *Caesar's Calendar: Ancient Time and the Beginnings of History* (Berkeley, 2007), 227n99, Denis Feeney notes that in *De oratore* Cicero's "apprehension of temporal 'unlikeness' is not at all as developed" as in *Brutus*. See also Andrew Feldherr, "Cicero and the Invention of 'Literary' History," in *Formen römischer Geschichtsschreibung von den Anfängen bis Livius*, ed. Ulrich Eigler, Ulrich Gotter, Nino Luraghi, and Uwe Walter (Darmstadt, 2003), 196–212, esp. 206. On personal or individual difference in the formation of an intimate style from Cicero to Montaigne, see Eden, *Renaissance Rediscovery of Intimacy*, 119–24.

Comparable to the progressive stages in painting and sculpture, rhetorical style has evolved; and this evolution means that the artistic production of individual orators will be constrained or conditioned not only by an individual talent but also by a particular *tempus* or *aetas*.[29]

It is to deepen his interlocutors' (and thereby his readers') understanding of Cato's style as a product of *its* time that Cicero pointedly inserts this evolutionary or progressive model of the arts, including rhetoric.[30] Disregarded by the Atticists, despite a *subtilitas* or plain-speaking similar to Lysias's, and virtually unread by anyone except Cicero (*Brutus* 65), Cato, Cicero explains, was constrained by "the way they spoke then" (*Brutus* 68)—a circumstance he could not change. Unlike the virtuous action of Aristotle's ethical agent, in other words, Cato's style, understood from a historical perspective, was not freely chosen. Even so, Cicero hypothesizes, with only a few adjustments or "corrections" in composition and rhythm designed to update an outmoded style, contemporary audiences, conditioned by their own time, would find the archaic (*pervetus*) Cato entirely to their liking (*Brutus* 68–69).

29. On the evolutionary (or progressive) dimension of Cicero's thinking about the arts, see E. H. Gombrich, "Renaissance Conception of Artistic Progress and Its Consequences," who traces the "new humanist idea of artistic progress" back to a number of Roman works unavailable before the fifteenth century, including Cicero's *Brutus*; and see, in addition, Sander M. Goldberg, *Epic in Republican Rome* (Oxford, 1995), 6–9; Dugan, *Making a New Man*, 250; and Feldherr, "Cicero and the Invention of 'Literary' History," who contends that Cicero's "progressive view of Roman development where the new triumphs over the old comes about only when evaluation is based on style, not on information content, or more importantly, on the transmission of social prestige" (202). Elsewhere the notion of progress is identified with modernity. See, for instance, Everson Marks, *Relativist and Absolutist: The Early Neoclassical Debate in England* (New Brunswick, NJ, 1955), 92–114, and Reinhart Koselleck, "Historia Magistra Vitae: The Dissolution of the Topos into the Perspective of a Modernized Historical Process," in *Futures Past: On the Semantics of Historical Time*, trans. Keith Tribe (New York, 2004), 26–42. On progress as an ancient idea, see Ludwig Edelstein, *The Idea of Progress in Classical Antiquity* (Baltimore, 1967), and E. R. Dodds, *The Ancient Concept of Progress and Other Essays on Greek Literature and Belief* (Oxford, 1973), 1–25.

30. For Cicero on Cato's style, see Narducci, "*Brutus*," 401–25, esp. 413–14, and *Cicerone e l'eloquenza romana* (Rome, 1997), 136–40, in which he notes that "rifiutandosi di giudicare Catone come un proprio contemporaneo, Cicerone arriverebbe praticamente a introdurre il concetto del carattere storicamente condizionate dei canoni estetici, e della loro sostanziale relatività" (137).

Cicero's historicizing hypothesis is so unexpected that even his best friend Atticus mistakes it for irony (*Brutus* 293–97)—a mistake that serves Cicero well. For it allows him not only to make Atticus the mouthpiece of an embarrassing bit of self-praise (296–97) but also to round out at the appropriate moment in his history the evolutionary model that much earlier in the dialogue accounted for the limitations of Cato's oratory. According to the predictable progress of the arts, Cicero eventually perfects what Cato has invented—each in keeping with the circumstances of his own time. Prodded by Atticus's accusation of ironic indirection, Cicero can repeat with a further analogy between painting and rhetoric that Cato's oratory lacked only those rhetorical techniques or colors (*colores*) that had not yet been invented (*quae inventa nondum errant*, 298). Far from using Socratic irony to discredit Cato for failing to fulfill a promise, as Socrates himself did against the sophists mentioned by Atticus, Cicero genuinely admires Cato's style, even if his admiration is infused with an attitude that would later come to be called *historicism* or *historical consciousness*.[31]

In keeping with his criticism of Atticus for mistaking historical awareness for irony, Cicero chastises Ennius for disdaining the older poet Naevius, who, like Myron in the passage quoted above, skillfully deployed all the artistic resources of his day to beautiful effect (*Brutus* 75). Directly addressing the ungrateful Ennius as if he were an interlocutor in the dialogue, Cicero charges him with either failing to repay his debt to his accomplished predecessor or even stealing from him (76). On the other hand, Cicero praises this same Ennius for celebrating the accomplishments of first-generation orator Marcus Cornelius Cethegus, whose *suaviloquia* or sweet eloquence was highly esteemed in his own time—a celebration punctuated by the repetition of the temporizing adverb *tum* (57–59).[32]

But Cicero does not reserve his historicizing attitude for his great Roman predecessors. Like Cato, Cicero tells us, Thucydides too sometimes failed in subsequent generations to attract readers (*Bru-*

---

31. For different readings of Atticus's accusation of irony, see Dugan, *Making a New Man*, 204–12; Hösle, "Cicero's Plato," 167–80; and Christopher van den Berg, "The Invention of Literary History in Cicero's *Brutus*," *Classical Philology* 114 (2019): 573–603, esp. 583–90. For one closer to my own, see Narducci, *Cicerone e l'eloquenza romana*, 138–40.

32. I am grateful to Joseph Farrell for flagging the importance of Cicero's treatment of Ennius in these two passages.

tus 66). And like Cato, Thucydides wrote in a style conditioned by his time (29). To foreground this temporality, Cicero once again resorts to a hypothesis: if Thucydides had lived at a later time, his style, accommodating this difference, would have been more mellow and less harsh (*Ipse enim Thucydides si posterius fuisset, multo maturior fuisset et mitior*, 288). Like Aristotle's lawgiver, in other words, Cicero's stylist in *Brutus*, whether Greek or Roman, must be granted leeway for responding to the resources of his art as he finds them. As these resources change, his style may require the kind of "correction" that necessitates not only hypothetical revivification but the application of equity.

Cicero's insistence in *Brutus* that assessments of style in all the arts must take account of the circumstances of production and allow for some "correction" combines with this hypothesis to set in high relief how much a historicizing attitude shares with an equitable judgment. For Aristotle's lawgiver is unlike his moral agent in the *Nicomachean Ethics* and *Rhetoric*. Whereas the moral agent is defined by making choices, the lawgiver is characterized by being constrained: on the one hand, he must formulate laws that are general to deal with actions that are particular and, on the other, he must formulate these laws knowing full well that unforeseen circumstances in times to come will require the laws' correction through the mechanism of equity. Rather than being allowed to rest in peace, he will need to come back to life on a regular basis to make the necessary adjustments or accommodations. That Cicero fully appreciates the resurrected lawgiver's role in these accommodations is clear from his youthful *De inventione*, where, in laying out the arguments for upholding the intention of the *scriptor* over his *scriptum*, Cicero invokes the lawgiver, who, "if he should rise from the dead, would approve this act, and would have done the same if he had been in a similar situation" (*De inv.* 2.139).[33]

Tethering his stylistic theory to his ethical theory, as we have seen, Aristotle also suggests—if he does not explicitly state—the homology between equity and *decorum* as the "rule" of accommodation to particular circumstances that trumps all other "rules" (or laws). Like equity, a historicizing attitude to style shares its conceptual DNA with *decorum*. More precisely, historicism, as a hermeneutic principle, is

---

33. On the homologies between the historicized reading and the equitable judgment, see Eden, *Hermeneutics and the Rhetorical Tradition*, 17–19 and 66–78.

the counterpart to *decorum* as a rhetorical principle—a relationship that remains tacit in *Brutus* but is openly theorized, as we will see, by Erasmus in his *Ciceronianus*.[34] Whereas the orator must construct his speech in keeping with the times, places, and persons involved, the historian of oratory who takes a historicizing attitude toward these speeches must understand them in this same context. If Cicero downplays the stylistic virtue of *decorum* in *Brutus*, preferring, as we have seen, to emphasize *Latinitas* and *ornatus* in pitting himself against Caesar, he nevertheless features its hermeneutic counterpart as the appropriate attitude of the historian.

Despite the commonalities that invite comparison between the histories of Greek and Roman oratory, Cicero also addresses head-on in *Brutus* the relativism implicit in a historicizing attitude.[35] And he does so in relation to temporality itself. For the very concepts of "old" and "new" or "recent" cannot be understood in fixed or absolute terms but only relative to a particular chronology, whether Roman (the *aetas populi Romani*) or Greek (the *Atheniensium saecula*) (*Brutus* 39). Whereas Pisistratus is a mere youngster (*adulescens*) in terms of the Athenian timeline, he is an elder (*senis*) in regard to the Roman (*Brutus* 39). In the next *saeculum*, Themistocles is similarly "very ancient [*perantiquus*] . . . by our standards, but not so old [*non ita sane vetus*] by the Athenians'" (41). Even the *pervetus* Cato is so only "in our chronological scheme [*ad nostrorum temporum rationem*]" (69). Just as Cicero considers all style subject to temporal constraints, in other words, he considers time-related qualities themselves as inherently relative—in Aristotle's terms, *pros hēmas* rather than *kat'auto to pragma*.

---

34. In "On the Scope and Function of Hermeneutical Reflection," trans. G. B. Hess and R. E. Palmer, in *Philosophical Hermeneutics*, ed. David E. Linge (Berkeley, 1976), Gadamer insists that "the rhetorical and hermeneutical aspects of human linguisticality completely interpenetrate each other" (25). For the homologies between equity and *decorum*, see Wesley Trimpi, "Horace's 'Ut Pictura Poesis': The Argument for Stylistic Decorum," *Traditio* 34 (1978): 29–73, and *Muses of One Mind*, 83–240, and Eden, *Hermeneutics and the Rhetorical Tradition*, 14–18, 26–27, 66–78.

35. In *Caesar's Calendar*, 26–28, Feeney notes that "In the masterpieces of the 50's, Cicero's use of transcultural parallels between Greece and Rome is very different from what we see later in the *Brutus*" (26).

QUINTILIAN AND TACITUS

Roman stylistic theory after Cicero responds directly to *Brutus*. In the *Institutio oratoria*, for instance, Quintilian offers his own mini-catalogues of stylists, sometimes repeating Cicero's characterizations (10.1.115), at other times picking up where Cicero, who refused to consider contemporary orators with the exception of Caesar and Marcellus, left off (12.10.7, 12.10.10–12, cf. 10.1.38). Like Cicero in *Brutus*, Quintilian both contrasts Attic style with Asian and Rhodian style and liberates it from the narrow confines of Calvus and his cohort (12.10.17–19). For Quintilian, as for Cicero, *Attice dicere* is synonymous with *optime* (or *bene*) *dicere* (12.10.26).

Also like Cicero in *Brutus*, Quintilian acknowledges the *temporal* as well as the *personal* and *local* constraints on style. In addition to rehearsing both the frequently invoked anecdote about Isocrates and his pupils Ephorus and Theopompus, whose individual natures required different training (10.1.75, cf. 2.8.11), and the old woman's outing of the foreigner Theophrastus in the marketplace (8.1.2), Quintilian introduces an anecdote of his own about the advice a caring uncle, Julius Florus, gives to his struggling nephew, Julius Secundus, to accept his personal limitations. "Do you really want to speak better than you can?" the uncle asks, to which Quintilian himself replies, "There lies the truth of the whole matter" (10.3.12–15, cf. 10.2.19).[36] Elsewhere (e.g., 10.1.97, 12.10.2), Quintilian questions whether such deficiencies belong to times as well as to persons—a question he answers in the context of the historical development of painting and sculpture, complete with more or less the same who's who of artists featured in *Brutus* (12.10.3–9). It is these very personal and temporal (and local) considerations, Quintilian seems to agree with Aristotle as well as Cicero, that distinguish style or *elocutio*, the third *officium* of the art of rhetoric, from the first two, invention and disposition (12.10.27). Unlike the production of proofs, the production of style re-

---

36. In "The Concept of Nature and Human Nature in Quintilian's Psychology and Theory of Instruction," *Rhetorica* 13 (1995): 125–36, Elaine Fantham explores various dimensions of *natura* in the *Institutio oratoria* without addressing it as a constraint, except to say that Quintilian "has not fully worked out the binary system of *natura* and *voluntas*" (132).

quires not only a history but a historicizing attitude to be adequately understood.

If Quintilian rehearses here and there the historicism of *Brutus*, Tacitus's *Dialogue on Orators* not only deploys its strategies but pushes its boundaries.[37] When Tacitus has the contrarian Aper take up the case for the style of the moderns against that of the ancients (16–23), for instance, he prefaces his defense with the same argument for the inherent relativism of time-related terms that Cicero, as we have seen, makes to friends Atticus and Brutus.[38] For Aper's opponents, the advocates of antique style, claim Cicero as an ancient, when, according to a time frame based on the lifespan of a single human being, Cicero rightly belongs in the camp of the moderns, along with Caesar, Calvus, and Brutus. Using Cicero's relative contemporaneity at the beginning of his argument as evidence to refute the opposition's arbitrary division between the ancients and the moderns, Aper returns to Cicero's modernity at the end of his argument, only this time the standard of measure is not some inevitably relative timeline but

37. On the historical consciousness of this early work of Tacitus, see Gadamer, *Truth and Method*, 288, and Struever, *Language of History in the Renaissance*, 32.

38. For the influence of *Brutus* on the *Dialogus*, see the edition, used throughout for the Latin and cited parenthetically in the text, by Roland Mayer (Cambridge, UK, 2001), 12–13, his notes to 8.3, 9.1, 21.1, 21.5, 24.4, and 18.1: "[Aper's] inspiration will have been the *Brutus* of Cicero, especially in this regard: neither Cicero nor Aper accounts for change of taste and style as a product of altered social and political institutions" (144). See also Alain M. Gowing, *Empire and Memory: The Representation of the Roman Republic in Imperial Culture* (Cambridge, UK, 2005), 109–20; D. S. Levene, "Tacitus' *Dialogus* as Literary History," *Transactions of the American Philological Association* 134 (2004): 157–200, esp. 178; and Étienne Borzsák, "Le 'Dialogue' de Tacite et le 'Brute' de Cicéron," *Bulletin de l'Association Guillaume Budé* 3 (1985): 289–98. In "Histoire de la querelle des anciens et des modernes," in *Oeuvres complètes* (Paris, 1859), 1: 13, H. Rigault cites Horace's Epistle to Augustus (Ep. 2.1) as the source for Aper's position on modernity. On the influence of *Brutus* on this Horatian epistle, see Denis Feeney, "*Una cum scriptore meo*: Poetry, Principate and the Traditions of Literary History in the Epistle to Augustus," in *Traditions and Contexts in the Poetry of Horace*, ed. Tony Woodman and Denis Feeney (Cambridge, UK, 2002), 172–87, esp. 177–81. See also T. J. Luce, "Reading and Response in the *Dialogus*," in *Tacitus and the Tacitean Tradition*, ed. T. J. Luce and A. J. Woodman (Princeton, 1993), 35n77. On the influence of *De oratore* on the *Dialogus*, see Sander M. Goldberg, "Appreciating Aper: The Defence of Modernity in Tacitus' *Dialogus de oratoribus*," *Classical Quarterly* 49 (1998): 224–37, esp. 233–35, and Luce, "Reading and Response in the *Dialogus*," 12–13, 26–28.

Cicero's own assessment of his stylistic credentials. "[Cicero] had the same battle with his contemporaries," Aper claims, "as I have with you. They admired the ancients, he preferred the eloquence of his own day [*suorum temporum*]. And there is nothing in which he outstripped the orators of that period [*eiusdem aetatis*] more decisively than in his judgment" (22.1).[39] According to Aper, in other words, Cicero not only judged the style "of his day" better suited to his duties as an orator but actually considered himself a modern.

Aper also insists that Cicero's style did more than change over time. It improved.[40] The early speeches lack the signature blend of polish and passion that characterizes Cicero's mature oratory (*Dialogus* 22). Through practice and experience (*usuque et experimentis*), Cicero gradually learned which style of speaking would work best (*quod optimum dicendi genus esset*, 22.2). Not that Cicero's mature style was perfect in any absolute sense. For Aper concludes his argument by returning to the stylistic imperfections of the master, and especially to those imitated by indiscriminate admirers (23). Earlier in his argument, Aper agreed with both Calvus, who criticized Cicero's style as "lax and spineless" (*solutum et enervem*), and Brutus, who found it "feeble and hamstrung" (*fractum atque elumbem*, 18.5). "If you ask me," Aper concurs, "*all* these criticisms were true" (18.6).

Aper takes pains, then, to distinguish Cicero's *personal* develop-

---

39. *Dialogue on Orators*, trans. Michael Winterbottom, in *Ancient Literary Criticism*, ed. D. A. Russell and M. Winterbottom (Oxford, 1972), 432–59, here and hereafter cited parenthetically in the text. And see Luce, "Reading and Response in the *Dialogus*," 34–35. Some important recent readers of Tacitus's dialogue dismiss Aper's argument out of hand. In *The Art of Rhetoric in the Roman World* (Princeton, 1972), 520, for instance, George Kennedy calls it "trivial," and in "The Significance of Tacitus' *Dialogus de oratoribus*," *Harvard Studies in Classical Philology* 90 (1986): 237–38, Timothy Barnes observes that "it is silly and is meant to look silly." In Aper's defense, see C. D. N. Costa, "The *Dialogus*," in *Tacitus*, ed. T. A. Dorey (London, 1969), 19–34, esp. 31; Goldberg, "Appreciating Aper"; Donald Martin, *Tacitus* (London, 1981), 62–66; and Gordon Williams, *Change and Decline: Roman Literature in the Early Empire* (Berkeley, 1978), 26–51, esp. 49, where he grants Aper "a deep sense of historical relativity."

40. In this regard, Cicero differs from Calvus, who had the will but not the way—neither the *ingenium* nor the *vires*—to improve his style (21.2). On the relation between Cicero and Calvus, see G. L. Hendrickson, "Cicero's Correspondence with Brutus and Calvus on Oratorical Style," *American Journal of Philology* 47 (1926): 234–58.

ment as an orator from the *historical* development of Roman oratory.[41] Unlike Messalla, as we will see momentarily, Aper rejects the evolutionary model of the arts, including the discursive arts, featured in *Brutus*. Although the orator Gaius Gracchus is fuller and richer than the elder Cato, according to Aper, and Crassus is more refined and decorative than Gracchus, Cicero is both more witty and sublime than these and less gentle and sweet than Corvinus (18). For Aper, in other words, Cicero does not represent, as he does for the advocates of antiquity, the full development of Roman oratory. "I'm not looking for the most eloquent among them," Aper insists:

> I am for the moment content with proving that eloquence has no single face [*unum eloquentiae vultum*]. In those you call "ancients," too, more than one type can be discerned, and a thing isn't automatically worse because it's different [*diversum*]. (18.3)[42]

Like *De oratore* and *Brutus*, then, Tacitus's *Dialogue* focuses on difference. And yet all three dialogues take different stands on this key issue. Whereas the difference addressed in *De oratore*, as we have seen, is primarily the *personal* difference among contemporaries due to the diversity of *ingenia* or *naturae*, the difference featured in *Brutus* is rather the *historical* distinctions among *aetates* or *tempora*. But Cicero's refusal to extend his history to living orators besides Caesar, Marcellus, and himself shields him from confronting—let alone charting—Roman oratory's inevitable decline.[43] Even his brief corre-

41. For a reading of the *Dialogus* that foregrounds the *personal* element, see Antonia Syson, "Born to Speak: Ingenium and Natura in Tacitus' *Dialogue on Orators*," *Arethusa* 42 (2009): 45–75, esp. 61–62.

42. The identification of style with the face, both *vultus* and *facies* in Latin, is an important part of the history of style. See Kathy Eden, "Facebook *avant la lettre*: Communicating Renaissance-Style in Montaigne's *Essais*," in *Montaigne in Transit: Essays in Honour of Ian Maclean*, ed. Neil Kenny, Richard Scholar, Wes Williams (Cambridge, UK, 2016), 61–76.

43. On Cicero's decision to stick to the dead, see Douglas, *M. Tulli Ciceronis Brutus*, xi, and Dugan, *Making a New Man*: "By so yielding to the forces of history, Cicero also avoids a pitfall implied in his periodic notion of the development of oratorical history, a model which necessitates Cicero's own obsolescence. Cicero's teleological model for oratory's development does not account for how oratory, apart from extraneous political forces, might decline, and thus it leaves Cicero at the apex of that tradition. The end of oratorical history, in its own gloomy way,

sponding history of Athenian oratory shies away from identifying the *suavitas* of Demetrius of Phaleron (*Brutus* 38), after Demosthenes' perfection (*Brutus* 35), with inevitable devolution.

At the outset of the *Dialogue*, in contrast, Tacitus announces that he *will* address the very question of decline. For he introduces the dialogue as an effort to answer Justus Fabius's complaint that "while earlier periods [*priora saecula*] were brightened by the luster and talent of so many outstanding orators, our own times [*nostra aetas*] should find themselves barren, bereft of distinction in eloquence—scarcely even retaining the name 'orator'" (1.1). Indicative of this barrenness, that is, the term *orator* no longer applies to contemporary speakers— the speakers of *haec tempora*, who are called rather lawyers, advocates, or attorneys (1.1). The question of decline, in other words, not only presupposes but privileges the circumstance of time, here featured in a cluster of terms that recalls the preoccupations of *Brutus*: *tempus*, *aetas*, and *saeculum*.[44] And if the conversation begins with a heightened awareness of temporality, it closes with this same awareness, as Tacitus puts in the mouth of Aper's first opponent, Maternus, defender of poetry over and against oratory, a version of the historicizing hypothesis of a Thucydides *redivivus* that served Cicero's turn in his own history of style.[45] "Believe me, my excellent friends, who are as eloquent as our day requires," Maternus proclaims,

> if you had been born in earlier ages [*prioribus saeculis*] and those men we so much admire had been born in our times, some god having suddenly switched round your lives and periods [*tempora*], you would not have missed the highest distinction in eloquence— and they would not have failed to observe moderation. (41.5)

Like men in general, Maternus reminds us, orators are as the times are. No other circumstance conditions or constrains them more.

Aper's second opponent, Messalla, similarly acknowledges the decisive factor of time, even if his acknowledgment lacks the poet

---

assures Cicero's position as the ultimate *telos* of that narrative" (250). For Cicero on oratory's inevitable decline, see *Tusc. Disp.* 2.2.5.

44. For Tacitus's reluctance to answer the question of decline in his own voice, see Goldberg, "Appreciating Aper," 225.

45. On the interlocutors of Tacitus's dialogue, see Mayer's edition, 44–47.

Maternus's sense of drama. Rehearsing the Ciceronian legacy of a fundamentally Aristotelian rhetoric, Messalla argues that "he only is a true orator [*is est orator*] who can speak on any question brilliantly and splendidly and persuasively [*pulchre et ornate et ad persuadendum apte dicere*], with equal regard for the importance of the subject, the circumstances of the time, and the pleasure of the audience" (30.5). Whereas Aristotle, as we have seen, limits the virtues of style to only two and rounds out the triad including *logos* (the subject) and *pathos* (the audience) with the *ēthos* of the speaker, Messalla settles on three stylistic excellences (*pulchre*, *ornate*, and *apte dicere*) and tellingly drops *ēthos* for the more compelling factor of time: *utilitas temporum*. Like Aper in "leaving out of account supreme and perfect oratory" (26.1), Messalla nevertheless prefers the *aetas* or age of orators that includes Gaius Gracchus and Crassus, who belong to the *gradus* or stage of development preceding Cicero, over those who follow Cicero, such as Maecenas and Gallio (26.1). While Cicero's predecessors exhibit the inevitable flaws of an *eloquentia* "still growing and adolescent" (25.7), Messalla concedes in evolutionary terms, Cicero's successors represent a Roman oratory "broken and enfeebled" (*fracta et diminuta*)—in decline (26.8; cf. 25.3).

Messalla and Aper agree, then, on style as a historical concept—one that needs to be understood according to a *ratio temporum*. But they part ways on the kind of *historicism* that orients their understanding. Aper assumes a more thoroughgoing—arguably a more radical—historicist perspective grounded in turn in the assumption that as circumstances continue to change over time, style will change to accommodate them: "as times change [*cum condicione temporum*] and audiences vary," Aper maintains, "the style and appearance of oratory [*formam quoque ac speciem orationis*] must change too" (*Dialogus* 19.2).[46] While Messalla, like other admirers of the ancients (19.1), associates Cassius Severus with the *aetas* of oratory's decline, Aper, rejecting this standard of better and worse, applauds the same orator for his unflinching commitment to *decorum* (19.1–2). For Aper, difference—even differing from Cicero—does not constitute decline;

---

46. On the unchanging *forma et species* of Cicero's final, Platonizing work on style, so antithetical to Aper's position, see *Orator* 2, 9, 10, 43, 101; Fantham, "On the Use of *Genus*-Terminology," 452–53; and Burrow, *Imitating Authors*, 185–86, 214–18, and 250–53.

every age differs from every other. If *Brutus* subordinates *De oratore*'s *personal* difference to *historical* difference, Tacitus's *Dialogue* insists that there are, in turn, different understandings of *historical* difference.

CICERONIAN CONTROVERSIES

The sharp focus on stylistic difference offered by these newly recovered ancient texts, along with their differing versions of difference, shapes Renaissance discussions of style, and especially those engaged in the so-called Ciceronian controversy, which centered on two pressing questions: whose style to imitate and how.[47] While all participants in this ongoing debate rely more or less on the same ancient authorities to support their positions, including Aristotle, Cicero, Quintilian, and Tacitus, they refract these authors through very different lenses, depending, for instance, on whether they hold that imitation is absolutely essential to good writing and, if it is, whether imitators should follow one best model or multiple models. Whereas Angelo Poliziano in a brief letter to Paolo Cortesi famously asserts his writerly intention in the 1480s to express himself rather than apishly imitate Cicero or anyone else, Cortesi responds with a comparable respect for difference that, echoing *De oratore* (3.6.22, quoted above), nevertheless insists on a single art of eloquence with a single form or image (*una forma, una imago*) of stylistic excellence embodied in Cicero.[48] Many of the most accomplished stylists in antiquity, Cortesi argues, have imitated this single best model without forfeiting their diversity (2.4). Aligning themselves early in the next century with opposing sides of this disagreement, Gianfrancesco Pico and Pietro Bembo deepen the

47. On these two questions, see McLaughlin, *Literary Imitation in the Italian Renaissance*, and Burrow, *Imitating Authors*. On the Ciceronian controversy, see Remigio Sabbadini, *Storia del Ciceronianismo e di altre questioni letterarie nell' età della Renascenza* (Turin, 1885), and John Monfasani, "The Ciceronian Controversy," in *The Cambridge History of Literary Criticism*, vol. 3: *The Renaissance*, ed. G. P. Norton (Cambridge, UK, 1999), 395–401.

48. *Ciceronian Controversies*, ed. JoAnn DellaNeva, trans. Brian Duvick (Cambridge, MA, 2007), 2.2. All references to the letters of Poliziano, Cortesi, Pico, and Bembo are to this edition and will be cited in the text. For the refutative agenda of Erasmus's dialogue and Cortesi's lack of skill on this score, see chap. 2 above, p. 91.

divide. They do so, moreover, by scoring many of the same points made in Cicero's mature treatises on style—without assuming, as we will see, the historicizing attitude of *Brutus*.[49]

In the first of two letters to Bembo (1512), Pico makes his case for *personal* difference in matters of style by deploying a number of the strategies crucial to the stylistic theory of both the late Cicero and his Roman protégés Quintilian and Tacitus. From these protégés in particular, Pico learns that Cicero's contemporaries considered his style deficient on several counts (3.10)—although Pico himself considers not only Cicero's orations but even his *De oratore* and *De claris oratoribus* (or *Brutus*) flooded with eloquence (3.23). In keeping with his advocacy of what he calls one's own *genius* and *propensio naturae* (3.8), moreover, Pico makes a case against imitating a single model or any flesh-and-blood model, for that matter. Instead, he echoes Cicero's *Orator* in calling for a *forma et species*, an *idea* of eloquence (3.10) as a pattern to follow.[50] In mounting his argument in favor of this *idea*, on the other hand, Pico frequently turns to *Brutus*, if not to its historicizing agenda.

It is in this late Ciceronian dialogue (*Brutus* 51), for instance, that Pico finds three locations—Athens, Asia, and Rhodes—as the places of origin of three different styles. And like Cicero, Pico extends the three stylistic types to include a fourth. Unlike Cicero, however, Pico enlists local difference in the cause of personal (rather than historical) difference. "Because of his own natural bent [*ingenio*]," Pico contends, "one man will love Laconic brevity, another will be eager for

49. On the exchange between Pico and Bembo, see McLaughlin, *Literary Imitation in the Italian Renaissance*, 249–74, and Burrow, *Imitating Authors*, 207–11. For the difficulties presented by this historicizing attitude to Erasmus's contemporaries, see G. W. Pigman III, "Imitation and the Renaissance Sense of the Past: The Reception of Erasmus' *Ciceronianus*," *Journal of Medieval and Renaissance Studies* 9 (1979): 155–77.

50. On the importance of differing concepts of *forma* to Pico and Bembo, see Burrow, *Imitating Authors*: "To put the opposition in crude terms, Pico appears to have regarded 'forma' as a principle of structuration that is intrinsically inimitable, so each orator should look to his own nature, read widely and develop his own 'idea' (or quasi-Platonic 'form') of writing which would suit his own genius, and from which he might produce works which manifested that 'form'. For Bembo, on the other hand, the 'form' of a piece of writing is intrinsic to it and nothing can be added to it or taken away. Hence the only viable imitation is of a single author, whose individual 'forma' would be the object of *imitatio*" (210–11).

Asiatic richness. This man will burn for that golden Attic mean, that one will prefer Rhodian moderation" (3.26). Pico similarly appropriates the "garment of style" metaphor, so ready, as we have seen with Erasmus, to serve a historicizing aim, for the single-minded focus of his letter, warning that the footprints of the ancients will be either too big or too small for a modern stylist—a warning that culminates in a sartorial version of a frequently repeated adage: "But the ancients had as many shoes as they had feet" (3.19).[51] Even his reference to the differences between Aristotle and Cicero on the question of prose rhythm—differences comparable to habits of dress—gives way to the conclusion that some moderns willingly don "garments woven from Cicero's broad warp and Pliny's tight woof," while others "pilfer [*surripiant*] a robe to suit themselves" (3.26). Like fashion differences, in other words, differences in literary style point resolutely for Pico to personal differences between stylists. To those who apishly imitate Cicero by pilfering a rare word or two that he may or may not have actually used, Pico issues the further warning that "if Cicero were revived from the dead he would deny that they had taken [*surripiant*] those words from him" (3.12).[52] While Cicero's Thucydides *redivivus* in *Brutus*, as noted earlier, reinforces the temporality inherent in style, Pico's Cicero *redivivus* advertises the dangers of "pilfering" from any one ancient writer whose corpus is inevitably both corrupt and incomplete.

Bembo's reply to Pico opens with a polite disclaimer that he has not written a *refellatio* of his learned friend's position offered so graciously in the spirit of *sermo*—refutation's opposite.[53] And yet, Bembo writes, he must reject Pico's claim, rooted in the Platonically oriented *Orator*, that each skilled stylist patterns his compositions after an *idea*

51. There are, in fact, two adages combined here: one is *quot homines, tot sententiae* (I.iii.7, CWE 31: 240–41; ASD II-1, 319–20), which appears in various versions at *De oratore* 3.34, *Orator* 53, and *Institutio oratoria* 12.10.10; the other belongs to a cluster concerning the different sizes and shapes of feet, each requiring accordingly its own shoe, including II.v.46, II.ix.18, and IV.iv.56. For Erasmus's disdain for the cobbler who stiches "a shoe of the same shape for every foot," see above, p. 122.

52. For Leonardo Bruni's use of a similar formula regarding Plato (Ep. 1.1), see DellaNeva, *Ciceronian Controversies*, 243n43.

53. On the traditional opposition between the adversarial nature of refutation and the amicability of conversation, see chap. 2 above, pp. 68–71.

of eloquence firmly fixed in his own mind. On the contrary, Bembo argues on the basis of both personal experience and the authority of another Ciceronian treatise, *Ad Herennium*, successful imitation requires, logically as well as practically, devotion to a single best model.[54] Whereas Pico features throughout his letter the many *personal* differences among stylists that would undermine such a practice, Bembo aligns himself with those promising imitators who "through care and diligence" can "inflect our style in whatever direction we wish [*volumus*]" (4.7). And who would not wish to write like Cicero, despite those few flaws noted by his contemporaries and recorded in the newly recovered works of Quintilian and Tacitus? Like Aristotle's moral agent in the *Nicomachean Ethics* and his speaker in the *Rhetoric*, but unlike the orators showcased in *Brutus*, Bembo's stylist is noteworthy for his freedom to make choices.

Strikingly indifferent to the constraints imposed on style by time and place as well as natural bent, all featured in *Brutus*, Bembo rehearses one of its key passages on the arts of painting and sculpture, *Brutus* 70, quoted above. More precisely, Bembo adapts its list of artists to the agenda he shares with *Ad Herennium*.[55] "It is as if an artist who has learned to paint in the style of Apelles," Bembo explains without identifying the two sources he combines,

> also was made to consult the paintings of Polygnotus and Timanthes by whom Apelles was taught; or a sculptor who imitated Lysippus's excellent and famous art of statuary also had to contemplate the stiff figures of Calamis or even stiffer ones of Canachus. (4.4)

54. On the authenticity of the pseudo-Ciceronian *Ad Herennium*, first challenged by Lorenzo Valla and increasingly rejected as authentic in the course of the sixteenth century, see DellaNeva, *Ciceronian Controversies*, 249n15 and Erasmus, *Ciceronianus*, CWE 28: 363–64, where Bulephorus refers to the treatise as a work "foisted upon Cicero and falsely claiming his parentage." See also CWE 28: 554n146.

55. See *Ad Her.* 4.6.9: "Not thus did Chares learn from Lysippus how to make statues. Lysippus did not show him a head by Myron, arms by Praxiteles, a chest by Polycleitus. Rather with his own eyes would Chares see the master fashioning all the parts; the works of the other sculptors he could if he wished study on his own initiative." On the importance of this passage, see Baxandall, *Giotto and the Orators*, 40–41.

Whereas Cicero provided these artistic genealogies in *Brutus*, as we have seen, to defend the style of Cato, which must be "corrected"— that is, historicized—in order to be judged equitably, Bembo, following the pseudo-Ciceronian text, invokes these Ciceronian genealogies to make an unrelated point: that one should take only the single most accomplished artist as a model to imitate.

When Bembo returns later in the letter to some of these same painters and sculptors, he also returns to *Brutus* and particularly to the conclusion that follows these genealogies in the ancient dialogue, namely, that "nothing has been both discovered and perfected all at once" (*Brutus* 71). Here again, however, it is Cicero's status as the one who perfects, if not the one who invents, that interests Bembo. Regarding Cicero's ambitious agenda to surpass his predecessors, Bembo remarks that "It is absurd to believe that we can invent a better way than Cicero's. He did not invent it himself, to be sure, but he did render richer and more brilliant what others had discovered" (4.28). Endorsing the doctrinaire position of *Ad Herennium* rather than the historicizing reflections of *Brutus*, Bembo nevertheless leverages his reading of the Ciceronian dialogue to bolster his case against Pico.

Despite Bembo's insistence that he has no intention of refuting a friend, Pico's reply (1513) registers the adversarial dimension of Bembo's letter, which, Pico notes, looks to disclose his contradictions and inconsistencies (5.2). Accordingly, no small part of Pico's agenda in his second letter, he tells Bembo, is "to refute [*refutandis*] your critique of my arguments about imitating many writers and the Idea that belongs to the soul" (5.17). To reaffirm the latter point regarding the idea of eloquence, Pico returns to the *Orator*, not only quoting it directly but rehearsing at length its main claims (*Orator* 2, 7, 8). "For that which is fashioned [*fingitur*] after the likeness [*exemplar*] of some image [*imago*]," Pico paraphrases Cicero, "if no external image exists, must necessarily be made after the very image of that which he bears in his mind, whoever the fashioner [*fictor*] might be" (5.6).[56] Pico's re-affirmation of *personal* difference, on the other hand, quotes Cicero's advice to his son Marcus in *De officiis* about the uniqueness of each individual (*De officiis* 1.110, quoted above). Here again, Pico bolsters quotation with paraphrase: "each individual bears his own distinc-

---

56. For the role of fiction in the formation of an ideal and its relation to the *qualitative* status, see chap. 1 above, p. 54.

tive character which he does not share with others" (*uniusquisque illo-rum proprium insigne gerat, quod non sit ei commune cum ceteris*, 5.12). Cicero's ethical agent as well as his stylist, Pico repeats, answers to a natural bent or *natura* that is entirely his own.

Staunchly opposed to Bembo, then, in his rejection of a single best model to imitate, Pico is like Bembo not only in leveraging his own reading of *Brutus* to support his position but in doing so without taking any notice of its historicizing attitude to style. Reprising the metaphor of the "garment of style" introduced in *Brutus* and invoked in his own earlier letter, Pico agrees to grant, for argument's sake, that Bembo could walk in Cicero's shoes. But what about the rest of the outfit? Given an inevitably incomplete and inaccurate understanding of antiquity, even the most devoted imitator runs the risk of "taking a military coat for a toga, a traveling cloak for a long coat . . . a tunic for a mantle" (5.22). Still echoing *Brutus*, Pico further grants that the finest painters brought back to life to create in turn a lifelike Cicero in his customary dress still could not endow their creative imitations with the soul (*animus*) from which Cicero derived the eloquence that his tongue expressed (5.22). Enlisted to drive home Pico's central point about the idea that animates style, the painterly Cicero *redivivus* is, like his counterpart in Pico's earlier letter, a far cry from Cicero's Thucydides *redivivus* in *Brutus*, who returns from the dead to set in high relief how style is necessarily conditioned by time and place. Pico's revivified Ciceros, in contrast, come back to life to underscore the impossibility of achieving stylistic excellence through slavish imitation.

CASTIGLIONE'S *COURTIER*

In Castiglione's *Book of the Courtier*, it is Count Ludovico da Canossa and Federico Fregoso who face off over the pros and cons of imitation, and they do so as part of the so-called *questione della lingua*, a lively debate of Castiglione's generation concerning the Italian vernacular—a debate in which the historical Bembo, unlike his fictional counterpart, is a high-profile participant.[57] Castiglione signals

57. On this debate and Castiglione's part in it, see Uberto Motta, "La 'questione della lingua' nel primo libro del *Cortegiano*: dalla seconda alla terza redazione," *Aevum* 72 (1998): 693–732; Giancarlo Mazzacurati, "Baldassar Castiglione

the centrality of this debate to his own artistic agenda in the letter he writes to Don Michel de Silva prefacing the 1528 *editio princeps* of his best-seller, where he cuts short his defense of his stylistic practices "bycause in thys point there is sufficyent talke in the first booke" (Hoby 13, Maier 75).[58] There, Federico Fregoso takes Bembo's position in championing a single best model. "Me seemeth then, who so will be out of doubt and wel assured," Federico tells Ludovico and the others, "it is requisite for him to determine with himselfe to follow one [*imitar uno*], that by all mens accorde is judged good, and to take him for a guide alwaies" (1.37, Hoby 52, Maier 133–34). In poetry, Federico clarifies, that guide is Petrarch; in prose it is Boccaccio.

In stark opposition to Federico, Ludovico entertains the extreme position attributed to Poliziano and Pico by their opponents that imitation is not a necessary condition of stylistic excellence, citing Homer as well as Petrarch and Boccaccio as writers who followed only "their own natural inclination and judgment" (*l'ingegno ed il lor proprio giudicio naturale*, 1.37, Hoby 61, Maier 147). Like Pico, then, Ludovico puts a premium on "natural bent"—a position Ludovico reinforces with the authority of Cicero's Antonius in *De oratore*, who not only questions the necessity of imitating but, according to Ludovico, "affirmeth also that maisters should consider the nature of their scholers, and taking it for their guide, direct and prompt them in the way that their wit and naturall inclination moveth them unto" (1.37, Hoby 62, Maier 149). Whereas Cicero's Crassus, as we have seen, identifies this pedagogical practice with Isocrates (3.36, see above), Ludovico appropriates it for Crassus's principal rival in the discussions that take place in his gardens in Tusculum.

---

e la teoria cortegiana: ideologia di classe e dottrina critica," *Modern Language Notes* 83 (1968): 16–66; and McLaughlin, *Literary Imitation in the Italian Renaissance*, 268–74. In "The Enduring Word: Language, Time, and History in *Il Libro del Cortegiano*," in *Castiglione*, ed. Hanning and Rosand, 69–90, Wayne Rebhorn notes that "Castiglione rigs the debate against poor Federico by having the only two actual Tuscans in the group (i.e., Giuliano de' Medici and Bernardo Bibbiena) speak against him" (69).

58. On the various redactions of the *Cortegiano* and the addition of the prefatory letter, see Ghino Ghinassi, "Fasi dell' elaborazione del *Cortegiano*," *Studi di filologia italiana* 25 (1967): 155–96. In *Imitating Authors*, 188, Burrow reminds us that the "sufficyent talke" of the final version, which Emilia Pia cuts short, was in the first redaction a brief reference to the need to accommodate the times.

Ludovico also looks to *De oratore* for the related arguments in favor of *personal* difference. Whereas Crassus showcases this difference in the context of the pantheon of great painters and sculptors (3.26), Ludovico makes the same point with the help of the current art scene in Italy:

> Behold in painting Lenard Vincio, Mantegna, Raphael, Michelãgelo, George of Castelfranco: they are all most excellent doers, yet are they in working unlike, but in any of them a man would not judge that there wanted ought in his kinde of trade: for everie one is knowne to bee of most perfection after his manner. (1.37, Hoby 62; Maier 148)[59]

When he turns his attention to this same variety of practitioners in oratory, on the other hand, Ludovico reverts to his Ciceronian model, citing Isocrates, Lysias, Aeschines, Laelius, Galba, Sulpicius, Cotta, Antonius, and Crassus (1.37, Hoby 62, Maier 148)—a list that leads Ludovico to a version of the same adage that struck Cicero's Crassus and Pico on similar occasions: "so many Orators, so manie kindes of speach" (1.37, Hoby 62, Maier 149).[60] Giving nature (*natura, ingegno*) its due and taking account of the multitude of accomplished artists, both verbal and visual, Ludovico argues against Federico's proposition "that everye man should bee compelled to follow onely Petrarca and Boccaccio" (1.37, Hoby 63, Maier 149). Indeed, the best practices of the courtier in regard to speaking and writing should conform to his apian approach to his activities in stealing "from eche one, that parcell that shall be most worthie prayse" (1.26, Hoby 45, Maier 123).[61]

---

59. On the influence of this passage on the artistic theory of subsequent centuries, see Sauerländer, "From Stilus to Style," 257–58. On the humanists' reliance on painting to theorize style in the verbal arts, see Baxandall, *Giotto and the Orators*, 51–66. On Castiglione's increasing investment in the visual arts during the long period of the dialogue's composition, see Olga Zorzi Pugliese, "La scrittura dell'arte nel *Libro del Cortegiano*," *Letteratura & Arte* 3 (2005): 23–33.

60. For Cicero's discussion of these orators, see G. V. Sumner, *The Orators in Cicero's "Brutus": Prosopography and Chronology* (Toronto, 1973). For the adage, see above, p. 152.

61. On the famous similitude of the bee, see Burrow, *Imitating Authors*, 85, 108–10, 145–46, 186–87, and the introduction, above. See also Erasmus, *Ciceronianus*, CWE 28: 402; ASD I-2, 652 ll. 13–21.

But Ludovico's case against Federico looks to *Brutus* as well as *De oratore*, especially when the difference at stake is *temporal* rather than *personal*.[62] For orators "have always had such a diversitie among them, as (in a manner) every age [*ogni età*] hath brought forth and set by one sorte of Orators peculiar for that time [*peculiar di quel tempo*]," rendering them different from their predecessors as well as from each other (1.37, Hoby 62, Maier 148). No small part of this diversity is occasioned by the inevitable changes in language over time—changes that lead Ludovico to speculate that such prehistoric worthies as Evander and Turnus "spake otherwise" than did the last kings of Rome and the first consuls (1.32, Hoby 55, Maier 137). Like theorists of style since Aristotle, then, Ludovico appreciates the historical dimension of all languages, including not only Latin but Greek, whose evolution he outlines in brief (1.35, Hoby 58, Maier 142–43). And what is true for these ancient tongues is also true of the vernaculars, whose words, more or less attached to their Latin roots, come into and fall out of use.[63]

On the evidence of *Brutus*, moreover, Ludovico argues that the ancients themselves "forsooke many wordes that had beene used among their predecessors" (1.32, Hoby 55, Maier 138), with Antonius, Crassus, Hortensius, and even Cicero rejecting on occasion the language they found in Cato. The failure of Sergius Galba—whom Hoby mistranslates as Gibda (Hoby 55)—to do the same, Ludovico claims on Cicero's authority (*Brutus* 82), leaves his orations with an odor of antiquity, while Ennius, at the other extreme, "set litle by his pre-

---

62. In "Assumed Simplicity and the Critique of Nobility: Or, How Castiglione Read Cicero," *Renaissance Quarterly* 54 (2001): 460–86, Jennifer Richards laments that "Castiglione's claim to have followed Cicero's *De oratore* and *Orator* in the writing of *Il libro del cortegiano* is well known, but not always taken seriously" (460). See also her *Rhetoric and Courtliness*, which makes the case as well for the crucial role of Cicero's *De officiis*. As this chapter aims to show, Castiglione's reliance on *Brutus* is similarly overlooked. See, in addition, Kathy Eden, "Cicero *Redivivus* and the Historicizing of Renaissance Style," in *Inventing a Path: Studies in Medieval Rhetoric in Honour of Mary Carruthers*, ed. Laura Iseppi De Filippis, *Nottingham Medieval Studies* 56 (2012): 143–69. For Castiglione's personal collection of ancient texts, including the works of Cicero, see Guido Rebecchini, "The Book Collection and Other Possessions of Baldassarre Castiglione," *Journal of the Warburg and Courtauld Institutes* 61 (1998): 17–52. On the notable differences between *De oratore* and the *Cortegiano*, see Daniel Javitch, *Poetry and Courtliness*.

63. On the expansion over time of Ludovico's case regarding the historicity of language, see Motta, "La 'questione della lingua,'" 713–25.

decessors" (Hoby 55; cf. *Brutus* 76), including, as we have seen, the poet Naevius. Taking his cue from Cicero's history of style, in other words, Ludovico refutes Federico's position on the grounds of its inherent contradictions, which he puts paradoxically as "if wee will follow them of old time, we shall not follow them" (1.32, Hoby 55, Maier 138). For these ancients most certainly did not slavishly imitate a single model or even multiple models without weighing the effectiveness of their imitation.

With *Brutus* in mind, Castiglione also has Ludovico agree with the speculation of Giuliano de' Medici, Il Magnifico, who echoes Cicero's defense of the style of Cato when he suggests that Petrarch and Boccaccio, "if they were alive now," would write differently than they did then (1.31, Hoby 53, Maier 135). "I believe therefore (as the Lord Magnifico hath saide)," Ludovico repeats, "that were Petrarca and Boccaccio at this present in life, they woulde not use many words that we see in their writings" (1.36, Hoby 60, Maier 145). Unlike Pico in his correspondence with the historical Bembo, then, Ludovico revivifies the dead to press a historicizing agenda. While Cicero's invocation of a Thucydides *redivivus* in *Brutus*, as we have seen, serves to excuse both the Greek historian and the Roman orator Cato for elements of their style that alienated later readers, Castiglione's appropriation of this Ciceronian strategy defends those, like himself, who reject a slavish imitation of a single author that includes the use of outdated language.[64] In his prefatory letter to de Silva, he states forthrightly that he avoids "in my writing to use wordes of Boccaccio which are used no more in Tuscane" (Hoby 13, Maier 75). In line with Pico and his own Ludovico, moreover, Castiglione faults Boccaccio for giving too little latitude to his own "witt" and "natural inclination" (Hoby 11, Maier 72).

Ludovico's attention to the conditioning factor of time in matters of style is complemented by a corresponding attention to place. Here again, his principal source is *Brutus*, where, as we have seen, Cicero illustrates the ineradicability of regional differences in not only word choice but pronunciation and intonation with the anecdote about the

---

64. Rebhorn refers his readers to the many metaphors of resurrection in the *Cortegiano* without mentioning the strategy featured here ("Enduring Word," 85–86). Rebhorn also considers Castiglione's complex relation to history without taking up the issue of historicism.

outing of the proud foreigner Theophrastus. Ludovico lightly touches on this anecdote when he commends those who stick to their own "natural speech" rather than affecting the privileged dialect, whether Attic or Tuscan, contrasting them with "such as would appeare over mere Athenians" and were blamed for it (1.35, Hoby 58, Maier 143). In his prefatory letter to de Silva, Castiglione spells out the reasons for this blame, insisting that he "wil not do as Theophrastus did, which for speaking tomuch the mere Athenian tongue, was of a simple olde woman knowen not to be of Athens" (Hoby 13, Maier 75). Steering clear of speaking "tomuch Tuscan" (Hoby 13, Maier 75), Castiglione claims pride in being a Lombard speaking Lombard.

ERASMUS'S *CICERONIANUS*

Both a historicizing attitude toward style and the practice of imitating multiple models, strikingly on display in Castiglione's *Book of the Courtier*, shape Erasmus's *Ciceronianus*, also first published in 1528.[65] Whereas Castiglione takes his most audible cues from Cicero and Boccaccio, however, Erasmus looks to Cicero and, as we have seen in some detail in chapter 2, Plato. And while the Ciceronian dialogue foremost in Castiglione's mind is arguably *De oratore*, it is *Brutus* that presides over the pages of the *Ciceronianus*.[66] Bulephorus openly ad-

65. In "La 'questione della lingua,'" n. 87, Motta notes that both works argue against a strict imitation that fails to imitate but insists that Castiglione was unaware of Erasmus's satire. In "Castiglione and Erasmus: Towards a Reconciliation?" *Journal of the Warburg and Courtauld Institutes* 61 (1998): 258–60, Guido Rebecchini concludes that "the evidence brought to light by Castiglione's inventories shows that Erasmus was the best represented contemporary in his library" (260). On the other hand, Castiglione may be among the four silly Italians whom Bulephorus derides (CWE 28: 406, 572n488) and who disparaged Erasmus's style as insufficiently Ciceronian (Ep. 1791, *Opus epistolarum*, ed. Allen, 6: 471–75, CWE 12: 479–81). On Erasmus's reference to Castiglione, see Chomarat, *Grammaire et rhétorique*, 2: 816.

66. For the acknowledgment by Erasmus's contemporaries that *Brutus* is his model, see Izora Scott, *Controversies over the Imitation of Cicero* (New York, 1910; rpt. Davis, CA, 1991), 40, who quotes Vives to Erasmus (Ep. 990), regarding the catalogue of Ciceronians, "It is not astonishing that you forgot [to include Vives in the list], busied as you were in gathering so many names of every rank and class in fact in running through that there came into my mind what Atticus said of

vertises this connection when he invokes the *perlongus catalogus oratorum* (CWE 28: 408; ASD I-2, 657 ll. 2–3) that Cicero lays out for friends Atticus and Brutus before launching into his own lengthy *catalogus tullianorum* (CWE 28: 429; ASD I-2, 690 ll. 8–9) that stretches from Seneca to Sadoleto—without any of the stylists mentioned meeting Nosoponus's high standards. None, that is, except the hapless Longueil, whose early death Bulephorus compares to the untimely end of Calvus, tethering an extreme Attic purity rejected in *Brutus* to its Ciceronian counterpart (CWE 28: 345, ASD I-2, 608 ll. 16–19).[67]

Bulephorus also begins the conversation, as we have seen in the introduction, by complimenting Nosoponus's eloquence in terms that *Brutus* records were reserved for Pericles (*Brutus* 59), on whose lips Persuasion herself sat enthroned (CWE 28: 344; ASD I-2, 607 ll. 28–29). And Nosoponus himself mines *Brutus* for compliments, according the singular praise Cicero showered on Quintus Scaevola and Lucius Crassus (cf. *Brutus* 145)—one the best speaker among jurists, the other the best jurist among speakers—to Andrea Alciati, one of the many contenders for the title of Ciceronian in Bulephorus's catalogue (CWE 28: 419; ASD I-2, 669 ll. 11–14).[68] Like Nosoponus, moreover, Bulephorus adapts the insights and attitudes of *Brutus* as needed. For instance, Cicero comments, as part of his case for the importance of writing in oratorical training, that Laelius's written speeches more accurately preserved his style of speaking than Galba's did Galba's because Laelius was a proficient writer (*Brutus* 93–94). Bulephorus repurposes this comment to underscore his objections, voiced, as we have seen, by Pico and Castiglione, to slavishly following a single model, even one as worthy of imitation as Cicero. "Cicero wrote that the mind of Laelius breathed in Laelius' written word," Bulephorus

---

Cicero's making a review of orators." See also CWE 28: 332. In "Imitation and the Renaissance Sense of the Past," Pigman notes both Vives's (and Melanchthon's) understanding of Erasmus's "historical decorum," which constitutes the major contribution of the dialogue (161, 167–68), and the lack of such understanding in most other early modern readers, for whom the catalogue was the point.

67. On Christophe de Longueil, see CWE 28: 324–30 and Peter G. Bietenholz, *Contemporaries of Erasmus: A Biographical Register of the Renaissance and Reformation*, 3 vols. (Toronto, 1985–87), 2: 342–45. For Longueil on Erasmus's style, see Erasmus's response, Ep. 935, CWE 6: 286–88; *Opus epistolarum*, ed. Allen, 3: 520–22.

68. On Alciati, see Bietenholz, *Contemporaries of Erasmus*, 1: 23–26.

recalls (CWE 28: 402; ASD I-2, 652 ll. 1–3), "but it is stupid to try deliberately to write in another man's humour and endeavour to have Marcus Tullius' mind breathing in what you write." The aim of writing, on the contrary, is to express oneself—a writerly agenda that readers of the *Ciceronianus* have recognized as one of its signal contributions to rhetorical theory and literary practice.[69]

The stupidity or *stultitia* (folly) of trying to write with the *stomachus* or "humour" of another speaks directly to the personal difference that Cicero theorizes in his later discussions of style (as well as in *De officiis*). In these late works, as we have seen, *natura* or *ingenium* is as constraining as it is enabling. Bulephorus warns Nosoponus of these constraints (CWE 28: 396–97; ASD I-2, 647 ll. 36–38): "Every one of us has his own inborn characteristics, and these have such force that it is useless for a person fitted by nature for one style of speaking to strive to achieve a different one." Here as elsewhere (cf. CWE 28: 376), Bulephorus compares this struggle to battling against the gods. He also compares it, as did Pico, to treading awkwardly in another's footsteps (CWE 28: 445–46)—awkward, that is, because of the different shapes and sizes of our feet. And he repeats Quintilian's anecdote, without attribution and stripped of proper names, about a student (Julius Secundus) who labors for days without success to craft his introduction, adding that the young man is "rightly twitted for trying to speak better than he could" (CWE 28: 407; ASD I-2, 656 ll. 2–4, see above, p. 144). "It is foolish [*stultum*]," Bulephorus repeats at the end of the *Ciceronianus*, "to pursue something you cannot achieve" (CWE 28: 448; ASD I-2, 709 l. 33).[70]

In *De oratore*, as we have seen, Cicero's Crassus makes his case for

---

69. On Bulephorus's case in the *Ciceronianus* for self-expression, see especially Cave, *Cornucopian Text*, 39–49, and Chomarat, *Grammaire et rhétorique*, 2: 833–41.

70. Like Pico, Erasmus echoes *De officiis* 1.110 regarding personal limitations (CWE 28: 603n448). On the similarities in the positions of Pico and Erasmus, see Sabbadini, *Storia del Ciceronianismo*, 63–64, and Eden, "Cicero *Redivivus*," 164–65. In the prefatory letter to the second edition (CWE 28: 341), Erasmus claims to have discovered the exchange between Bembo and Pico after the publication of the first edition. In this second edition (CWE 28: 379), Erasmus adds a number of lines that suggest to readers that Bembo was the model for Nosoponus (CWE 28: 560n260)—a suggestion complicated by Erasmus's insistence in the prefatory letter that he is largely in agreement with Bembo. In the third edition, Erasmus has the interlocutors draw further attention to this exchange by at once praising

personal difference with the help of the visual and plastic arts, noting the equal if various excellences of sculptors Myron, Polyclitus, and Lysippus alongside painters Zeuxis, Aglaophon, and Apelles. In *Brutus*, as we have also seen, Cicero adapts this analogy between the visual and verbal arts to feature the *temporal* or *historical* difference, rooted in an evolving technology, between a statue by Myron, which lacks a perfected naturalness, and one by Polyclitus, which achieves this perfection. Similarly, the *forma et liniamenta* of a painting by Zeuxis pale when it is compared to one by Apelles. Throughout the *Ciceronianus*, Bulephorus relies on this same analogy to drive home not just the method of following multiple models, echoing the young Cicero of *De inventione*, but, more to the point of this chapter, the decisive impact of temporality (or history) on style; and he does so by coupling the analogy between rhetorical and painterly style with the comparison between rhetorical style and dress, also introduced, as we have seen, in *Brutus*.

In the alignment of these two analogies, Bulephorus, ever the good therapist, follows Nosoponus's lead. For it is the lovesick Ciceronian who responds to his interlocutor's claim, noted earlier, that "language is a sort of dress" (*orationem quasi vestem esse*, CWE 28: 381; ASD I-2, 635 l. 5) with the alternative comparison to painting, allowing Bulephorus to applaud their joint rejection of "clothes which aren't suitable [*accommodum*] for the wearer" and "a painting which isn't appropriate [*aptam*] to the subject" (CWE 28: 382; ASD I-2, 636 ll. 14–15). In the course of this coupling, Bulephorus brings Nosoponus face to face with the key concept of *decorum*, which takes account, as we have seen, of persons, times, and places—but especially times. Elsewhere Bulephorus refers to this principle as "the doctrine of the fitting and appropriate [*decorum et aptum*]" (CWE 28: 373; ASD I-2, 628 l. 38–629 l. 1). Although the interlocutors easily agree, with this doctrine in mind, that the clothing for a child ill befits an old man and dress for a wedding is out of place at a funeral, the core of the controversy between them concerns the continued appropriateness of rhetorical style, and especially Ciceronian style, over time. In an effort to settle the question, Bulephorus turns to Apelles and, more to the point, to an Apelles *redivivus*, who, Nosoponus agrees, could

---

Pico as a great man and disqualifying him as a Ciceronian on the grounds of his own words to Bembo (CWE 28: 416; ASD I-2, 664 ll. 3–4; cf. CWE 28: 581n613).

not paint Germans in the same dress as he once painted Greeks unless he were resigned to paint *non apte* (CWE 28: 381; ASD I-2, 635 l. 25), indecorously—an unthinkable misstep for a supreme artist.

Bulephorus's recourse at this moment in the conversation to the strategy of an Apelles *redivivus* reprises not only his own earlier efforts at revivification but those of *Brutus*. Like Cicero in his dialogue on the history of style, Erasmus appreciates a broad range of motives for bringing the dead back to life, from the elegiac and histrionic to the properly historicist. In *Brutus*, for instance, Cicero amplifies his own nostalgia for Rome's better days with the hypothesis that if his friend and fellow pleader Hortensius, recently deceased, "were alive" (*si viveret*), he too would decry the loss of freedoms in the forum (*Brutus* 6).[71] In a satiric rather than elegiac key, in contrast, Erasmus has Nosoponus make hyperbolically vivid the quiet he requires for cranking out his Ciceronian compositions by bringing Pythagoras back to life (*si viveret*) to listen to the music of the spheres (CWE 28: 350; ASD I-2, 612 l. 18). Hoping to cure Nosoponus of this and other fixations, Bulephorus aligns *his* efforts to revivify Cicero with Cicero's own production of a historicized Thucydides *redivivus* in the *Brutus*.

Fully in keeping with his ancient model, Bulephorus hypothesizes that if Cicero had lived in the age of Cato, Scipio, or Ennius, his speech would have accommodated their *aetas* or *seculum* rather than his own (CWE 28: 381; ASD I-2, 635 ll. 1–2). "You agree, I think," Bulephorus repeats with increasing pressure on Nosoponus, "that Cicero's style would not have met with approval in the time of Cato the Censor [*seculo Catonis censorii*], as it was too elaborate and fancy to suit the standards of that age [*illius aetatis moribus conveniebat*]" (CWE 28: 404; ASD I-2, 653 ll. 36–38). And what holds true for an earlier age pertains as well to a later age, including an *aetas Christiana*. "But I won't have it that a man is speaking in Ciceronian manner [*dicit Ciceroniane*]," Bulephorus insists, "if, being a Christian, he speaks to Christians on

---

71. On the elegiac dimension of *Brutus*, see Alain Gowing, "Memory and Silence in Cicero's *Brutus*," *Eranos* 98 (2000): 39–64, and Steel, "Cicero's *Brutus*," 195–211. Whereas *Brutus* plays down the recent death of Calvus in favor of commemorating Hortensius, the *Ciceronianus* similarly minimizes the death of Longueil but remembers in its prefatory letter to the second edition (1529) the passing of Jakob Wimpfeling (CWE 28: 338–41), who, like Hortensius, "could have been counted happy if his old age had not coincided with these very troubled times" (339).

a Christian subject in the way that Cicero, being a pagan, once spoke to pagans on non-Christian subjects; but only if he speaks as Cicero would be likely to speak if he were living today as a Christian among Christians [*dicturus esset hodie Christianus apud Christianos si viveret*]" (CWE 28: 392; ASD I-2, 643 l. 36–644 l. 7).[72] Just as Thucydides' style would have been "more mellow and less harsh" if he had lived at a later time, Cicero posits to Atticus and Brutus, so Cicero himself, if he had lived in a later, Christian age, Bulephorus reprises for Nosoponus, would have accommodated time and place and written like a Christian.

Accommodation to time and place—that is, *decorum*—effectively defines Bulephorus's version of Ciceronian style, *Ciceroniane dicere*, which he identifies with *apte dicere*, one of the four traditional virtues of style. In *Brutus*, as we have seen, Cicero deploys a similar strategy in adding *Attice dicere* to these traditional four—an addition that not only does not escape Bulephorus's notice but motivates his own identification. For Bulephorus draws an explicit analogy between Cicero's case for *Attice dicere* and his own call for *Ciceroniane dicere* insofar as both champion difference—even if an ever so slightly different difference. For just as (*Quemadmodum*) "speakers may vary very much among themselves, and yet all be Atticists," Bulephorus builds on *Brutus* by way of a similitude (CWE 28: 443; ASD I-2, 705 ll. 31–33), so (*ita*) "speakers may all be classed as Ciceronians, even if their styles are very different, if they are equals in oratorical ability [*dicendi virtutibus*]." Whereas Nosoponus associates speaking like Cicero with *ornate dicere* and so concentrates obsessively on words, figures, and rhythms, Bulephorus opts for a different, arguably deeper, imitation of the *princeps eloquentiae* with his concentration on *decorum*.[73]

To illustrate his point, Bulephorus singles out the rhetorical accomplishments of Jacopo Sadoleto.[74] Unlike the more rigid Cicero-

---

72. For Erasmus's use of this strategy of recalling Cicero to life in his correspondences around the time of the publication of the *Ciceronianus*, see Pigman, "Imitation and the Renaissance Sense of the Past," 159–61.

73. For Nosoponus's emphasis throughout on *ornatus*, enumerated as words, figures, and rhythm (*voculae, figurae, numeri*) (ASD I-2, 637 l. 8), see CWE 28: 383, 391, 438, 443, 446. In the third edition, Nosoponus compares *grammatice dicere* with *tulliane loqui*, a telling alternative to *Ciceroniane dicere* (CWE 28: 348; ASD I-2, 610n11).

74. On Sadoleto, see Bietenholz, *Contemporaries of Erasmus*, 3: 183–87.

nians, including Bembo, whom Nosoponus admires, the bishop of
Carpentras (later secretary to Pope Leo X) is not deterred from using
properly Christian language in his writings. "Well then, did [Sado-
leto] not employ a Ciceronian style [*Tulliano more*] when speaking?"
Bulephorus asks, before answering:

> He did not. Or rather, he did—because he spoke as Cicero prob-
> ably would speak on occasions if he were alive now [*si viveret dic-
> turum esse Ciceronem*], that is, in a Christian manner on Christian
> topics. (CWE 28: 436; ASD I-2, 698 ll. 8–11)

In the last of multiple variations on the revivification strategy in the
Ciceronianus, Erasmus has Bulephorus showcase his preferred stylistic virtue by means of a *correctio* that sets in high relief the paradox
featured in the second chapter (see above, p. 91): to write *unlike* Cicero, given the changes in time and place, is to write *like* him precisely
by accommodating the particularities of a different time and place.

Like Ludovico in *The Book of the Courtier*, then, Bulephorus appreciates the historical awareness that informs Cicero's history of style.[75]
And like Ludovico, he adapts its revivification strategy. But unlike
Ludovico, Bulephorus binds the unnamed hermeneutical principle
required for understanding the writing of the past to its rhetorical
counterpart. Whereas the Count and others, including Federico
Fregoso in book 2, agree that *decorum* rules every aspect of the successful courtier's behavior, Bulephorus puts the conceptual force of
this rule as a founding principle of style behind what comes to be
called historicism.

Leading Nosoponus to this insight only gradually, in keeping with
a Socratic-style refutation (see above, pp. 88–92), Bulephorus begins to approach his goal by bringing Cicero back to life with another
agenda in mind: making the case for multiple models. "Suppose [*Fin-
gamus*] that Cicero were alive today," Bulephorus announces with
emphasis on the fictionalizing required:

---

75. Erasmus alerts his reader to the historicized attitude advanced in the *Ciceronianus* with the prefatory letter of the second edition to Johann von Vlatten,
where Erasmus commends Wimpfeling's historical understanding of Augustine
in contrast to that of the naïve Augustinians who represent their founder "with a
long beard, a black habit and a leather belt" (CWE 28: 340).

and that there were someone like Trachalus. Would you go to Cicero for modulation of the voice, or to Trachalus? I imagine you would go to the one who was held to be preeminent in this aspect of the art. For an example of discretion and control would you prefer to go to Crassus, if he were alive [*si viverit*], or to Cicero? (CWE 28: 361; ASD I-2, 619 l. 29–620 l. 3)

Leveraging once again his reading of *Brutus* (158), where Cicero recalls Crassus's moderate demeanor in court, Bulephorus has also learned the lessons of the last books of the *Institutio oratoria*.[76] There Quintilian not only commends Trachalus for his exceptional sonority (10.1.119, 12.10.11) but makes clear that Cicero himself followed the Zeuxian method of imitating multiple models in his mature oratorical practice as well as in his early rhetorical theory (10.1.108–9). Despite its commitment to this approved method, however, Cicero's oratory is not free of faults, as a number of his contemporaries record, prompting Quintilian to rehearse the record. These critics, including Calvus, Brutus, and the younger Cato, find Cicero's style "bombastic, Asiatic, redundant, given to excessive repetition, liable at times to be pointless in [its] witticisms, sensuous, extravagant and (an outrageous accusation!) almost effeminate in [its] rhythm" (12.10.13). In the *Dialogue on Orators*, as we have seen, Aper confirms these criticisms (18.5–6), noting, in addition, that the changes in legal procedure under the Empire have rendered a Ciceronian-style oratory ineffective (20.2, 37.4–8). In *Brutus*, moreover, Cicero remembers his own early shortcomings in appearance and delivery (313).

Bulephorus's attention in the course of the conversation to each and every one of these flaws prompts Nosoponus's complaint that "You seem to have come here determined to find fault with Cicero" (CWE 28: 360).[77] On the contrary, Bulephorus assures him, his intention is to plead "not only Cicero's case, but ours too" (CWE 28: 360; ASD I-2, 619 ll. 6–7). For those who apishly imitate the prince of eloquence by reproducing his words rather than his underlying principles, and especially *decorum*, advocate through their slavish imita-

76. On the impact of Quintilian on the *Ciceronianus*, see Burrow, *Imitating Authors*, 174–83.

77. For both Cicero's faults and the futility of his kind of pleading in a sixteenth-century context, see CWE 28: 359–60, 369, 404–5, 430.

tions a judgment on his style according to the letter (of the law).[78] Representing Cicero's style badly by copying his words, they also diminish his reputation. Bulephorus, by contrast, calls for an equitable judgment on Cicero's style, one that looks beneath the words to grasp the animating spirit, the intention or *mens* behind the words. Whereas Ciceronians like Nosoponus are keen to imitate even the master's faults, Bulephorus prefers to excuse these faults in light of mitigating or extenuating circumstances, among which are times, places, and persons. Cicero himself, as we have seen, rendered just such an equitable judgment of Cato's style in *Brutus*. And he did so because all style is conditioned by not just *personal* but *temporal* and *local* factors outside the stylist's control. Fully in keeping with this legal (and ethical) framework for judging stylistic matters, Bulephorus also follows Cicero in reviving the dead. More to the point, the strategy of revivification, as we have seen, proves indispensable to making the case for a number of stylists of former times, clarifying in the process just how different rhetorical treatments of *style* in the Renaissance are from rhetorical treatments of *proof*, despite the noteworthy overlaps by such crossover strategies as the similitude. But Bulephorus, like Castiglione's Ludovico and Castiglione himself, insists on making the case for present (and future) as well as past stylists—for moderns as well as ancients, Christians as well as pagans, for us as well as Cicero; and in an earlier, very different kind of publication, Erasmus helps us understand why.[79]

CONCLUSION

More than a decade before the *Ciceronianus* rubbed Erasmus's contemporaries the wrong way, his edition of Jerome (1516) sowed the seeds of not only satiric impatience with ineffective imitation but firm commitment to stylistic difference.[80] Calling out the "half-witted noisy

78. For Erasmus's contrast in the *Ciceronianus* between Nosoponus's literalizing understanding of Cicero and Bulephorus's spiritual, equitable, and historicized understanding, see Eden, *Hermeneutics and the Rhetorical Tradition*, 67–78.

79. For Erasmus on the revivified Paul understanding his own words equitably, see Eden, *Hermeneutics and the Rhetorical Tradition*, 75–78.

80. On the collaborative composition of the nine volumes of the works of Jerome published by Froben in 1516, see CWE 61, xi, xxii–xxx. On Erasmus's focus

fellow" who for so many centuries passed his own inept writings off as those of the desert father (CWE 61: 12, 23), Erasmus takes the time to brandish the weapon he wields against the shameless forger: style. For style is the surest sign, the "Lydian stone" of *personal* difference, more capacious, here as in the *Ciceronianus*, than mere words, figures, and rhythms. On the contrary, as cited in the introduction (p. 12), style not only "comprehends a multiplicity of things" but marks the difference between talents, "as numerous as men themselves" (CWE 61: 78). Rehearsing an adage used in various versions by both his ancient and early modern predecessors, introduced here to argue against the kind of slavish imitation identified with forgery, Erasmus advertises the confidence he has in the elements of expression that allow him to judge the works in Jerome's corpus as genuine or spurious.[81] And here as in the *Ciceronianus*, Erasmus calls for an equitable judgment— one that is "predisposed towards acquittal rather than conviction" (CWE 61: 83).

Taking up arms against false imitators, Erasmus the editor also does battle with readers of Jerome who misunderstand and even ridicule his notorious self-identification as a Ciceronian.[82] These readers fail to take mitigating circumstances into account. "They pay no attention," Erasmus complains, "to the times in which Jerome has written, to the person addressed, to the occasion, or to the spirit of his composition. Nor do they discuss what preceded it or what follows it or what he wrote on the same subject in another place" (CWE 61: 132). Like Nosoponus in undervaluing the hermeneutic force of the rhetorical principle of *decorum*, these readers neglect not only textual but historical context.[83] Whereas the forger underestimates the telltale signs of *personal* difference, readers unresponsive to fairness or equity overlook *historical* difference, insensitive to the lesson

---

on stylistic difference in the prefatory material, see Eden, *Renaissance Rediscovery of Intimacy*, 87–89, 119–20.

81. On the relation between imitation and forgery, see, for instance, the essays in Hall Bjørnstad, ed., *Borrowed Feathers: Plagiarism and the Limits of Imitation in Early Modern Europe* (Oslo, 2008).

82. On Jerome's equivocation regarding his famous dream and the witty reply of Theodore Gaza to Cardinal Bessarion regarding Jerome's credentials as a Ciceronian, see CWE 61: 35, 50–51, 54–55, 131.

83. On these two aspects of context and Erasmus's role in establishing their hermeneutic importance, see Eden, *Hermeneutics and the Rhetorical Tradition*.

that all revivified lawmakers know and that Bulephorus, as we have seen, drives home in the *Ciceronianus*. "Indeed, what else is it to be Ciceronian," Erasmus asks in the prefatory *Life of Jerome*, "than to use language in the best way, even if one should use it differently? For indeed Cicero himself would have had to change his language if he were Jerome" (CWE 61: 58). Whether writing in Cato's time (the past) or in Jerome's (the future), Cicero, like Cato himself in *Brutus*, would have written differently *pro ratione temporis*, in keeping with the times. Contextualizing the letters with the life, Erasmus uses the prefatory material of the Froben edition of Jerome's writings to plead Jerome's case.[84]

Part and parcel of this pleading is the brief rhetorical commentary (*artis annotatio*) attached to the opening letter of the volume of letters edited by Erasmus. Unmatched anywhere else in the edition, this singular commentary serves to explain (and even defend) the exuberant style of an earnest young Jerome exhorting a dear friend (Heliodorus) to join him in the desert.[85] It also speaks not just to the four discrete chapters of this book but to their underlying integration and so will serve as its conclusion. For Erasmus is eager to have Jerome's early modern readers appreciate, as a shaping feature of this letter, its refutative agenda in combating his friend's deep-seated reservations about becoming an eremite—reservations rooted in his natural affection for his family.

To refute these "fetters," which Heliodorus would "plead as hindrances" to the eremitic life (CWE 61: 111), Erasmus explains in terms that foreground the legal framework, Jerome first establishes that the question the letter raises is one of *quality*—the third of the three *status* questions, the one that is "drawn from the notion of what is right" (CWE 61: 129).[86] Were Heliodorus to leave his family behind, Jerome invites his addressee to imagine, the case against him would turn not

---

84. In the prefatory letter to the 1516 *Annotations*, Erasmus closes by calling for a fair hearing from his reader—on deserving "the same measure of equity as the courts give to those accused of murder and sacrilege" (CWE 41: 792).

85. On the singularity of this commentary, see CWE 61: 264n39; Chomarat, *Grammaire et rhétorique*, 1: 536–40; and see CWE 25: 97, where Erasmus characterizes the letter itself as "an epitome of all the rules for this class [of letter]."

86. For the *qualitative status* in deliberative oratory, see Quintilian 7.4.2: "Under the same head of quality fall questions whether certain things should be done or not and certain objects sought or avoided: such topics are specially adapted for

on a *conjectural* or *definitive* but a *qualitative* issue: not *if* he should leave loved ones behind or whether that "leaving" constitutes, say, "abandonment" but whether the act would be defensible or indefensible, praiseworthy or blameworthy. To resolve this "question of quality" (CWE 61: 129), Erasmus contends, Jerome draws out an implicit comparison between the devoted servant of Christ and the military man who fulfills his official duty regardless of emotional pressure to shirk it.[87] And Jerome does so, Erasmus further asserts, by framing the comparison "in the manner of Cicero" (*more Tulliano*),[88] as a series of rhetorical questions that elevate the style and thus intensify the feelings it arouses.[89]

But Jerome's comparison does more, Erasmus insists, than raise the stylistic register. It also advances the argument, which Erasmus distills for his reader's ready comprehension to the conventional formula of a similitude. "One can explain [the *parabola*] as follows," Erasmus writes:

> just as [*sicut*] the soldier in that hour of danger ignores his mother's tears, so [*ita*] the Christian does not regard the feelings of his parents when it is a matter of his eternal life.[90]

Whereas Jerome demonstrates his stylistic virtuosity by complicating the usual two-part formula of the similitude for heightened effect, Erasmus, ever building on the lessons of *De copia*, deconstructs the complexity to reveal the rhetorical nuts and bolts within. For such rhetorical hardware in the hands of a master craftsman like Jerome can easily escape a reader's detection. And the same is true, as I have tried to show, of the skilled handiwork of Petrarch, Castiglione, Montaigne, and Erasmus himself. If rhetorical theory, ancient as well as early modern, doggedly treats *status* as a matter of *inventio*, refutation as part of *dispositio*, the similitude as a crossover with both proba-

---

deliberative themes, but occur with some frequency in controversial themes as well, the only difference being that in the latter we deal with what is past and in the former with the future." And see Chomarat, *Grammaire et rhétorique*, 1: 538n162.

87. For Erasmus's reliance, like Jerome's, on the figure of the Christian soldier, see, for instance, the *Enchiridion militis christiani*, CWE 66.

88. CWE 61: 129; *Hieronymi opera omnia* (Basel, 1516), vol. 1, 4C.

89. See, for instance, Cicero's strategy in *Pro Milone*, discussed above, p. 25.

90. CWE 61: 129; *Hieronymi opera omnia*, vol. 1, 4C.

tive and stylistic dimensions, and style itself as a complex mix of factors conditioned in no small measure by times, places, and persons, Renaissance writers, including the most esteemed among them, ply these (and other) rhetorical threads, as we have seen, to weave their apparently seamless masterworks—literary monuments to a rhetorical renaissance.

ACKNOWLEDGMENTS

The chapters of this book are the product of classes taught at Columbia University and Princeton University and papers delivered at the University of Pennsylvania, Freie Universität Berlin, the University of Cambridge, the University of Chicago, the Center for Medieval and Renaissance Studies at the State University of New York at Binghamton, Indiana University, the Ancient and Medieval Studies Colloquium at the Massachusetts Institute of Technology, and the Dutch Royal Academy of Arts and Sciences. For asking probing questions, offering helpful suggestions, and/or reading written versions of what they heard, I owe special thanks to Hall Bjørnstad, Vladimir Brljak, Rita Copeland, Joseph Farrell, Stephanie Frampton, Lorna Hutson, Jesse James, Joachim Küpper, Micha Lazarus, Timothy Lundy, D. S. Mayfield, Charles McNamara, Subha Mukherji, Lodi Nauta, Shankar Raman, Kara Schechtman, Jane Siegel, Richard Strier, Emily Vasiliauskas, Sonia Velazquez, Arnoud Visser, and Dorothea von Mücke. Colin Burrow and Armando Maggi provided critical readings for the University of Chicago Press that proved especially helpful.

This book is dedicated to my students at Columbia over the past forty or so years, some of whose names are included above.

*

Earlier versions of parts of two of the four chapters have appeared as "From the Refutation of Drama to the Drama of Refutation" in *Rhetoric and Drama*, ed. D. S. Mayfield (Berlin, 2017), 55–70, and "Cicero

Redivivus and the Historicizing of Renaissance Style" in a special volume (56) of *Nottingham Medieval Studies* entitled *Inventing a Path: Studies in Medieval Rhetoric in Honour of Mary Carruthers*, ed. Laura Iseppi De Filippis (Turnhout, 2012), 143–69.

BIBLIOGRAPHY OF
SECONDARY SOURCES

Adams, Don. "Elenchos and Evidence." *Ancient Philosophy* 18 (1998): 287–307.

Adamson, Sylvia. "Synonymia: or, in Other Words." In *Renaissance Figures of Speech*, ed. Sylvia Adamson, Gavin Alexander, and Katrin Ettenhuber, 17–35. Cambridge, UK, 2007.

Aldrete, Gregory S. *Gestures and Acclamations in Ancient Rome*. Baltimore, 1999.

Altman, William H. F. "Womanly Humanism in Cicero's *Tusculan Disputations*." *Transactions of the American Philological Association* 139 (2009): 407–41.

Ausland, Hayden W. "Socratic Induction in Plato and Aristotle." In *The Development of Dialectic from Plato to Aristotle*, ed. J. L. Fink, 224–50. Cambridge, UK, 2012.

Baldwin, T. W. *William Shakspere's Small Latine & Lesse Greeke*. 2 vols. Urbana, IL, 1944.

Baraz, M. "Les images dans les *Essais* de Montaigne." *Bibliothèque d'humanisme et Renaissance* 27 (1965): 361–94.

Barish, Jonas. "The Prose Style of John Lyly." *English Literary History* 23 (1956): 14–35.

Barkan, Leonard. *Mute Poetry, Speaking Pictures*. Princeton, 2013.

Barnes, T. D. "The Significance of Tacitus' *Dialogus de oratoribus*." *Harvard Studies in Classical Philology* 90 (1986): 225–44.

Baron, Hans. *Petrarch's "Secretum": Its Making and Its Meaning*. Cambridge, MA, 1985.

Bartholin, Erasmus, and Lynda Gregorian Christian. "The Figure of Socrates in Erasmus' Works." *Sixteenth Century Journal* 3 (1972): 1–10.

Baxandall, Michael. *Giotto and the Orators: Humanist Observers of Painting in Italy and the Discovery of Pictorial Composition, 1350–1450*. Oxford, 1971; rpt. 2006.

Bennett, Camille. "The Conversion of Vergil: The *Aeneid* in the *Confessions*." *Revue des Études Augustiniennes* 34 (1988): 47–69.

Benson, Hugh H. "The Priority of Definition and the Socratic Elenchus." *Oxford Studies in Ancient Philosophy* 8 (1990): 19–65.

Berkowitz, Beth A. "Decapitation and the Discourse of Antisyncretism in the Babylonian Talmud." *Journal of the American Academy of Religion* 70 (2002): 743–69.

Bernard, John. "'Formiamo un cortegian': Castiglione and the Aims of Writing." *Modern Language Notes* 115 (2000): 34–63.

Bettini, Maurizio. "Guardarsi in faccia a Roma: le parole dell'apparenza fisica nella cultura latina." In *Le orecchie di Hermes: studi di antropologia e letterature classiche*, 314–56. Turin, 2000.

Billanovich, Giuseppe. "Petrarca e il Ventoso." *Italia medioevale e umanistica* 9 (1966): 389–401.

Black, Robert. *Humanism and Education in Medieval and Renaissance Italy.* Cambridge, UK, 2001.

———. "The New Laws of History." *Renaissance Studies* 1 (1987): 126–56.

Borzsák, Étienne. "Le 'Dialogue' de Tacite et le 'Brutus' de Cicéron." *Bulletin de l'Association Guillaume Budé* 3 (1985): 289–98.

Boskoff, Priscilla S. "Quintilian in the Late Middle Ages." *Speculum* 27 (1952): 71–78.

Boutcher, Warren. "The Origins of Florio's Montaigne: 'Of the Institution and Education of Children, to Madame Lucy Russell, Countess of Bedford.'" *Montaigne Studies* 24 (2012): 7–32.

———. *The School of Montaigne in Early Modern Europe.* 2 vols. Oxford, 2017.

Bouwsma, William J. "The Two Faces of Humanism: Stoicism and Augustinianism in Renaissance Thought." In *Itinerarium Italicum: The Profile of the Italian Renaissance in the Mirror of Its European Transformations*, ed. Heiko A. Oberman and Thomas A. Brady Jr., 3–60. Leiden, 1975.

Bovey, Muriel. "Le *Dialogus de oratoribus* de Tacite et les manuels de rhétorique." *Latomus* 59 (2000): 353–63.

Boyle, Marjorie O'Rourke. "Erasmus' Prescription for Henry VIII: Logotherapy." *Renaissance Quarterly* 31 (1978): 161–72.

Braet, Antoine. "The Classical Doctrine of *Status* and the Rhetorical Theory of Argumentation." *Philosophy and Rhetoric* 20 (1987): 79–93.

Brennan, Joseph X. "The *Epitome Troporum ac Schematum*: The Genesis of a Renaissance Rhetorical Text." *Quarterly Journal of Speech* 46 (1960): 59–71.

———. "Joannes Susenbrotus: A Forgotten Humanist." *PMLA* 75 (1960): 485–96.

Breslin, Charles. "Philosophy or Philology: Auerbach and Aesthetic Historicism." *Journal of the History of Ideas* 22 (1961): 369–81.

Brink, C. O. "History in the 'Dialogus de Oratoribus' and Tacitus the Historian: A New Approach to an Old Source." *Hermes* 121 (1993): 335–49.

Burke, Peter. *The Fortunes of the Courtier: The European Reception of Castiglione's Cortegiano.* University Park, PA, 1995.

———. "The Renaissance Dialogue." *Renaissance Studies* 3 (1989): 1–12.

Burnyeat, Miles F. "Protagoras and Self-Refutation in Later Greek Philosophy." *Philosophical Review* 85 (1976): 44–69.

Burrow, Colin. *Imitating Authors: Plato to Futurity.* Oxford, 2019.

Bynum, Caroline. *Dissimilar Similitudes: Devotional Objects in Late Medieval Europe.* New York, 2020.

Caron, Elisabeth. "Saint Augustin dans les *Essais.*" *Montaigne Studies* 2 (1990): 17–33.

Carter, Michael. "*Stasis* and *Kairos*: Principles of Social Construction in Classical Rhetoric." *Rhetoric Review* 7 (1988): 97–112.

Castagnoli, Luca. *Ancient Self-Refutation: The Logic and History of the Self-Refutation Argument from Democritus to Augustine.* Cambridge, UK, 2010.

Cavarzere, Alberto. "La funzione di Ortensio nel prologo del *Brutus*" *Lexis* 16 (1998): 149–62.

Cave, Terence. *The Cornucopian Text: Problems of Writing in the French Renaissance.* Oxford, 1979.

Celenza, Christopher S. "Petrarch, Latin, and Italian Renaissance Latinity." *Journal of Medieval and Early Modern Studies* 35 (2005): 509–36.

Chomarat, Jacques. "Érasme et Platon." *Bulletin de l'Association Guillaume Budé* 1 (1987): 25–48.

———. *Grammaire et rhétorique chez Érasme.* 2 vols. Paris, 1981.

Cian, Vittorio. *La lingua di Baldassarre Castiglione.* Florence, 1942.

Clark, Carol. "Erasmus and the Four-Part Simile in Sixteenth-Century Vernacular Writing." In *Neo-Latin and the Vernacular in Renaissance France*, ed. Grahame Castor and Terence Cave, 216–26. Oxford, 1984.

———. *The Web of Metaphor: Studies in the Imagery of Montaigne's "Essais."* Lexington, KY, 1978.

Classen, C. Joachim. "The Rhetorical Works of George of Trebizond and Their Debt to Cicero." *Journal of the Warburg and Courtauld Institutes* 56 (1993): 75–84.

Cole, A. Thomas. "The Relativism of Protagoras." *Yale Classical Studies* 22 (1972): 19–45.

Compagnon, Antoine. *Literature, Theory, and Common Sense.* Trans. Carol Cosman. Princeton, 2004.

Connolly, Joy. *The State of Speech: Rhetoric and Political Thought in Ancient Rome.* Princeton, 2007.

Copeland, Rita. "The History of Rhetoric and the *Longue Durée*: Ciceronian Myth and Its Medieval Afterlives." *JEGP* 106 (2007): 176–202.

Corbeill, Anthony. "Ciceronian Invective." In *Brill's Companion to Cicero: Oratory and Rhetoric*, ed. James M. May, 197–217. Leiden, 2002.

———. "Rhetorical Education in Cicero's Youth." In *Brill's Companion to Cicero: Oratory and Rhetoric*, ed. James M. May, 23–48. Leiden, 2002.

Costa, C. D. N. "The *Dialogus*." In *Tacitus*, ed. T. A. Dorey, 19–34. London, 1969.

Cox, Virginia. *The Renaissance Dialogue: Literary Dialogue in Its Social and Political Contexts, Castiglione to Galileo.* Cambridge, UK, 1992.

Craig, Christopher P. "The Structural Pedigree of Cicero's Speeches *Pro Archia, Pro Milone*, and *Pro Quinctio*." *Classical Philology* 80 (1985): 136–37.

Croll, Morris W. *Style, Rhetoric, and Rhythm.* Ed. J. Max Patrick, Robert O. Evans, John M. Wallace, and R. J. Schoeck. Princeton, 1966.

Cummings, Brian. "Autobiography and the History of Reading." In *Cultural Reformations: Medieval and Renaissance in Literary History*, ed. Brian Cummings and James Simpson, 635–57. Oxford, 2010.

———. "Encyclopaedic Erasmus." *Renaissance Studies* 28 (2014): 183–204.

———. "Erasmus, Sacred Literature, and Literary Theory." In *Erasmus on Literature: His* Ratio *or 'System' of 1518/1519*, ed. Mark Vessey, trans. Robert D. Sider, 48–62. Toronto, 2021.

Curtius, Ernst Robert. *European Literature and the Latin Middle Ages*. Trans. Willard R. Trask. New York, 1953; rpt. 1963.

De Angelis, Francesco. "Pliny the Elder and the Identity of Roman Art." *RES* 53/54 (2008): 79–92.

Délègue, Yves. "Les comparaisons dans les *Essais* de Montaigne." *Revue d'Histoire Littéraire de la France* 66 (1966): 593–618.

Della Corte, Francesco. "La scoperta del Tacito minore." In *La fortuna di Tacito dal sec. XV ad oggi: atti del colloquio, Urbino 9–11 ottobre 1978*, ed. Franco Gori and Cesare Questa, 13–45. Urbino, 1979.

Dihle, Albrecht. *The Theory of Will in Classical Antiquity*. Berkeley, 1982.

Di Mauro, Damon. "L'unité religieuse des Tragédies Sainctes de Louis des Masures." *Bibliothèque d'Humanisme et Renaissance* 64 (2002): 271–94.

Dolven, Jeff. "Reading Wyatt for the Style." *Modern Philology* 105 (2007): 65–86.

Douglas, A. E. "A Ciceronian Contribution to Rhetorical Theory." *Eranos* 55 (1957): 18–26.

———. "Form and Content in the *Tusculan Disputations*." In *Cicero the Philosopher*, ed. J. G. F. Powell, 197–218. Oxford, 1995.

———. "Oratorum Aetates." *American Journal of Philology* 87 (1966): 290–306.

Dugan, John. *Making a New Man: Ciceronian Self-Fashioning in the Rhetorical Works*. Oxford, 2005.

Durling, Robert. "The Ascent of Mont Ventoux and the Crisis of Allegory." *Italian Quarterly* 18 (1974): 7–28.

Edelstein, Ludwig. *The Idea of Progress in Classical Antiquity*. Baltimore, 1967.

Eden, Kathy. "Cicero *Redivivus* and the Historicizing of Renaissance Style." *Nottingham Medieval Studies* 56 (2012): 143–69.

———. "Cicero's Portion of Montaigne's Acclaim." In *Brill's Companion to the Reception of Cicero*, ed. William H. T. Altman, 39–55. Leiden, 2015.

———. "Erasmus on Dogs and Baths and Other Odious Comparisons." *Erasmus Studies* 38 (2018): 1–20.

———. "Facebook avant la lettre: Communicating Renaissance-Style in Montaigne's *Essais*." In *Montaigne in Transit: Essays in Honour of Ian Maclean*, ed. Neil Kenny, Richard Scholar, and Wes Williams, 61–76. Cambridge, UK, 2016.

———. "Forensic Rhetoric and Humanist Education." In *The Oxford Handbook of English Law and Literature, 1500–1700*, ed. Lorna Hutson, 23–40. Oxford, 2017.

———. *Friends Hold All Things in Common: Tradition, Intellectual Property, and the "Adages" of Erasmus*. New Haven, 2001.

———. *Hermeneutics and the Rhetorical Tradition: Chapters in the Ancient Legacy and Its Humanist Reception*. New Haven, 1997.

———. *Poetic and Legal Fiction in the Aristotelian Tradition*. Princeton, 1986.

———. *The Renaissance Rediscovery of Intimacy*. Chicago, 2012.

Edwards, Robert R. "Petrarchan Narratives: Representation and Hermeneutics." *Modern Language Notes* 130 (2015): 1–23.

Engelhardt, George John. "Mediæval Vestiges in the Rhetoric of Erasmus." *PMLA* 63 (1948): 739–44.

Fahnestock, Jeanne, and Marie Secor. "The Stases in Scientific and Literary Argument." *Written Communication* 5 (1988): 427–43.

Fantham, Elaine. "The Concept of Nature and Human Nature in Quintilian's Psychology and Theory of Instruction." *Rhetorica* 13 (1995): 125–36.

———. "On the Use of *Genus*-Terminology in Cicero's Rhetorical Works." *Hermes* 107 (1979): 441–59.

———. "*Orator* 69–74." *Central States Speech Journal* 35 (1984): 123–25.

———. *Roman Readings: Roman Response to Greek Literature from Plautus to Statius and Quintilian.* Berlin, 2011.

———. *The Roman World of Cicero's* De oratore. Oxford, 2004.

———. "*Varietas* and *Satietas*: *De oratore* 3.96–103 and the limits of *ornatus*." *Rhetorica* 6 (1988): 275–90.

Feeney, Denis. *Caesar's Calendar: Ancient Time and the Beginnings of History.* Berkeley, 2007.

———. "*Una cum scriptore meo*: Poetry, Principate and the Traditions of Literary History in the Epistle to Augustus." In *Traditions and Contexts in the Poetry of Horace*, ed. Tony Woodman and Denis Feeney, 172–87. Cambridge, UK, 2002.

Feldherr, Andrew. "Cicero and the Invention of 'Literary' History." In *Formen römischer Geschichtsschreibung von den Anfängen bis Livius*, ed. Ulrich Eigler, Ulrich Gotter, Nino Luraghi, and Uwe Walter, 196–212. Darmstadt, 2003.

Frame, Donald M. *Montaigne's Essais: A Study.* Englewood Cliffs, NJ, 1969.

Franklin, James. *The Science of Conjecture: Evidence and Probability before Pascal.* Baltimore, 2001.

Freedman, Joseph S. "Cicero in Sixteenth- and Seventeenth-Century Rhetoric Instruction." *Rhetorica* 4 (1986): 227–54.

Fumaroli, Marc. *L'âge de l'éloquence: rhétorique et 'res literaria' de la Renaissance au seuil de l'époque classique.* Paris, 1980.

Funkenstein, Amos. "Collective Memory and Historical Consciousness." *History and Memory* 1 (1989): 5–26.

———. *Theology and the Scientific Imagination from the Middle Ages to the Seventeenth Century.* Princeton, 1986.

Gadamer, Hans-Georg. *Truth and Method.* Trans. Joel Weinsheimer and Donald G. Marshall. New York, 1975; rpt. 1992.

Gaines, Robert. "Cicero's Response to the Philosophers in *De oratore*, Book 1." In *Rhetoric and Pedagogy: Its History, Philosophy, and Practice*, ed. Winifred Bryan Horner and Michael Leff, 43–56. Mahwah, NJ, 1995.

Gaisser, Julia Haig. "Teaching Classics in the Renaissance: Two Case Histories." *Transactions of the American Philological Association* 131 (2001): 1–21.

Gallo, Ernest. "Geoffrey of Vinsauf and Erasmus' *De copia*." *American Notes and Queries* 9 (1970): 38–39.

Garin, Eugenio. "Erasmo e l'umanesimo italiano." *Bibliothèque d'Humanisme et Renaissance* 33 (1971): 7–17.

Gerlo, A. "The *Opus de Conscribendis Epistolis* of Erasmus and the Tradition of the *Ars Epistolica*." In *Classical Influences on European Culture, A.D. 500–1500*, ed. R. R. Bolgar, 103–14. Cambridge, UK, 1971.

Ghinassi, Ghino. "Fasi dell'elaborazione del *Cortegiano*." *Studi di filologia italiana* 25 (1967): 155–96.

Gilbert, Neal W. "The Concept of Will in Early Latin Philosophy." *Journal of the History of Philosophy* 1 (1963): 17–35.

Gill, Christopher. "Personhood and Personality: The Four-*Personae* Theory in Cicero, *De officiis* I." *Oxford Studies in Ancient Philosophy* 6 (1988): 169–99.

———. *The Structured Self in Hellenistic and Roman Thought*. Oxford, 2006.

Ginzburg, Carlo. "History and/or Memory: On the Principle of Accommodation." In *Thinking Impossibilities: The Intellectual Legacy of Amos Funkenstein*, ed. Robert S. Westman and David Biale, 193–206. Toronto, 2008.

———. "The Letter Kills: On Some Implications of 2 Corinthians 3:6." *History and Theory* 49 (2010): 71–89.

———. "Style as Inclusion, Style as Exclusion." In *Picturing Science, Producing Art*, ed. Caroline A. Jones and Peter Galison, 27–54. New York, 1998.

Giuliani, Alessandro. "The Influence of Rhetoric on the Law of Evidence and Pleading." *Juridical Review*, 2nd ser., 7 (1962): 216–51.

Glenn, Cheryl. "Remapping Rhetorical Territory." *Rhetoric Review* 13 (1995): 287–303.

Goh, Ian. "An Asianist Sensation: Horace on Lucilius as Hortensius." *American Journal of Philology* 139 (2018): 641–74.

Goldberg, Sander M. "Appreciating Aper: The Defence of Modernity in Tacitus' *Dialogus de oratoribus*." *Classical Quarterly* 49 (1999): 224–37.

———. *Epic in Republican Rome*. Oxford, 1995.

Goldhill, Simon. "Literary History without Literature: Reading Practices in the Ancient World." *SubStance* 28, no. 1 (1999): 57–89.

Gombrich, E. H. "The Debate on Primitivism in Ancient Rhetoric." *Journal of the Warburg and Courtauld Institutes* 29 (1966): 24–38.

———. "The Renaissance Conception of Artistic Progress and Its Consequences." In *Norm and Form: Studies in the Art of the Renaissance*, 1–10. London, 1966.

———. "Vasari's *Lives* and Cicero's *Brutus*." *Journal of the Warburg and Courtauld Institutes* 23 (1960): 309–11.

Görler, W. "From Athens to Tusculum: Gleaning the Background of Cicero's *De oratore*." *Rhetorica* 6 (1988): 215–35.

Gorman, Robert. *The Socratic Method in the Dialogues of Cicero*. Stuttgart, 2005.

Gougenheim, Georges. *Les mots français dans l'histoire et dans la vie*. Vol. 1. Paris, 1966.

Goumarre, Pierre. "La morale et la politique: Montaigne, Cicéron et Machiavel." *Italica* 50 (1973): 285–98.

Gowing, Alain. *Empire and Memory: The Representation of the Roman Republic in Imperial Culture*. Cambridge, UK, 2005.

———. "Memory and Silence in Cicero's *Brutus*." *Eranos* 98 (2000): 39–64.

Goyet, Francis. *Le sublime du "lieu commun": l'invention rhétorique dans l'Antiquité et à la Renaissance*. Paris, 1996.

Grafton, Anthony, and Lisa Jardine. *From Humanism to the Humanities*. Cambridge, MA, 1986.

Gray, Hanna H. "Renaissance Humanism: The Pursuit of Eloquence." *Journal of the History of Ideas* 24 (1963): 497–514.

Green, Jeffrey Martin. "Montaigne's Critique of Cicero." *Journal of the History of Ideas* 36 (1975): 595–612.

Green, Lawrence D. "The Reception of Aristotle's *Rhetoric* in the Renaissance." In *Peripatetic Rhetoric after Aristotle*, ed. William W. Fortenbaugh and David C. Mirhady, 320–48. New Brunswick, NJ, 1994.

Greene, Thomas M. "*Il Cortegiano* and the Choice of a Game." In *Castiglione: The Ideal and the Real in Renaissance Culture*, ed. Robert W. Hanning and David Rosand, 1–15. New Haven, 1983.

Grendler, Marcella, and Paul Grendler. "The Survival of Erasmus in Italy." *Erasmus in English* 8 (1976): 2–22.

Grossi, Paolo, and Juan Carlos D'Amico, eds. *De la politesse à la politique*. Caen, 2001.

Grube, G. M. A. *The Greek and Roman Critics*. London, 1965.

Guérin, Charles. "Définir l'*ars dicendi*: enjeux et méthode de la réflexion cicéronienne dans le *De oratore*." In *La rhétorique au miroir de la philosophie*, ed. Barbara Cassin, 175–90. Paris, 2015.

———. "Référence aux orateurs et usages de la citation chez Cicéron et Sénèque le rhéteur." *Papers on Rhetoric* 10, ed. Lucia Calboli Montefusco, 141–56. Rome, 2010.

Gumbrecht, Hans Ulrich. "A History of the Concept 'Modern.'" In *Making Sense in Life and Literature*, trans. Glen Burns, 79–110. Minneapolis, 1992.

Hamlyn, D. W. "Aristotelian Epagoge." *Phronesis* 21 (1976): 167–84.

Hampton, Timothy. *Writing from History: The Rhetoric of Exemplarity in Renaissance Literature*. Ithaca, 1990.

Hankins, James. *Plato in the Italian Renaissance*. 2 vols. Leiden, 1990.

Hanning, Robert W. "Castiglione's Verbal Portrait: Structures and Strategies." In *Castiglione: The Ideal and the Real in Renaissance Culture*, ed. Robert W. Hanning and David Rosand, 131–41. New Haven, 1983.

Heath, Malcolm. "The Substructure of *Stasis*-Theory from Hermagoras to Hermogenes." *Classical Quarterly* 44 (1994): 114–29.

Hendrickson, G. L. "Cicero *De optimo genere oratorum*." *American Journal of Philology* 47 (1926): 109–23.

———. "Cicero's Correspondence with Brutus and Calvus on Oratorical Style." *American Journal of Philology* 47 (1926): 234–58.

———. "Literary Sources in Cicero's *Brutus* and the Techniques of Citation in Dialogue." *American Journal of Philology* 27 (1906): 184–99.

Henry, Madeleine M. *Prisoner of History: Aspasia of Miletus and Her Biographical Tradition*. Oxford, 1995.

Herrick, Marvin T. "The Early History of Aristotle's *Rhetoric* in England." *Philological Quarterly* 5 (1926): 242–57.

Hobbs, Catherine L. *Rhetoric on the Margins of Modernity: Vico, Condillac, Monboddo*. Carbondale, 2002.

Hohmann, Hanns. "The Dynamics of Stasis: Classical Rhetorical Theory and Modern Legal Argumentation." *American Journal of Jurisprudence* 34 (1989): 171–97.

Hölscher, Tonio. "Greek Styles and Greek Art in Augustan Rome: Issues of the Present versus Records of the Past." In *Classical Pasts: The Classical Traditions of Greece and Rome*, ed. James I. Porter, 237–69. Princeton, 2006.

Holtsmark, Erling B. "Quintilian on Status: A Progymnasma." *Hermes* 96 (1968): 356–68.

Hösle, Vittorio. "Cicero's Plato." *Wiener Studien* 121 (2008): 145–70.

Hunter, G. K. *John Lyly: The Humanist as Courtier.* London, 1962.

Huppert, George. "The Renaissance Background of Historicism." *History and Theory* 5 (1966): 48–60.

Hutson, Lorna. *Circumstantial Shakespeare.* Oxford, 2015.

———. *The Invention of Suspicion.* Oxford, 2007.

Iggers, Georg G. "Historicism: The History and Meaning of the Term." *Journal of the History of Ideas* 56 (1995): 129–52.

Innes, D. C. "Theophrastus and the Theory of Style." *Rutgers University Studies* 2 (1985): 251–67.

Isager, Jacob. "*Humanissima ars*: Evaluation and Devaluation in Pliny, Vasari, and Baden." In *Ancient Art and Its Historiography*, ed. A. A. Donohue and Mark D. Fullerton, 48–68. Cambridge, UK, 2003.

Ivanoff, Nicola. *Il concetto dello stile nella letteratura artistica del' 500.* Trieste, 1955.

Javitch, Daniel. *Poetry and Courtliness in Renaissance England.* Princeton, 1978.

Johnson, W. R. *Luxuriance and Economy: Cicero and the Alien Style.* Berkeley, 1971.

Jones, Howard. *Master Tully: Cicero in Tudor England.* Nieuwkoop, 1998.

Jordan, Constance. "Montaigne on Property, Public Service, and Political Servitude." *RQ* 56 (2003): 408–35.

Kacprzak, Agnieszka. "Rhetoric and Roman Law." In *The Oxford Handbook of Roman Law and Society*, ed. Paul J. du Plessis, Clifford Ando, and Kaius Tuori, 200–213. Oxford, 2016.

Kahn, Charles H. "Drama and Dialectic in Plato's *Gorgias*." *Oxford Studies in Ancient Philosophy* 1 (1983): 75–121.

Kahn, Victoria. "The Figure of the Reader in Petrarch's *Secretum*." *PMLA* 100 (1985): 154–66.

———. *Rhetoric, Prudence and Skepticism in the Renaissance.* Ithaca, 1985.

Kallendorf, Craig. "The Historical Petrarch." *American Historical Review* 101 (1996): 130–41.

Kastely, James L. *Rethinking the Rhetorical Tradition: From Plato to Postmodernism.* New Haven, 1997.

Kelly, Donald H. "Hermes, Clio, Themis: Historical Interpretation and Legal Hermeneutics." *Journal of Modern History* 55 (1983): 644–68.

Kemp, Martin. "'Equal excellences': Lomazzo and the Explanation of Individual Style in the Visual Arts." *Renaissance Studies* 1 (1987): 1–26.

Kennedy, George. *The Art of Persuasion in Greece.* Princeton, 1963.

———. "Cicero's Oratorical and Rhetorical Legacy." In *Brill's Companion to Cicero: Oratory and Rhetoric*, ed. James M. May, 481–501. Leiden, 2002.

———. "The Evolution of a Theory of Artistic Prose." In *The Cambridge History of Literary Criticism: Classical Criticism*, ed. George A. Kennedy, 184–99. Cambridge, UK, 1989.

———. *Greek Rhetoric under Christian Emperors.* Princeton, 1983.

Kenny, Neil. *The Uses of Curiosity in Early Modern France and Germany.* Oxford, 2004.

Kessler, Eckhard. "Petrarch's Contribution to Renaissance Historiography." *Res publica litterarum* 1 (1978): 129–49.

King, James. "Elenchus, Self-Blame and the Socratic Paradox." *Review of Metaphysics* 41 (1987): 105–26.

Kinney, Daniel. "More's Letter to Dorp: Remapping the Trivium." *Renaissance Quarterly* 34 (1981): 179–210.

Klosko, George. "The Refutation of Callicles in Plato's *Gorgias*." *Greece and Rome* 31 (1984): 126–39.

Koselleck, Reinhart. *Futures Past: On the Semantics of Historical Time*. Trans. Keith Tribe. New York, 2004.

Krans, Jan. *Beyond What Is Written: Erasmus and Beza as Conjectural Critics of the New Testament*. Leiden, 2006.

Kries, Douglas. "On the Intention of Cicero's *De Officiis*." *Review of Politics* 65 (2003): 375–93.

Kumaniecki, K. "La tradition manuscrite du 'De oratore.'" *Revue des études latines* 44 (1966): 204–18.

La Bua, Giuseppe. "Cicero's *Pro Milone* and the 'Demosthenic' Style: *De optimo genere oratorum* 10." *Greece and Rome* 61 (2014): 29–37.

Lanham, Richard A. *The Motives of Eloquence*. New Haven, 1976.

Laurays, Marc. "Per una storia dell'invettiva umanistica." *Studi umanistici piceni* 23 (2003): 9–30.

Lecointe, Jean. *L'idéal et la différence: la perception de la personnalité littéraire à la Renaissance*. Geneva, 1993.

Lee, Alexander. *Petrarch and Saint Augustine: Classical Scholarship, Christian Theology, and the Origins of the Renaissance in Italy*. Leiden, 2012.

Lee, Dwight E., and Robert N. Beck. "The Meaning of 'Historicism.'" *American Historical Review* 59 (1954): 568–77.

Leeman, A. D. *Orationis ratio: The Stylistic Theories and Practice of Roman Orators, Historians, and Philosophers*. Amsterdam, 1986.

Leff, Michael. "Decorum and Rhetorical Interpretation: The Latin Humanist Tradition and Contemporary Critical Theory." *Vichiana* 1 (1990): 107–26.

Legros, Alain. "Les *Ombrages* de Montaigne et d'Augustin." *Bibliothèque d'humanisme et Renaissance* 55 (1993): 547–63.

Levene, D. S. "Tacitus' *Dialogus* as Literary History." *Transactions of the American Philological Association* 134 (2004): 157–200.

Lipking, Lawrence. "The Dialectic of *Il Cortegiano*." *PMLA* 81 (1966): 355–62.

Lloyd-Jones, Kenneth. "Erasmus and Dolet on the Ethics of Imitation and the Hermeneutic Imperative." *International Journal of the Classical Tradition* 2 (1995): 27–43.

Lovejoy, Arthur O., and George Boas. *Primitivism and Related Ideas in Antiquity*. New York, 1965.

Lowrie, Michèle. "Cicero on Caesar or Exemplum and Inability in the *Brutus*." In *Notions of the Self in Antiquity and Beyond*, ed. Alexander Arweiler and Melanie Möller, 131–54. Berlin, 2008.

Lucarini, Carlo M. "I due stili asiani e l'origine dell'Atticismo letterario." *Zeitschrift für Papyrologie und Epigraphik* 193 (2015): 11–24.

Luce, T. J. "Reading and Response in the *Dialogus*." In *Tacitus and the Tacitean Tradition*, ed. T. J. Luce and A. J. Woodman, 11–38. Princeton, 1993.

Mac Carthy, Ita. *The Grace of the Italian Renaissance.* Princeton, 2020.

Mack, Peter. "The Dialogue in English Education of the Sixteenth Century." In *Le dialogue au temps de la Renaissance,* ed. M. T. Jones-Davies, 189–212. Paris, 1984.

———. *Elizabethan Rhetoric: Theory and Practice.* Cambridge, UK, 2002.

———. *A History of Renaissance Rhetoric, 1380–1620.* Oxford, 2011.

———. *Renaissance Argument: Valla and Agricola in the Traditions of Rhetoric and Dialectic.* Leiden, 1993.

Mackenzie, Mary Margaret. *Plato on Punishment.* Berkeley, 1981.

Maclean, Ian. "Montaigne and the Truth of the Schools." In *The Cambridge Companion to Montaigne,* ed. Ullrich Langer, 142–62. Cambridge, UK, 2005.

———. "The Place of Interpretation: Montaigne and Humanist Jurists on Words, Intention and Meaning." In *Neo-Latin and the Vernacular in Renaissance France,* ed. Grahame Castor and Terence Cave, 252–72. Oxford, 1984.

MacPhail, Eric. "Philosophers in the New World: Montaigne and the Tradition of Epideictic Rhetoric." *Rhetorica* 30 (2012): 22–36.

———. "Praising the Past: Novelty and Nostalgia in Machiavelli, Castiglione, and Montaigne." *Romanic Review* 101 (2010): 639–54.

———. *The Sophistic Renaissance.* Geneva, 2011.

Magnien, Michel. "Un écho de la querelle cicéronienne à la fin du XVIᵉ siècle: éloquence et imitation dans les *Essais*." In *Rhétorique de Montaigne: Actes du Colloque de la Société des Amis de Montaigne (Paris, 14 et 15 décembre 1984),* ed. Frank Lestringant, 85–99. Paris, 1985.

Mann, Nicholas. "From Laurel to Fig: Petrarch and the Structures of the Self." *Proceedings of the British Academy* 105 (2000): 17–42.

Margolin, Jean-Claude. "L'analogie dans la pensée d'Erasme." *Archiv für Reformationsgeschichte* 69 (1978): 24–49.

Marks, Emerson R. *Relativist and Absolutist: The Early Neoclassical Debate in England.* New Brunswick, NJ, 1955.

Marsh, David. *The Quattrocento Dialogue: Classical Tradition and Humanist Innovation.* Cambridge, MA, 1980.

Martin, Andrew John. "Giorgione e Baldassar Castiglione: proposte per l'interpretazione di un passo fondamentale del *Cortegiano*." *Venezia Cinquecento* 3 (1993): 57–66.

Mathieu-Castellani, Gisèle. "Dire, signifier. la figure de la *Significatio* dans les *Essais*." *Montaigne Studies* 3 (1991): 68–81.

May, James M. "The *Ethica Digressio* and Cicero's *Pro Milone*: A Progression of Intensity from *Logos* to *Ethos* to *Pathos*." *Classical Journal* 74 (1979): 240–46.

———. *Trials of Character: The Eloquence of Ciceronian Ethos.* Chapel Hill, 1988.

Mazzacurati, Giancarlo. "Baldassar Castiglione e la teoria cortigiana: ideologia di classe e dottrina critica." *Modern Language Notes* 83 (1968): 16–66.

McCall, Marsh H. *Ancient Rhetorical Theories of Simile and Comparison.* Cambridge, MA, 1969.

McConica, James. "Humanism and Aristotle in Tudor Oxford." *English Historical Review* 94 (1979): 291–317.

McCormick, Samuel. "Argument by Comparison: An Ancient Typology." *Rhetorica* 32 (2014): 148–64.

McGowan, Margaret M. *Montaigne's Deceits: The Art of Persuasion in the* Essais. Philadelphia, 1974.

McKenna, Stephen J. *Adam Smith: The Rhetoric of Propriety*. Albany, 2006.

McLaughlin, Martin. "Alberti e le opere retoriche di Cicerone." In *Alberti e la tradizione: per lo "smontaggio" dei "mosaici" Albertiani. Atti del Convegno internazionale del Comitato Nazionale VI centenario della nascita di Leon Battista Alberti, Arezzo, 23–24–25 settembre 2004*, ed. Roberto Cardini and Mariangela Regoliosi, 181–210. Florence, 2007.

———. "*Il Cortegiano* in Inghilterra: la traduzione latina di Bartholomew Clerke (1571)." In *Una lingua morta per letterature vive: il dibattito sul latino come lingua letteraria in età moderna e contemporanea: atti del convegno internazionale di studi (Roma, 10–12 dicembre 2015)*, ed. Valerio Sanzotta, 41–64. Supplementa Humanistica Lovaniensia 45. Leuven, 2020.

———. "Histories of Literature in the Quattrocento." In *The Languages of Literature in Renaissance Italy*, ed. Peter Hainsworth, Valerio Lucchesi, Christina Roaf, David Robey, and J. R. Woodhouse, 63–80. Oxford, 1988.

———. "Humanist Concepts of Renaissance and Middle Ages in the Tre- and Quattrocento." *Renaissance Studies* 2 (1988): 131–42.

———. *Literary Imitation in the Italian Renaissance: The Theory and Practice of Literary Imitation in Italy from Dante to Bembo*. Oxford, 1995.

———. "Petrarch and Cicero: Adulation and Critical Distance." In *Brill's Companion to the Reception of Cicero*, ed. William H. F. Altman, 19–38. Leiden, 2015.

———. "*Renascens ad superos* Cicero: Ciceronian and Anti-Ciceronian Styles in the Italian Renaissance." In *The Afterlife of Cicero*, ed. Gesine Manuwald, 67–81. London, 2016.

McNally, James Richard. "*Dux Illa Directrixque Artium*: Rudolph Agricola's Dialectical System." *Quarterly Journal of Speech* 52 (1966): 337–47.

McNamara, Charles. "*Certum atque confessum*: Lorenzo Valla on the Forensics of Certainty." *Rhetorica* 36 (2018): 244–68.

McPherran, Mark L. "Socratic *Epagōgē* and Socratic Induction." *Journal of the History of Philosophy* 45 (2007): 347–64.

Meerhoff, Kees. "The Significance of Philip Melanchthon's Rhetoric in the Renaissance." In *Renaissance Rhetoric*, ed. Peter Mack, 46–52. London, 1994.

Megill, Allan. "Why Was There a Crisis of Historicism?" *History and Theory* 36 (1997): 416–29.

Migliorini, Bruno. *Storia della lingua italiana*. 2 vols. Florence, 1988.

Mommsen, Theodor E. "Rudolph Agricola's Life of Petrarch." *Traditio* 8 (1952): 367–86.

Monfasani, John. "The Ciceronian Controversy." In *Cambridge History of Literary Criticism*, vol. 3: *The Renaissance*, ed. G. P. Norton, 395–401. Cambridge, UK, 1999.

———. "Humanism and Rhetoric." In *Renaissance Humanism: Foundations, Forms, and Legacy*, ed. Albert Rabil Jr., 3: 171–235. 3 vols. Philadelphia, 1988.

Montefusco, Lucia Calboli. *La dottrina degli "status" nella retorica greca e romana*. Hildesheim, 1986.

Morgan, Kathryn. "Plato's Goat-Stags and the Uses of Comparison." In *Plato and the Power of Images*, ed. P. Destree and R. G. Edmonds III, 179–98. Leiden, 2017.

Motta, Uberto. "La 'questione della lingua' nel primo libro del *Cortegiano*: dalla seconda alla terza redazione." *Aevum* 72 (1998): 693–732.

Moyn, Samuel. "Amos Funkenstein on the Theological Origins of Historicism." In
Thinking Impossibilities: The Intellectual Legacy of Amos Funkenstein, ed. Robert S.
Westman and David Biale, 143–66. Toronto, 2008.

Murphy, James J. *Rhetoric in the Middle Ages: A History of Rhetorical Theory from
Saint Augustine to the Renaissance*. Berkeley, 1974.

Nadeau, Ray. "Some Aristotelian and Stoic Influences on the Theory of Stases."
Speech Monographs 26 (1959): 248–54.

Nadel, George H. "Philosophy of History before Historicism." *History and Theory* 3
(1964): 291–315.

Narducci, Emanuele. "*Brutus*: The History of Roman Eloquence." Trans. James M.
May. In *Brill's Companion to Cicero: Oratory and Rhetoric*, ed. James M. May,
401–25. Leiden, 2002.

———. *Cicerone e l'eloquenza romana*. Rome, 1997.

Nederman, Cary J. "The Union of Wisdom and Eloquence before the Renaissance:
The Ciceronian Orator in Medieval Thought." *Journal of Medieval History* 18
(1992): 75–95.

Norman, Larry F. *The Shock of the Ancient: Literature and History in Early Modern
France*. Chicago, 2011.

North, Helen F. "Combing and Curling: *Orator Summus Plato*." *Illinois Classical Studies* 16 (1991): 2001–19.

O'Brien, John. "Montaigne and Antiquity: Fancies and Grotesques." In *The Cambridge Companion to Montaigne*, ed. Ullrich Langer, 53–77. Cambridge, UK, 2005.

O'Connell, Michael. "Authority and the Truth of Experience in Petrarch's 'Ascent of
Mount Ventoux.'" *Philological Quarterly* 62 (1983): 507–19.

O'Malley, John. *Praise and Blame in Renaissance Rome*. Durham, NC, 1979.

Onians, John. "Quintilian and the Idea of Roman Art." In *Architecture and Architectural Sculpture in the Roman Empire*, ed. Martin Henig, 1–9. Oxford, 1990.

O'Sullivan, Neil. *Alcidamas, Aristophanes, and the Beginnings of Greek Stylistic Theory*.
Stuttgart, 1992.

Parker, Patricia. *Literary Fat Ladies: Rhetoric, Gender, Property*. London, 1987.

Paternoster, Annick. *Aptum. retorica ed ermeneutica nel dialogo rinascimentale del
primo Cinquecento*. Rome, 1998.

———. "La controversia nel *Libro del Cortegiano* di Baldassar Castiglione: retorica
della conflittualità a corte." *Lettere Italiane* 57 (2005): 209–36.

———. "Decorum and Indecorum in the *Seconda Redazione* of Baldassare Castiglione's *Libro del Cortegiano*." *MLR* 99 (2004): 622–34.

Pfeiffer, Douglas S. *Authorial Personality and the Making of Renaissance Texts: The
Force of Character*. Oxford, 2021.

Pigeaud, Jackie, ed. *Winckelmann et le retour à l'antique: Actes du colloque, 9–12 juin
1994*. Nantes, 1995.

Pigman, G. W., III. "Barzizza's Studies of Cicero." *Rinascimento* 21 (1981): 123–63.

———. "Imitation and the Renaissance Sense of the Past: The Reception of Erasmus'
Ciceronianus." *Journal of Medieval and Renaissance Studies* 9 (1979): 155–77.

Plett, Henrich F. *Rhetoric and Renaissance Culture*. Berlin, 2004.

Pohlenz, Max. "*To Prepon*: Ein Beitrag zur Geschichte des griechischen Geistes." *Philologisch-historische Klasse* 1 (1933): 53–92.

Quillen, Carol E. *Rereading the Renaissance: Petrarch, Augustine, and the Language of Humanism*. Ann Arbor, MI, 1998.

Quint, David. "Humanism and Modernity: A Reconsideration of Bruni's *Dialogues*." *Renaissance Quarterly* 38 (1985): 423–45.

Rawson, Elizabeth. "Cicero the Historian and Cicero the Antiquarian." *Journal of Roman Studies* 62 (1972): 33–45.

Rebecchini, Guido. "The Book Collection and Other Possessions of Baldassarre Castiglione." *Journal of the Warburg and Courtauld Institutes* 61 (1998): 17–52.

———. "Castiglione and Erasmus: Towards a Reconciliation?" *Journal of the Warburg and Courtauld Institutes* 61 (1998): 258–60.

Rebhorn, Wayne A. "Baldesar Castiglione, Thomas Wilson, and the Courtly Body of Renaissance Rhetoric." *Rhetorica* 11 (1993): 241–74.

———. *Courtly Performances: Masking and Festivity in Castiglione's "Book of the Courtier."* Detroit, 1978.

———. "The Enduring Word: Language, Time, and History in *Il Libro del Cortegiano*." In *Castiglione: The Ideal and the Real in Renaissance Culture*, ed. Robert W. Hanning and David Rosand, 69–90. New Haven, 1983.

Ricci, Pier Giorgio. "La tradizione dell'invettiva tra il Medioevo e l'Umanesimo." *Lettere Italiane* 26 (1974): 405–14.

Richards, Jennifer. "Assumed Simplicity and the Critique of Nobility: Or, How Castiglione Read Cicero." *Renaissance Quarterly* 54 (2001): 460–86.

———. *Rhetoric and Courtliness in Early Modern Literature*. Cambridge, UK, 2003.

Rigault, H. *Histoire de la querelle des anciens et des modernes*. In *Œuvres complètes*, vol. 1. Paris, 1859.

Rigolot, François. "Problematizing Renaissance Exemplarity: The Inward Turn of Dialogue from Petrarch to Montaigne." In *Printed Voices: The Renaissance Culture of Dialogue*, ed. Jean-François Vallée and Dorothea B. Heitsch, 3–24. Toronto, 2004.

Ringler, William. "The Immediate Source of Euphuism." *PMLA* 53 (1938): 678–86.

Robathan, Dorothy M. "A Fifteenth-Century History of Latin Literature." *Speculum* 7 (1932): 239–48.

Robertson, D. W., Jr. "A Note on the Classical Origin of 'Circumstances' in the Medieval Confessional." *Studies in Philology* 43 (1946): 6–14.

Robinson, Edward A. "The Date of Cicero's *Brutus*." *Harvard Studies in Classical Philology* 60 (1951): 137–46.

Robinson, Richard. *Plato's Earlier Dialectic*. Oxford, 1953.

Rosand, David. "The Portrait, the Courtier, and Death." In *Castiglione: The Ideal and the Real in Renaissance Culture*, ed. Robert W. Hanning and David Rosand, 91–129. New Haven, 1983.

Rowland, Ingrid D. *The Culture of the High Renaissance: Ancients and Moderns in Sixteenth-Century Rome*. Cambridge, UK, 1998.

Rubini, Rocco. *Posterity: Inventing Tradition from Petrarch to Gramsci*. Chicago, 2021.

Russell, D. A. *Greek Declamation*. Cambridge, UK, 1983.

Sabbadini, Remigio. *Le scoperte dei codici latini e greci ne' secoli XIV e XV.* 2 vols. Florence, 1905, 1914.

———. *Storia del Ciceronianismo e di altre questioni letterarie nell'età della Renascenza.* Turin, 1885.

Saccone, Eduardo. "The Portrait of the Courtier in Castiglione." *Italica* 64 (1987): 1–10.

Salmon, J. H. M. "Cicero and Tacitus in Sixteenth-Century France." *American Historical Review* 85 (1980): 307–31.

Sauerländer, Willibald. "From Stilus to Style: Reflections on the Fate of a Notion." *Art History* 6 (1983): 253–70.

Sayce, R. A. "The Style of Montaigne: Word-Pairs and Word-Groups." In *Literary Style: A Symposium,* ed. Seymour Chatman, 383–405. London, 1971.

Scaglione, Aldo. "The Humanist as Scholar and Politian's Conception of the Grammaticus." *Studies in the Renaissance* 8 (1961): 49–70.

Schiffman, Zachary Sayre. "Renaissance Historicism Reconsidered." *History and Theory* 24 (1985): 170–82.

Schlitt, Melinda. "'Anticamente Moderna et Modernamente Antica': Imitation and the Ideal in 16th-Century Italian Painting." *International Journal of the Classical Tradition* 10 (2004): 377–406.

Schütrumpf, Eckart. "Platonic Elements in the Structure of Cicero *De oratore* Book 1." *Rhetorica* 6 (1988): 237–58.

Sebastiani, Valentina. "Gli *Antibarbari* di Erasmo e il programma editoriale della Stamperia Froben." *Bruniana & Campanelliana* 19 (2013): 385–95.

Serjeantson, R. W. "Testimony: The Artless Proof." In *Renaissance Figures of Speech,* ed. Sylvia Adamson, Gavin Alexander, and Katrin Ettenhuber, 181–94. Cambridge, UK, 2007.

Shapiro, Barbara. "Presumptions and Circumstantial Evidence in the Anglo-American Legal Tradition, 1500–1900." In *The Law of Presumptions: Essays in Comparative Legal History,* ed. R. H. Helmholz and W. David H. Sellar, 153–87. Berlin, 2009.

Shorey, Paul. "Phusis, Melete, Episteme." *Transactions of the American Philological Association* 40 (1909): 185–201.

Shuger, Debora K. *Sacred Rhetoric: The Christian Grand Style in the English Renaissance.* Princeton, 1988.

Simone, Franco. "Il Petrarca e la sua concezione ciclica della storia." In *Arte e storia. studi in onore di Leonello Vincenti,* 387–428. Turin, 1965.

Skinner, Quentin. *Forensic Shakespeare.* Oxford, 2014.

———. *Reason and Rhetoric in the Philosophy of Hobbes.* Cambridge, UK, 1996.

Smith, Barbara Herrnstein. "Unloading the Self-Refutation Charge." In *Self and Deception: A Cross-Cultural Philosophical Enquiry,* ed. Roger T. Ames and Wimal Dissanayake, 143–60. Albany, 1996.

Sohm, Philip. "Ordering History with Style: Giorgio Vasari on the Art of History." In *Antiquity and Its Interpreters,* ed. Alina Payne, Ann Kuttner, and Rebekah Smick, 40–54. Cambridge, UK, 1999.

———. *Style in the Art Theory of Early Modern Italy.* Cambridge, UK, 2001.

Solmsen, Friedrich. "The Aristotelian Tradition in Ancient Rhetoric." *American Journal of Philology* 62 (1941): 35–50, 169–90.

———. "Aristotle and Cicero on the Orator's Playing upon the Feelings." *Classical Philology* 33 (1938): 390–404.

Sonnino, Lee. *A Handbook to Sixteenth-Century Rhetoric.* London, 1968.

Stachon, Markus. "Evolutionary Thinking in Ancient Literary Theory: Quintilian's Canon and the Origin of Verse Forms." *Classical World* 110 (2017): 237–55.

Steel, C. E. W. "Cicero's *Brutus*: The End of Oratory and the Beginning of History?" *Bulletin of the Institute of Classical Studies of the University of London* 46 (2002–3): 195–211.

Steinmetz, David C. "Divided by a Common Past: The Reshaping of the Christian Exegetical Tradition in the Sixteenth Century." *Journal of Medieval and Early Modern Studies* 27 (1997): 245–64.

Stillman, Robert E. *Philip Sidney and the Poetics of Renaissance Cosmopolitanism.* Aldershot, 2008.

Strier, Richard. "Paleness versus Eloquence: The Ideologies of Style in the English Renaissance." *Explorations in Renaissance Culture* 45 (2019): 91–120.

———. *The Unrepentant Renaissance: From Petrarch to Shakespeare to Milton.* Chicago, 2011.

Struever, Nancy. *The Language of History in the Renaissance: Rhetoric and Historical Consciousness in Florentine Humanism.* Princeton, 1970.

Stull, William. "*Deus ille noster*: Platonic Precedent and the Construction of the Interlocutors in Cicero's *De oratore*." *Transactions of the American Philological Association* 141 (2011): 247–63.

Stump, Eleonore. "Augustine on Free Will." In *The Cambridge Companion to Augustine*, ed. Eleonore Stump and Norman Kretzmann, 124–47. Cambridge, UK, 2001.

Sugg, Ellen. "A Ciceronian Context for Polyvalent Metaphor in 'Du parler prompt ou tardif.'" *Montaigne Studies* 2 (1990): 81–97.

Sumner, G. V. *The Orators in Cicero's "Brutus": Prosopography and Chronology.* Toronto, 1973.

Syson, Antonia. "Born to Speak: *Ingenium* and *Natura* in Tacitus' *Dialogue on Orators*." *Arethusa* 42 (2009): 45–75.

Tapper, Colin. *Cross and Tapper on Evidence.* 12th ed. Oxford, 2010.

Tarrant, Harold. "Socratic Method and Socratic Truth." In *A Companion to Socrates*, ed. Sara Ahbel-Rappe and Rachana Kamtekar, 254–72. London, 2005.

Taylor-Briggs, Ruth. "Reading between the Lines: The Textual History and Manuscript Transmission of Cicero's Rhetorical Works." In *The Rhetoric of Cicero in Its Medieval and Early Renaissance Commentary Tradition*, ed. Virginia Cox and John O. Ward, 77–108. Leiden, 2006.

Thompson, Wayne N. "*Stasis* in Aristotle's *Rhetoric*." *Quarterly Journal of Speech* 58 (1972): 134–41.

Tilley, Morris Palmer. *Elizabethan Proverb Lore in Lyly's Euphues and in Pettie's "Petite Palace."* New York, 1926.

Tournon, André. "Les prosopopées ironiques dans les *Essais*." In *Rhétorique de Montaigne. Actes du Colloque de la Société des Amis de Montaigne (Paris, 14 et 15 décembre 1984)*, ed. Frank Lestringant, 113–21. Paris, 1985.

Tracy, James D. *Erasmus of the Low Countries.* Berkeley, 1996.

Trafton, Dain A. "Structure and Meaning in *The Courtier*." *English Literary Renaissance* 2 (1972): 283–97.

Traninger, Anita. "Erasmus' *personae* between Rhetoric and Dialectics." *Erasmus Studies* 37 (2017): 5–22.

———. "Taking Sides and the Prehistory of Impartiality." In *The Emergence of Impartiality*, ed. Kathryn Murphy and Anita Traninger, 33–63. Leiden, 2014.

Trimpi, Wesley. "Horace's 'Ut Pictura Poesis': The Argument for Stylistic Decorum." *Traditio* 34 (1978): 29–73.

———. *Muses of One Mind: The Literary Analysis of Experience and Its Continuity.* Princeton, 1982.

———. "Reason and the Classical Premises of Literary Decorum." *Independent Journal of Philosophy* 5/6 (1988): 103–11.

Trinkaus, Charles. "A Humanist's Image of Humanism: The Inaugural Orations of Bartolommeo della Fonte." *Studies in the Renaissance* 7 (1960): 90–147.

———. *In Our Image and Likeness: Humanity and Divinity in Italian Humanist Thought.* 2 vols. Chicago, 1970.

———. *The Poet as Philosopher: Petrarch and the Formation of Renaissance Consciousness.* New Haven, 1979.

Trousdale, Marion. "Recurrence and Renaissance: Rhetorical Imitation in Ascham and Sturm." *English Literary Renaissance* 6 (1976): 156–79.

Tuve, Rosemund. *Elizabethan and Metaphysical Imagery.* Chicago, 1947.

van den Berg, Christopher S. "Intratext, Declamation, and Dramatic Argument in Tacitus' *Dialogus de oratoribus*." *Classical Quarterly* 64 (2014): 298–315.

———. "The Invention of Literary History in Cicero's *Brutus*." *Classical Philology* 114 (2019): 573–603.

Vickers, Brian. *In Defence of Rhetoric.* Oxford, 1988.

———. "Rhetoric and Poetics." In *The Cambridge History of Renaissance Philosophy*, ed. Charles Schmitt and Quentin Skinner, 715–45. Cambridge, UK, 1988.

———. "Rhetorical and Anti-rhetorical Tropes: On Writing the History of *Elocutio*." *Comparative Criticism* 3 (1981): 105–32.

———. "Some Reflections on the Rhetoric Textbook." In *Renaissance Rhetoric*, ed. Peter Mack, 81–102. London, 1994.

Vlastos, Gregory. "The Socratic Elenchus." *Oxford Studies in Ancient Philosophy* 1 (1983): 27–58.

———. "Was Polus Refuted?" *American Journal of Philology* 88 (1967): 454–60.

Voegelin, Eric. *Plato.* Baton Rouge, 1966.

Watson, Gerard. "Plato's *Gorgias* and Aristotle." *Maynooth Review* 14 (1989): 51–66.

Wenzel, Siegfried. "Petrarch's *Accidia*." *Studies in the Renaissance* 8 (1961): 36–48.

White, Hayden V. "The Burden of History." In *Tropics of Discourse: Essays in Cultural Criticism*, 27–50. Baltimore, 1978.

———. "Foucault's Discourse: The Historiography of Anti-humanism." In *The Content of the Form: Narrative Discourse and Historical Representation*, 104–41. Baltimore, 1987.

———. "On History and Historicisms." In *From History to Sociology: The Transition in German Historical Thinking*, by Carlo Antoni, trans. Hayden V. White, xv–xxviii. Detroit, 1959.

Whitman, Jon. "Fable and Fact: Judging the Language of Scripture (Judges 9:8–15) from Antiquity to Modernity." *Harvard Theological Review* 113 (2020): 149–85.

Wilcox, Donald J. *The Measure of Times Past: Pre-Newtonian Chronologies and the Rhetoric of Relative Time.* Chicago, 1987.

Williams, Gordon. *Change and Decline: Roman Literature in the Early Empire.* Berkeley, 1978.

Williams, Robert. "Leonardo's Modernity: Subjectivity as Symptom." In *The Life and the Work: Art and Biography*, ed. Charles G. Salas, 34–44. Los Angeles, 2007.

Winterbottom, Michael. "Fifteenth-Century Manuscripts of Quintilian." *Classical Quarterly* 17 (1967): 339–69.

Wisse, Jakob. "*De oratore*: Rhetoric, Philosophy, and the Making of the Ideal Orator." In *Brill's Companion to Cicero: Oratory and Rhetoric*, ed. James M. May, 375–400. Leiden, 2002.

———. *Ethos and Pathos from Aristotle to Cicero.* Amsterdam, 1989.

———. "Greeks, Romans, and the Rise of Atticism." In *Greek Literary Theory after Aristotle*, ed. J. G. J. Abbenes, S. R. Slings, and I. Sluiter, 65–82. Amsterdam, 1995.

———. "The Intellectual Background of Cicero's Rhetorical Works." In *Brill's Companion to Cicero: Oratory and Rhetoric*, ed. James M. May, 331–74. Leiden, 2002.

Witt, Ronald. *"In the Footsteps of the Ancients": The Origins of Humanism from Lovato to Bruni.* Leiden, 2000.

———. *The Two Latin Cultures and the Foundation of Renaissance Humanism in Medieval Italy.* Cambridge, UK, 2012.

Wolfe, Jessica. *Homer and the Question of Strife from Erasmus to Hobbes.* Toronto, 2015.

Zerba, Michelle. *Doubt and Skepticism in Antiquity and the Renaissance.* Cambridge, UK, 2012.

Zetzel, James. "Plato with Pillows: Cicero on the Uses of Greek Culture." In *Myth, History and Culture in Republican Rome*, ed. David Braund and Christopher Gill, 119–38. Exeter, 2003.

Zorzi Pugliese, Olga. "La scrittura dell'arte nel *Libro del cortegiano*." *Letteratura & arte* 3 (2005): 23–33.

INDEX